CANADIAN SOCIETY
A Sociological Analysis

CANADIAN SOCIETY

A Sociological Analysis

Harry H. Hiller

Department of Sociology
University of Calgary

PRENTICE-HALL OF CANADA, LTD.
Scarborough, Ontario

Canadian Shared Cataloguing in Publication Data
  Hiller, Harry H., 1942-
    Canadian society

  Bibliography: p.
  Includes index.
  ISBN 0-13-11333-2-2 bd.
  ISBN 0-13-11332-4-1 pa.

  1. Canada — Social conditions.   I. Title.
  HN103.H5   309.1'71

Prentice-Hall, Inc., Englewood Cliffs, New Jersey
Prentice-Hall International, Inc., London
Prentice-Hall of Australia, Pty., Ltd., Sydney
Prentice-Hall of India Pvt., Ltd., New Delhi
Prentice-Hall of Japan, Inc., Tokyo
Prentice-Hall of Southeast Asia (PTE.) Ltd., Singapore

ISBN 0-13-11332-4-1 *paperback*
ISBN 0-13-11333-2-2 *cloth*

Design by Julian Cleva

Typesetting by Better Creative Service Limited

Printed in Canada

    4   5   BP   80

To
Nathan Jeffrey
whose birth coincided
with the birth of this book.

Contents

Preface *ix*

Introduction *xiii*

1 Organismic Model *1*
   Societies as Organisms 3
   Describing a Human Society 5
   Functionalism and Social Cohesion 8
   Regional Variance: The Parts of the Social Organism 10
   From Regionalism to a National Society 37

2 Stratification and Internal Power Model *45*
   Objective Indices of Rank 47
   Subjective Indices of Rank 58
   Ethnic Stratification 59
   Social Mobility 63
   Social Power 67
   Poverty 73
   The Implications of a Stratified Society 75

3 External Power and Domination Model *83*
   The Notion of Colonialism 84
   The Nature of the External Societal Pressures 86
   Primary Factors Responsible for Canada's Subordinate Role 90
   Effects of External Pressures on Canadian Society 97

4 Ethnic Group Conflict Model *103*
   The Human Group 104
   Inter-group Relations 108
   The French-English Conflict 116
   The Native Indian - White Conflict 119
   Melting Pot or Mosaic? 120

5 Comparative Model *128*
  Problems of Societal Comparisons *129*

6 Identity Model *154*
  Identity as a Concept *155*
  The Concept of Nationalism *163*

7 Conclusion *175*

A Select Bibliography on Canadian Society *188*

Index *197*

Preface

Two or three decades of research by social scientists on various aspects of Canadian society has produced a growing body of literature containing valuable insights and information which should be brought together for two major reasons. One important reason is the necessity to integrate and to synthesize these insights in such a way that they provide a less fragmented and more comprehensive picture of Canadian society. This book is an attempt to summarize the results of important studies and technical observations in order to present an overview of Canadian society. Thus its primary purpose is to determine what sociological research has uncovered about the nature of Canadian society. My one regret with this approach is that the seemingly endless cataloguing of all appropriate studies has been a preoccupation to which critical assessment of all the material has taken second place.

The second reason this approach is warranted is that there is a need for the results of these numerous studies to be made available for wider public consumption. We have gone through an important phase in Canadian sociology when research articles written for professional journals were brought together into books of readings; these served as standard fare in sociology courses for many years. The professional and theoretical orientation of most of these readings made understanding difficult at the undergraduate level and contributed to the presentation of disjointed glimpses of Canadian society. My goal is to provide sufficient information to give the reader a macro view of Canadian society without becoming encyclopedic, while at the same time encouraging a more detailed interest in specific areas through significant bibliographic references for further study. Thus footnotes are frequent and sometimes more elaborate than necessary in order to help the interested reader to pursue specific issues in greater depth.

Another way of stating the objective of the book is to point out what it is *not* attempting to accomplish. I do not suggest that the book is a thorough introductory sociology textbook in itself, because it could be argued that many sociological principles and concepts are either left out or are not dealt with in all their complexities. From this point of view, the book might be more appropriately used in conjunction with a comprehensive introductory text. At the same time, I am not saying that the book cannot stand on its own. Concepts and principles are deliberately introduced in such a way that the reader who is new to sociology will find its perspective understandable. Undoubtedly, the book ought to be most useful in courses specifically focusing on Canadian society, for it is in this context that the idea for the manuscript was born.

It is also important to note that this work is *not* primarily history or economics but sociology. Others more qualified than I have written about Canada from a historical or economic perspective. History and economics certainly cannot be ignored for they are part of a good sociological analysis. Nevertheless, this study is couched within the framework of the discipline of sociology rather than that of other disciplines, and presents an analysis of one particular society from a sociological perspective.

Considerable research has already been made available in the areas chosen for analysis. The book does not aim to cover every possible aspect of Canadian society. The reader will always be able to think of areas which were not discussed in detail — in particular such institutions as the family, education, and politics. At least for the time being, I have felt that such information ought to be woven into discussions of other topical areas rather than to receive separate treatment in individual chapters. This policy was also consistent with my particular macro-sociological approach.

Thus the goal of my analysis is to give an integrated picture of the nature of Canadian society by examining its critical facets. Complex observations by other writers are frequently summarized in several sentences or a paragraph, and as a result their detailed research may be oversimplified. To the thorough academic, and indeed to the authors themselves, such an approach may appear all too cavalier, and undoubtedly is a limitation in writing this type of book. However, the hazards and advantages of this procedure notwithstanding, it is my hope that the book will serve as a catalyst for a more in-depth study by the reader. The footnotes and references cited ought to provide at least some of the tools for deeper probing.

Even though I accept full responsibility for the contents of this book, I acknowledge the research of others whose work I have attempted to represent faithfully in some instances or to interpret in others. In either case, every effort has been made to make appropriate references and credits. If any omissions have been made, it is due to the fact that the material has been so thoroughly internalized that it appears to be my own — a process that is both necessary and worthwhile, yet problematic.

My debts of gratitude begin with my students who have prompted this writing and stimulated me with their questions. I am also grateful to my colleagues, particularly Dr. Harvey Rich, for candid assessments of an earlier draft of this manuscript. The research assistance of Wayne Whittaker, Patty Beatty-Guenter, and Paul Pierzchalski helped immeasurably to lighten the load — particularly in the acquisition and compilation of materials. The demands of an author are felt perhaps most acutely by the secretarial staff and I am indebted to Rosie Handy and Myrtle Murray for their careful and meticulous typing. In addition, the editorial guidance of Jon Penman (Acquisitions Editor) and Marta Tomins (Production Editor) at Prentice-Hall greatly facilitated the publication of the manuscript. From a personal perspective, the accomplishment of this task was made possible by the patience and understanding of my wife, Beverly, who assumed additional responsibilities of motherhood during the period in which the manuscript was in preparation.

Harry H. Hiller

Introduction

A study of Canadian society requires a prior statement as to what the term "Canadian society" means. In order for any society to exist, individuals must first form relatively enduring networks of interrelationship and interaction. Such interaction may be primarily of a formal nature and mediated by bureaucracies and large-scale organizations which span sub-societies, or it may be of an informal nature as the result of frequent and mutual activity. When we speak of Canadian society, then, we assume that there must be some interaction among the residents of the nation-state, at least at the formal level.

But even though the term "Canadian society" implies this sociological aspect, it is dependent on geographic and political referents. The society is circumscribed by national boundaries, and the population contained within these boundaries forms the national society which we identify as Canadian society. Thus the organizing assumption of the book is that Canada is a national society, or that the society is coextensive with the nation-state because of the presupposition that its members will invariably have to interact in some way.

The notion that the population within Canada's boundaries forms a national society is fraught with numerous difficulties — many of which will be explored throughout the book. The most ponderous problem, at least from a historical perspective, as well as from the perspective of many Canadian contemporaries, is that Canadian society is not one society but essentially two: French-Canadian society and English-Canadian society. Those who believe this feel that the differences between the two societies are so striking and durable that the single society idea implicit in the notion of Canadian society is almost meaningless. I do not intend to take an opposite point of view and to suggest that the idea of two societies within one nation is tenable. However, it is my contention that national political boundaries force the population contained within these borders to interact and to be cognizant of each other at least in some minimal way merely because they share a common national territory and political system. Thus, we can use the term "Canadian society" to refer to the total population contained within the politico-national unit. We will have occasion to explore the concept of society in Chapter 1 and at that point can assess more carefully to what extent Canadian society in the sense described above actually is a society.

The material that follows is organized to offer a macro-sociological portrait of Canadian society. Each chapter is one picture or snapshot taken from a different perspective of the same basic entity. Just as a good photographer approaches his subject from numerous angles with each photograph stressing another aspect of the subject, so it is my intent to provide various pictures of Canadian society. Each picture will stress a different aspect of the society but contribute to an overall societal portrait.

The picture that each chapter gives of Canadian society is referred to as a particular *model* of the society. By *model* is meant a representation or replica on a small scale of very complex and human processes. Thus, the Stratification Model pictures Canadian society from one perspective by reducing all available data to a concise and accurate representation of complex differences in power among members of the society. Similarly, the Ethnic Group Conflict Model sketches the outlines of Canadian society by detailing the nature and impact of ethnic cleavages in the society. Caution should be exercised that the term "model" be assigned no additional meaning, for it is only intended to serve as an organizational category.

The six models or perspectives discussed in this book are merely conceptual frameworks through which sociological phenomena can be interpreted. They are categories whereby our portraits of the society can be ordered in a coherent way. Each of the following chapters isolates one central issue presently affecting Canadian society and discusses how that issue illuminates the nature of the society.

Perhaps it should also be pointed out that each model is not exclusive. Clearly there are elements of conflict in discussing stratification which may not be drawn out until a later chapter; or notions of external power may be included in a later discussion of identity. Materials in each chapter repeatedly overlap and the reader is encouraged to relate the perspective of each chapter to that of the other chapters.

Chapter 1 discusses Canada as a boundary-maintaining unit. Its position as the first chapter is not meant to construe a structural-functional bias maintained by the author either in that chapter or in the chapters to follow. It is useful to view Canadian society as a boundary-maintaining organism in order to understand the internal dynamics of the national preoccupation with retaining the nation intact. Given the fact that the nation is an independent political unit, the chapter discusses the demographic factors that put stress on relationships between parts of the society, and perhaps often even threaten the existence of the nation as a social unit. Although the chapter has no other purpose than to examine the national society as an interacting whole, it is not intended to suggest a hidden quest for social stability. If description and analysis are interpreted as grounds for prescription, the author leaves such action to the reader.

Chapter 2 deals with power (and the lack of power) in all of its dimensions. To what extent are there differences among members of a society in terms of income, education, or occupation? What is the nature of social class in Canada, and how does its existence affect the society?

Chapter 3 explores the effect of external forces on Canadian society and describes the nature of the domination. The fact that Canada maintains a strong dependency on other societies and foreign organizations has been the cause of considerable ferment within the society, and it is the goal of the chapter to clarify the issues and to discuss their impact.

Chapter 4 views Canadian society in terms of the ethnic identifications of her diverse population. The plurality of minorities and variations in group awareness implicitly involve suspicions and hostilities expressed in conflicts that have an ethnic base. The chapter describes the relationship between minorities and the society as a whole. In general, this is a well-researched area in Canadian society, and the material referenced in the chapter only scratches the surface.

Comparisons between societies must be undertaken with great care because of the danger of overemphasizing similarities within one society for the sake of comparing that society with another. However, Chapter 5 seeks to discover what can be learned about Canada from such comparisons. Published research is scattered and skimpy in this area, and often is highly questionable when value judgments and generalizations form the basis of comparison. Nevertheless, the chapter does give us a useful additional perspective on Canadian society.

In contrast to societal comparisons, an area that has received considerable attention through the years is the search for a Canadian identity. Chapter 6 analyzes the factors that have both retarded and contributed to this quest. The development of feelings of nationalism is also discussed in relation to the struggle for a national identity.

No social scientist is without his values and, if properly labelled, they ought not to interfere with an objective societal analysis. The personal biases in this book can be stated bluntly. While I do not perceive Canada's cultural heterogeneity as a social problem, I do view it as a fact which has significant consequences for societal interaction. Secondly, while I do not believe that there is a general desire for national integration, I do feel that Canadian society is still engaged in a perpetual search for a minimal level of consensus. Thirdly, I am personally distressed by the regional inequities and imbalances that exist in Canada and am appalled by the government policy that perpetuates such dominance. To that extent, I identify with regional protests and regional rights. Finally, I am convinced that each nation ought to have the right to retain its national sovereignty and independence, but not at the expense of the liberty of its own citizens. The research and reflection that have produced this book have only served to reaffirm this ideal — particularly for Canadian society as it continues to evolve.

1
Organismic Model

When we use the term "Canadian society", we imply that there exists a society with an independent identity and with unique traits that differentiate it as a society from other societies. The adjective "Canadian" prior to the word "society" is meant to indicate the nature of this qualitative distinction.

But is there really such a thing as a Canadian society? Could it not be that the strength of the various sub-societies in Canada precludes any meaningful discussion about Canadian society as a whole? Even a cursory analysis reveals great difficulty with a wholistic approach, for the relatively short history of Canada, coupled with considerably high immigration and emigration rates, has produced a continuously changing social unit. It could be argued further that Canada's continued reference group relationships with British, French, and American societies have engendered conflicting loyalties that have contributed to Canada's inability to develop as a society with traits all her own.

In spite of the fact that it is impossible to speak of Canadian society as a traditional, stable, and homogeneous unit with uniquely uniform traits, perhaps a wide-angle view of this society can still be instructive *and is necessary*. Canada exists as a nation by the political and legislative decree of the British North America Act passed in 1867. It is because of her legal delineation as an independent national unit that we are compelled to raise the sociological question regarding the nature and character of the people and their interaction within her geographic and political borders. Even though modern nations do not exist in complete isolation from external influence on the one hand, and are not free from the internal presence of numerous sub-societies on the other hand, the political or national entity can be a useful and workable unit for the description and analysis of human populations as societies.[1] Certainly it is the color and diversity contained within national boundaries and expressed through regionalism, ethnicity, occupational groups, and leisure-time activities that give a national society its character. In addition, the fact that the climate of one area may tend to attract older people; that the industry of another encourages increased settlement by professional and working class families; and that the underdevelopment of yet another region tends to produce a society of poverty — all these factors tell us something about the social dynamics present within a nation. So the intriguing and central question is this: In what way can we speak of the population within Canada's borders as a society?

Societies are not static entities. They change continuously through time. Hence, a description of Canadian society or of one of its regions at varying historical moments would produce different pictures of the same society. For instance, the 1930s stereotype of Alberta society as rural and agricultural changed considerably by 1971 when only 26% of the provincial population was classified as rural, and over 55% of the population lived in two census metropolitan areas.[2] Similarly, a view of Quebec thirty or forty years ago would have been considerably different from the picture of the industrial urban province that we know today. While the social change which Canada has experienced is significant, this chapter focuses on the social differentiation and social conflict presently found within the national society. Instead of painting portraits of the social landscape of Canada at significant points in history, I will sketch the character, composition, and nature of contemporary Canadian society.

Let us begin with the assumption that the existence of Canada as a national society implies a certain degree of interaction and interdependence among those residing within her boundaries. It is through such interaction that a national character is formed.[3] This is not to say that social cohesion (or a sense of belonging together) is necessarily found among the parts of the political unit, but that the efficient functioning of the national unit requires the development of a minimal network of social interaction.

It is the primary concern of this chapter to specify the differences among the interacting members of the Canadian social unit. To use an analogy, societal bodies may be likened to human bodies whose condition will be determined both by intrusions from without and by growths from within. Just as a medical researcher assesses the human body by studying the forces that retard or foster its efficient functioning, so the social scientist is concerned with diagnosis of the forces that affect the existence of human societies. But, where the physician's goal is to return the body to homeostasis, the social scientist is careful to point out that a healthy social order may not mean, and perhaps can never mean, the absence of social conflict. Therefore, my approach will be to specify some of the social bases of conflict within Canadian society as a means of clarifying the nature and form of the society.

Societies as Organisms

The analogy of societies with living organisms is an old tradition in sociology. In his quest for a perfect social order, the father of sociology, Auguste Comte (1798-1857), outlined the observable characteristics shared by societies and living organisms.[4] He perceived that as a collective organism, society had an adaptable structure of "functionally interrelated parts" that tended to develop more complex forms through time. However, it was the Social Darwinist Herbert Spencer (1820-1903) who made more explicit use of the analogy of society with the biological organism. In his work *The Principles of Sociology*[5], Spencer pointed out how a society changes and adapts through "natural selection" in order to meet its functional requirements, and how it evolves appropriate structures through "survival of the fittest".

While contemporary social theorists consider the direct organismic analogy of societies with biological organisms both too crude and dated, the structural-functional school within sociology makes use of some similar principles in its approach. But because functionalism overplays the quest for consensus, equilibrium, and harmony within social units and underplays the role of conflict, change, and the role of social actors as decision makers within a social system, it is presently also not a popular perspective for societal analysis. Therefore, other than in the more recent cybernetic approach to society as a complex adaptive system[6], sociologists have been less inclined to view societies wholistically, i.e. as units. Obviously, the great difficulty of such an endeavor is that its quest for societally valid generalizations easily minimizes internal diversity in an attempt to be all-encompassing and all-inclusive. Nevertheless, if the whole idea of Canadian society is to have any meaning, we must take this macro approach in order to understand the characteristics of the society and the nature of its functioning as a unit.

For lack of better terminology, we refer to the wholistic means of perceiving Canadian society as the Organismic Model. This perspective suggests that, in a unique way, residents of Canada form a social organism the boundaries of which are politically determined, and in which each part of the organism makes a different contribution to the existence of the whole. The implication is that the parts of the society become interdependent and interrelated, and contribute to the creation of the identity of the social organism. Just as the personal identity of a human being is related to specific attributes such as the power of his legs, the color of his hair, the use of his brain, and the dexterity of his hands, so the identity of a national society is related to the variant characteristics of the social and regional groupings within its constituent parts.

The French sociologist Emile Durkheim asked the perplexing

question, "How is social order possible?" in a period of French history marked by disorder and disharmony. In a similar era of Canadian history charged with the tensions and strains of social change, we can raise the same question. It is no easier to answer now than it was in Durkheim's day. What is it that holds the people of the political and geographic unit known as Canada together as a society? Are the parts of the unit all needed and are they functional to the existence of the whole? Or, there are perhaps the questions that systems theorists would ask: Can something more be said about Canadian society than that it is merely the sum of its parts? What is it that gives Canadian society its character?

The Organismic Model, then, is a way of looking at Canadian society as a social unit and of asking how, in spite of internal diversity, the national society can hang together. Such a question is certainly an awesome one — particularly in light of the sociological differences that divide the population (which we will explore).

Describing a Human Society

The question has been raised as to whether the term "society" is appropriately descriptive of Canada's population and we can now begin to assess the degree to which Canadian society (in my use of the term) approximates a human society in the full sense. From a sociological point of view, a human society must possess the following characteristics: locality, organization, durability, and self-identification.

Locality.   A society requires that its members share a common environment or locality. A common territory encourages and facilitates interaction that binds together the many smaller groups that exist within the area. Thus the experience of living together in a common locale is necessary for the formation of a society.

While it is true that Canadians share a common territory, it is also true that that territory is large, often sparsely settled, and made up of ethnically diverse population blocs frequently separated by great distances. Nevertheless, in spite of the factors that divide the population, it is often thought that the experience of living in Canada will knit those who have come to this location into a common pattern of interaction. In other words, living in one geographic location should provide the common "pot" for the melting of all the immigrants from other societies into one society — Canadian society.

However, the Canadian experience has shown that a developing sense of society has been retarded by a scattered population within an extremely large territorial unit. Regionalism continues to divide the national population and, furthermore, multicultural policies remind members of the society of issues that divide them. Thus locality has hindered societal interaction in Canada and certainly has not been conducive to cementing the society.

Organization. A society also requires that its members be organized in such a way that the division of labor enables the needs of all members of the society to be met. Roles and tasks must be distributed throughout the society in order to ensure its survival. Such organization unites the society's members in a web of interrelationships. In modern societies this organization usually becomes very complex as policies are made and decisions are carried out by specialized individuals (e.g. urban planners, customs officers, army personnel) on behalf of the entire society.

In Canada, the federal government joins large corporations and agencies in giving organization to the society. Through job specialization in the division of labor, members of the society learn to depend on each other for goods and services. The only problem is that many of the organizational dependencies and relationships have been somewhat superficially constructed. For example, geography has frequently predisposed organized interaction in Canada to move in a north-south direction across the U.S. border rather than in an east-west direction across Canada. As a means of establishing and reinforcing the organizational structure of Canadian society, the federal government has had to set up regulatory agencies and mechanisms such as tariffs and immigration rules to ensure intrasocietal interaction. Tariffs force consumers to turn to Canadian industries, and immigration laws prevent persons from crossing borders merely at the appearance of better opportunities. What societal organization exists is thus protected and solidified as the boundaries of the society are reaffirmed. Eventually, society-wide organization is even enlarged as the society is knit together and given greater cohesiveness.

Durability. A society requires that its organization of interaction be relatively permanent and durable. When generations of families have inhabited an area for years, and when interfamilial interaction takes place more or less continuously over a lifetime, familiar behavior patterns and a common heritage are likely to develop within the society.

Durability has been thwarted in Canada by repeated injections of immigrants into the society and by the reverse flow of out-migration which retard the emergence of traditions. When a society begins to develop durability, a sense of societal history becomes very important to facilitate the development of group consciousness. It is understandable, then, that the demand for textbooks using Canadian materials has recently become so acute.

The education system is the primary instrument for equipping youth with an understanding of their society. Canadian society's lack of this sense of durability because it is a young and recently populated nation, can be partially remedied by the schools' sociali-zation of the young into the society's heritage and development. Anglophone schools have been particularly weak in societal socialization — partially at least for want of materials dealing with Canadian society. Educational materials that use Canadian illus-trations and present a Canadian sense of history rather than a world-view of an alien society are integral to developing common reference points through which interaction can be facilitated with-in the society.

Self-identity. Lastly, a society must possess a self-identity or awareness of itself as a unique society, not merely as a shadow of other societies. Participants in one society must be differentiated from participants in another by an awareness of the society to which they belong.

Within the international social world, the member of Canadian society must be able to locate himself by clinging to the societal identity of being "Canadian". Customs, symbols, folk heroes, and important landmarks contribute to an awareness of societal iden-tity. For instance, the display of the maple leaf in public assists a Canadian in differentiating his society from other societies and helps him to establish his own identity.

Yet a collective Canadian identity has been slow to develop within the society. One of the most significant factors has been the presence of two distinct societies within the nation-state. For reasons which I will discuss in Chapter 4, French-Canadian society has always had a well-developed conception of itself as a society in contrast to the more diffuse image of Anglo-Canadian society. In any case, Québecois have been somewhat apprehensive about what Anglophone Canadians have in mind regarding an emerging nation-al society for fear it may mean the inevitable destruction of

Quebec society. And it is precisely the preservation of its own societal identity that each side has in mind.

In addition to the dual society idea, the so-called hyphenated-Canadian (Italian-Canadian, German-Canadian) terminology has persisted. Members of the society are repeatedly identified in terms of the society of their origin. While it could be argued easily that these social groupings of hyphenated Canadians have given Canada the collective identity that it does possess, there is no doubt that they reduce the society's ability to establish its own self-identity which all members of the society can recognize and in which they can participate.

"Canadian society" is thus a term which must be used with great care for there are certainly many problems in speaking of Canada's population as a society. It is only as Canada overcomes her spatial difficulties, develops more fully and naturally the web of social organization that binds her members together, creates relatively durable patterns of interaction among a permanent population, and fosters a sense of identification with the socio-political unit, that the population within her geographic boundaries will ever become a national society in the full sense of the term. Such a goal may never be desired by Canadians and indeed may even be impossible. But as long as this is the case, the term "Canadian society" must always be used cautiously.

Functionalism and Social Cohesion

We can hypothesize that a Canadian society has evolved because, just as in an organism, its parts have become functionally inter-related. Such a view of a society implies that all parts of a social system have important functions to fulfill in order to maintain the whole unit.

Functional analysis is preoccupied with the consequences or the effects that one part of a social system has on the entire unit; i.e., the part is viewed in terms of its function in relation to the whole unit. For example, a physician may explain the heart in terms of its functions or consequences in pumping blood and therefore nourishment to all parts of the body. The family might be described in terms of its societal functions of reproduction and socialization of children for the society. In relation to Canada, the Royal Canadian Mounted Police might be defined in terms of their function of preserving law and order in the early West as an honest and efficient police force. But whether something is functional or dysfunctional depends on one's point of view. The RCMP may have been functional to the business elite who wished to protect their markets and trade routes on the frontier. However, to Indians and Métis, the RCMP may have been the symbol of white exploitation and invasion and therefore dysfunctional to their own purpose of maintaining their way of life.[7]

Furthermore, what is defined by some as good for the social system as a whole may not be accepted positively by the individual units of the system; for it is a subject of some debate whether a social act is actually beneficial or functional for all segments of a society. For instance, if you were trapped in the Ukraine as a landless peasant, Canada's immigration policy may have been functional in giving you greater security and a new lease on life. Similarly, if you were a shareholder in the Canadian Pacific Railway, you may have lauded immigration as a great source of transportation revenues and increased profits. However, if you were a British patriot and loyal to the Queen, you may have viewed European immigration as dysfunctional in that it diluted the British majority with those whose allegiances were elsewhere, and thus retarded the development of national unity.

A further distinction can be made between a *manifest* and a *latent* function. An action has a manifest function if it has recognized and intended consequences. In contrast, an action has latent functions if its consequences are unintentional, unexpected, or immediately unrecognized. The manifest functions of large-scale immigration into Canada were the settlement of the land and the provision of needed skilled and unskilled labor. These were the intended consequences of immigration. However, the latent functions of this population invasion, or its unintended consequences, were ethnic hostilities, occupational arrogance and insecurity among professionals already in Canada, or perhaps a distraction from the development of Canadian nationalism.

It is clear, then, that the effect of particular social acts on Canadian society as a whole may be a debatable issue. Disputes often rage not only over whether an event is dysfunctional or not but also over whether the consequences of an action are really as latent or unintended as is officially reported. For example, while English-speaking Canadians often referred to the early twentieth-century European immigration as a necessity to populate the land, and so lessen fears of American conquest, French Canadians have viewed this immigration policy, not in terms of unintended consequences, but as a deliberate effort to overwhelm French Canadians with a large population group which would eventually assimilate to the English culture. What was functional and perhaps unintended by the English-speaking elite was considered dysfunctional by French Canadians, and deliberately intended to destroy the French-English balance of power. What is functional for one segment of a society may not be so for another part of the society. Therefore, it is very difficult ever to determine what is functional for the nation as a whole without noting its probable negative consequences for some segment of the society.

Many of the strains that Canadian society has felt have centered on disputes over what is functional and to whom it is functional. What is good for the nation and its social cohesiveness for some persons, may be dysfunctional or negatively evaluated by others within the same society. The protective tariff, for example, may function to strengthen Canadian industry in the Golden Horseshoe, but at the same time may force Maritime residents and western farmers to pay higher prices for manufactured goods. Thus the functionalist debate in Canada has remained heated, particularly along regional lines, as different parts of the national society evaluate and compare what is to their advantage. Regional self-interest and national interests are often divergent matters that become the fount of bitter controversy.

Regional Variance: The Parts of the Social Organism

I have argued that the use of an organismic model to understand Canadian society is meaningful because it focuses on the way in which interaction among the parts of the societal unit contributes to the character and existence of the total unit. Therefore, any significant changes within the unit have repercussions on the shape and condition of the societal organism. While it may be assumed that there is a usual predilection to maintain the society intact, revolutionary activity, even leading to secession, cannot be ruled out. Indeed, regular conflict may be endemic to a society at the same time that, for instance, the preservation of Canada as a national society is a pre-eminent goal. It is my contention that one useful perspective on Canadian society is to determine how regional population diversity has been a barrier to social cohesion (or to a sense of belonging together) without, at the same time, producing the dismemberment of the national unit. From a theoretical point of view, I am suggesting that we examine the bases for social conflict that exist within Canada as an organismic, boundary-maintaining social system.

The sociologist perceives these conflicts within the national society not primarily in terms of economic or political factors, but rather in terms of differences in the characteristics of a population. For example, the greater the degree of variance in ethnic background, religious tradition, occupation, place of residence, or degree of assimilation among a society's members, the greater will be the difficulty in obtaining social cohesiveness. It is my argument, from a wholistic perspective, that the stresses and conflicts that exist within the Canadian society are experienced largely as a result of variations in the characteristics of the population from region to region.[8] In Canada, cross-pressures within the national society frequently have a regional basis in that every region tends to possess a population with characteristics sufficiently different from those found in another region. Canadian society, then, is further differentiated and divided by sociological factors that have a regional referent.

The significance of regionalism is an oft-repeated theme in discussions concerning Canadian society. Geographers have made particular use of the concept in noting the effects of physiographic, climatic, economic, or resource factors in fostering the identification of regions as individual units.[9] Another approach has been to view regions as products of a network of interchange focused on singularly large urban centers.[10] In either case, a region implies a significant land area that possesses a recognized common identity based on at least one criterion of homogeneity or common interest which enables the establishment of some type of boundary.[11] Anthropolgists speak of regions in terms of culture areas in which specific cultures are directly associated with particular geographic environments.[12] However, the massive difficulty in defining boundaries with any precision and in determining whether sufficient homogeneity exists within a region has called the accurate use of the concept into question.

Sociologists have been somewhat reluctant to speak of regions from within their discipline because this would assume a homogeneity among the people of a region that seldom exists. Differences may be more significant than superficial similarities, for every region could probably be divided into numerous subregions based on variant population characteristics. It may be preferable to speak of regionalism in the geographic sense because it does not necessarily imply the existence of a region as a homogeneous social grouping.

Nevertheless, the sociological tradition possesses a sub-discipline known as *human ecology* that directly attempts to relate human interaction with environmental factors. Most discussions about Canadian society imply that the geographic divisions of Canada have affected social interaction. B.Y. Card, for example, notes that since social interaction takes place in different territories, it is natural that differences in the experiences, interests, and attitudes of Canadians will exist.[13] What is less clear is whether it is possible to speak of the social entities produced by geographic factors as regional societies. Is there such a thing as a Maritime or Prairie society with distinctive traits all its own? A positive response assumes that a region is a type of social gestalt.[14] Because each region has its own history, its own mixture of people, and its own culture, a unique pattern or social configuration is formed that is peculiar to that particular region. As a well-known student of the Great Plains region, Carl Kraenzel, has argued, it is the complexity of interrelationships that form within a region that builds social cohesion within the unit.[15]

It is my contention that regionalism in Canada is more a product of interaction among areas within the national society than interaction within an area itself. It is the interaction among regions that produces the need for interrelationships to coagulate within a region.[16] Therefore, I am rejecting the idea that regions are necessarily areas with considerable social homogeneity. They are instead *areas in which the residents have formed interrelationships primarily through frequent interaction in a common environment.* Gordon Merrill speaks of regionalism in terms of identity as "an awareness of belonging to a distinctive part of Canada".[17] In any case, from a sociological perspective, a region can be a convenient category for the study of social life in areal terms.[18]

It is my task to point out how the population differs from region to region within Canada. But the major obstacle to this discussion is the determination of what constitutes a region. The traditional regional units have usually been identified as the Atlantic provinces, Quebec, Ontario, the Prairies, British Columbia, and the Territories. Other than the Atlantic and Prairie regions, the other regions are merely provincial designations which may or may not be a good means to specify regionalism. Surely northern Ontario and southern Ontario are considerably different areas in many ways. However, it has been pointed out that because provinces are administrative units reinforced by sociopolitical interaction, they have become near synonyms for regions.[19] Vallee's plea to consider regions within provinces rather than provinces as regions is certainly well taken;[20] however, it ignores the fact that regional boundaries vary, depending on whether we are talking about ethnicity or occupation or any other variable. Being cognizant of the problem of determining boundaries and the difficulty in collecting statistics for comparison when boundaries of a region can easily be changed, and noting how provinces do tend to form their own social configurations as a result of internal social interaction, I am electing to use provincial units as the basis from which regional differences in Canada can be pointed out. Where appropriate, provinces can be clustered together when, for various reasons, they evidence similar patterns.

Two qualifications of the central role that has been given to regionalism must be made. First, as has been already suggested, regions are not necessarily socially homogeneous units. Some regions may be more homogeneous than others, but for the purposes of the perspective of this chapter, the significant point is not that differences exist within a region but that differences exist among regions. Second, there is no implication that regional differences ought to be eradicated and a society-wide homogeneity serve as the ultimate national goal. Regional variance here is referred to merely as a fact of Canadian life that gives the society its character but also forms the basis for societal strain. It is my purpose, therefore, to discuss the numerous sociological factors which produce societal conflict as a result of regional variance.

The branch of sociology that deals with the statistical study of human population in given areas is known as *demography*. I will use demographic data to illustrate the nature of regional differences in population under four main headings: population distribution, population composition, population change, and internal population shifts.

POPULATION DISTRIBUTION

The distribution of a population is the nature of its geographic dispersion over a given area. Where does the Canadian population tend to live? To what extent is the Canadian population spread over its national territory?

Canada's 1971 population of 21,568,311 was contained within a territory of 3,851,809 square miles. [21] Canada's land space is less than half the size of Russia but more than forty times the size of Great Britain, and eighteen times the size of France. China (including Taiwan) and Brazil are just slightly smaller in size than Canada, with 3,705,408 square miles and 3,286,488 square miles respec-

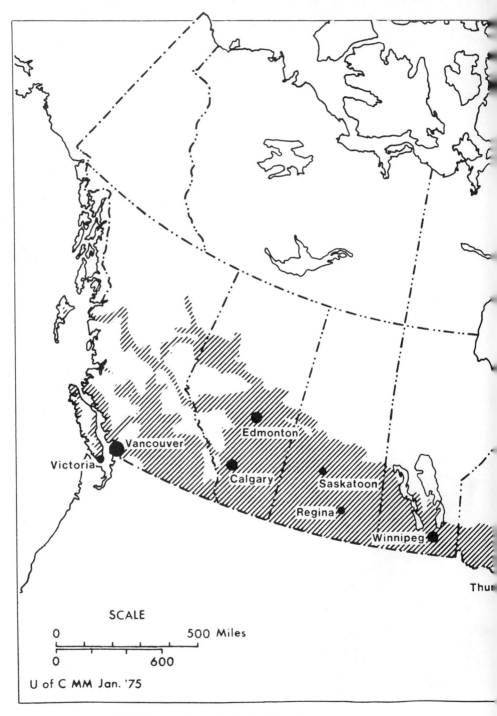

Source: Based on 1971 Census data, Statistics Canada.

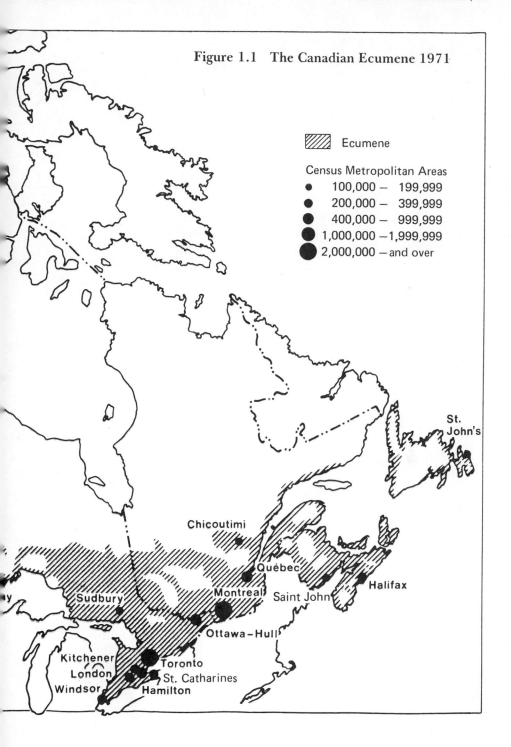

Figure 1.1 The Canadian Ecumene 1971

tively. It is interesting to note that while Brazil is slightly smaller in land size, her population is more than four times as large as Canada's. This perhaps gives us a clue that Canada has either a thinly dispersed population or that some factor makes a large geographic area of the nation less desirable or inhabitable. The latter in fact is the case. Both climate and terrain discourage significant settlement of over 85% of the land area.[22]

The term that is used to describe settled areas is *ecumene*, literally meaning inhabited space.[23] Population settlement is usually directly related to the land that is available for agriculture. It must be pointed out that in Canada less than 8% of the land surface is occupied farmland.[24] The fact that such a large percentage of the land is unavailable for agriculture results in sparse population settlement or no settlement at all on much of the land. Figure 1.1 illustrates the size of the *ecumene* in Canada. It can be seen easily that a relatively small strip lying adjacent to the U.S. border is the land area most heavily settled and utilized. Even though the northern areas are potentially habitable for activities other than agriculture, the slow movement of population to these locations produces a considerably uneven distribution of the population within Canada. Thus it becomes clear why north-south interaction across the border has frequently been more natural than east-west relationships within Canada.

If climate and terrain discourage settlement in some parts of Canada, they encourage it in other parts of Canada. Figure 1.2 shows how particular provinces have attracted larger population concentrations than others, and gives some indication of how history and climate have combined to disperse the population. Ontario possesses 35.7% of the total Canadian population and Quebec 27.9%. Together these two provinces contain 63.6% of the total Canadian population — an overwhelmingly dominant position within Confederation. British Columbia is next with 10.1%, the three Prairie provinces combined with 16.4%, and the four Maritime provinces with 9.5%. In spite of their earlier settlement, the Maritime provinces have failed to experience rapid growth and have even lost population to the industrial centers of Quebec and Ontario. The more favorable climate and terrain of southwestern British Columbia and southern Quebec and Ontario have attracted both farmers and industry. The development of a strong industrial base in these areas increased employment opportunities and furthered the population concentration by attracting both internal and external migrants. Certain provinces thus hold more powerful positions within the society by virtue of their claim to a larger per-

Figure 1.2 Percentage Distribution of the Population of Canada by Province, 1971

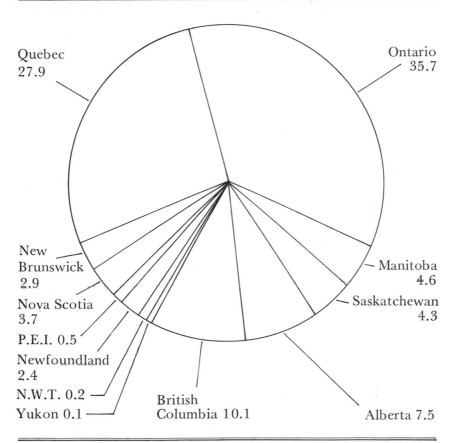

Quebec 27.9

Ontario 35.7

New Brunswick 2.9

Nova Scotia 3.7

P.E.I. 0.5

Newfoundland 2.4

N.W.T. 0.2

Yukon 0.1

British Columbia 10.1

Manitoba 4.6

Saskatchewan 4.3

Alberta 7.5

Source: Adapted from 1971 Census of Canada, Vol. I, Part 1, Statistics Canada, Cat. 92-702.

centage of the population. The uneven distribution of population reinforces the development of regionalism as smaller population aggregations attempt to counter the dominance of larger population aggregations.

The most densely populated areas in Canada are in those provinces that have been settled the longest. Because the Maritime provinces (except for Newfoundland) are the smallest in area, have the highest percentage of inhabited space, and have been settled the longest, they have the highest population density per square mile as shown by Table 1.3. Ontario follows very closely in density

Table 1.3 Population Density and Percentage Ecumene by Province, 1971

	Population	Density	% Ecumene*
Canada	21,568,311	6.06	12.4
Newfoundland	522,104	3.64	6.5
Prince Edward Island	111,641	51.08	100.0
Nova Scotia	788,960	38.67	49.7
New Brunswick	634,557	22.96	61.3
Quebec	6,027,764	11.50	11.6
Ontario	7,703,106	21.75	19.6
Manitoba	988,247	4.67	17.3
Saskatchewan	926,242	4.21	47.5
Alberta	1,627,874	6.61	30.0
British Columbia	2,184,621	6.34	14.4
Yukon	18,388	.09	.9
Northwest Territories	34,807	.03	.3

Source: Special Bulletin (SG-1), 1971 Census of Canada, Statistics Canada, Cat. 98-701. Reprinted by permission of Information Canada.

* Percentage of inhabited space within each province is adapted from R.T. Gajda, "The Canadian Ecumene — Inhabited and Uninhabited Areas", *Geographical Bulletin*, 15 (1960), p. 8. Gajda based his data on the *1958 Canada Yearbook*, and there has probably been a small increase in the size of the ecumene since then.

with 22.96 while Quebec, with a much larger land surface, follows with 11.50. The western provinces also have fairly large land surfaces but possess a much lower population density. The density differential points out another basis for regional variance within the nation.

Regional variance can also be expressed in the distribution of the population in rural and urban areas.[25] The lowest rates of urbanization in the country as shown by Table 1.4 are found in Prince Edward Island (38%) and Saskatchewan (53%). With these two exceptions, the percentage of the population that is urbanized in the Maritimes as a block is exactly 57%, while the Prairies hover around the low 70s. Quebec and Ontario are the most urbanized with percentages in the low 80s. It is surely a myth that Canada's population is rural and agricultural. Even provinces with a high rural population component, such as the Maritime provinces, consist predominantly of large, rural, non-farm populations often not

Table 1.4 Percentage of Urban, Rural Non-Farm, and Rural Farm Population by Province, 1971

	Urban	Rural Non-Farm	Rural Farm
Canada	76.1	17.3	6.6
Newfoundland	57.0	42.0	1.0
Prince Edward Island	38.0	43.0	19.0
Nova Scotia	57	40	3
New Brunswick	57	39	4
Quebec	81	14	5
Ontario	82	13	5
Manitoba	70	17	13
Saskatchewan	53	22	25
Alberta	74	12	14
British Columbia	76	21	3

Source: 1971 Census of Canada, Vol. I, Part 1, Statistics Canada, Cat. 92-709.

directly engaged in agriculture. While the heaviest concentration of agricultural activity is found in the Prairie provinces, it is these provinces that are also quite heavily urbanized. Clearly, while there are considerable degrees of urbanization within Canada, the distribution of Canada's population is concentrated in urban areas. A continuum would show that the Maritimes are the least urbanized, and Ontario and Quebec the most urbanized, with the Prairie provinces somewhere in between.

The significance of rural-urban differentials can be seen in Figures 1.5 and 1.6. Rural populations, as evidenced by the population pyramid, tend to be much younger with an especially large gap in the 20-40 year age group. Urban populations of 100,000 or more attract this age group into their opportunity and employment structure and swell their ranks with young employables and family units. This distinction is so marked that it points out the large void found in rural populations among young adults and the swollen ranks of the 20-40 year age group in urban populations. This leads us to conclude not only that some Maritime and Prairie provinces have experienced a considerable population drain of their most able people, but that provinces of large urban aggregations possess the necessary population to service industry and its subsidiary demands. Thus, regions with heavy urban concentra-

Figure 1.5   Distribution of Rural Farm Population by Age and
Sex, 1971

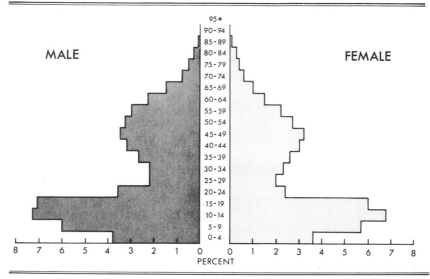

Source: Based on 1971 Census of Canada, Vol. 1, Part 2, Statistics
Canada, Cat. 92-715.

Figure 1.6   Distribution of Population in Urban Areas,
100,000 and Over, by Age and Sex, 1971

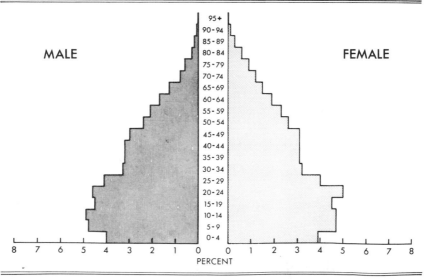

Source: Based on 1971 Census of Canada, Vol. 1, Part 2, Statistics Canada,
Cat. 92-715.

tions will contain a larger percentage of the distribution of the population in the 20-40 year age group.

The geographic dispersion of Canada's population within her national borders enables us to make some interesting observations qualified by regional variance.

1. Most of the population lives adjacent to the American border though climate and agriculture allow more northerly settlement in the Prairie provinces.
2. History, climate, and industry have favored the population growth and dominance of Ontario and Quebec so that they possess almost two thirds of the total Canadian population.
3. The smallest provinces with the most inhabitable territory have the highest population densities.
4. Contrary to an international myth, Canada's population is largely urban, with the lowest percentage of urbanization in the Maritimes and the highest in Ontario and Quebec.
5. Large urban areas possess a greater percentage distribution of the population in the younger and highly employable age group of 20-40 years.

POPULATION COMPOSITION

Not only is there considerable variation in the way in which the total population is distributed geographically within Canada's national territory, but there are also definite differences in the composition of the population in various parts of the country. It can be shown that regional distinctions are further compounded by differences in the characteristics of the inhabitants dwelling within each area.

A frequent characterization of Canadian society is that it is an ethnic mosaic. What is less frequently noted is that this mosaic varies with territoriality. If ethnic identities and traditions really do continue to persist within the society, then it is significant to note that the diversity of ethnic groups is rather unevenly dispersed throughout the nation. Regions tend to display considerable variance in terms of which ethnic peoples predominate and which ethnic groups are strong minorities. The variation in ethnic composition of the population from locale to locale within Canada has been a factor underlying regional difference and pressures on the national unit.

Table 1.7 illustrates the degree of ethnic variation from province to province. The dominance of one particular ethnic group is highest in Newfoundland (93.76% British), followed by Prince Edward Island (82.66% British), Quebec (78.95% French) and

Table 1.7 Percentage Composition of the Population by Specific Ethnic Groups for Each Province, 1971

	British Isles	French	German	Italian	Nether-lands	Polish	Scandi-navian	Ukrain-ian	Native Indian
Canada	44.62	28.65	6.10	3.38	1.97	1.46	1.78	2.69	1.36
Newfoundland	93.76	2.95	.45	.09	.12	.05	.22	.03	.23
Prince Edward Island	82.66	13.72	.85	.09	1.11	.09	.24	.11	.28
Nova Scotia	77.48	10.16	5.18	.47	1.88	.41	.51	.29	.56
New Brunswick	57.63	37.03	1.32	.21	.84	.10	.56	.09	.61
Quebec	10.61	78.95	.89	2.81	.20	.39	.14	.33	.54
Ontario	59.40	9.57	6.17	6.01	2.68	1.87	.78	2.07	.81
Manitoba	41.90	8.75	12.45	1.05	3.57	4.32	3.55	11.57	4.35
Saskatchewan	42.12	6.06	19.44	.30	2.05	2.90	6.38	9.27	4.36
Alberta	46.78	5.81	14.19	1.52	3.59	2.72	6.04	8.32	2.73
British Columbia	57.92	4.41	9.07	2.46	3.22	1.35	5.13	2.75	2.39
Yukon	48.65	6.66	8.45	.87	2.80	1.33	5.43	3.29	14.03
Northwest Territories	25.23	6.53	3.82	.70	.97	.77	2.58	1.80	20.62

Source: Adapted from Advance Bulletin, 1971 Census of Canada, Statistics Canada, Cat. 92-762.

Nova Scotia (77.48% British). With the exception of the Territories, the Prairie provinces of Manitoba, Saskatchewan, and Alberta possess the greatest diversity of ethnic group strength. In all three Prairie provinces, the British contribution to the population is less than 50% with strong representation from European nationality groups. In Ontario, British Columbia, and New Brunswick, almost 60% of the population is of British heritage in spite of the fact that the first two provinces possess considerable ethnic heterogeneity. New Brunswick is the exception to this pattern of one dominant ethnic group and a multi-ethnic minority in containing a stronger counterbalance of 37.03% French to the 57.63% British population than is found in any other province.

It is clear that while the Prairies have been dependent upon diverse European immigration to settle the land, the Maritimes have been more homogeneous as the result of growth from their British population base. The strength of the British ethnic majority continues throughout the Maritimes with the exception of that portion of New Brunswick bordering on Quebec where another ethnic majority, the French, dominates into Quebec and into the bordering areas of Ontario. From Ontario westward, numerous ethnic minorities proliferate in spite of the British centrality. The presence of large Italian, Ukrainian, and German minorities within each province, for example, has given these ethnic groups specific advantages which they are concerned to protect, and has contributed to a mosaic quite different from that of the Atlantic provinces.

Is it easy for the British-dominant Maritimes to understand and relate to the ethnic diversity of Manitoba with its strong Ukrainian contingent? Are their people not considerably different in terms of culture, tradition, and language from those of French Canada? How can the relatively mono-ethnic Quebec society identify nationally with Ontario, which has a high Italian concentration; or with Saskatchewan, which has a strong German contingent? These are all questions that emphasize the difficulty of relating the parts of the society to the whole. It is far more difficult to obtain social unity when ethnicity and its correlates of language, tradition, and world view are so diverse. The strains felt within the national society or conversely the lack of cohesion are directly related to this population heterogeneity. The fact that the expressions of ethnic diversity are regionally variant only compounds the unity problem.

Obviously the identification of intra-societal differences solely on the grounds of ethnic heritage is insufficient. In spite of our reluctance to accept the "melting pot" idea in Canada, ethnicity may no longer be as significant as the above data suggest. For example, according to the 1971 census, even though fairly large minorities in the Prairie provinces claimed languages such as German and Ukrainian as their mother tongue, English was still overwhelmingly the language most often spoken at home.[26] If historical statistics of the language most often spoken at home were available, no doubt they would show that the frequency of use of the mother tongue in the home was considerably greater in the past. The point is that, while ethnicity may have been and may still be a major aspect of differentiation within the society in terms of culture and traditions, assimilation and adjustment to the English language have provided at least a common medium for expression and communication.[27]

However, the emergence of English as the dominant language in some regions of Canada is countered by French as the dominant language in other parts of Canada. English is the language of the home for 99% of the Newfoundlanders;[28] however, it is the language of the home for only 67.9% of the residents of New Brunswick and for 14.7% of the residents of Quebec. Given the fact that it is in the home that language and tradition are nurtured, the 31.4% and 80.9% of the population of New Brunswick and Quebec that use French most often in the home are significant indeed. Thus, the region known as French Canada maintains its language in the face of other assimilationist pressures, and thereby increases its differentiation from other parts of the national society.

Table 1.8 Percentage Composition of Population by Official Language for Each Province, 1971*

	English Only	French Only	Both English & French	Neither English nor French
Canada	67.1	18.0	13.4	1.5
Newfoundland	98.0	0.1	1.8	0.1
Prince Edward Island	91.2	0.6	8.2	0.0
Nova Scotia	92.7	0.5	6.7	0.1
New Brunswick	62.6	15.9	21.4	0.1
Quebec	10.5	60.9	27.6	1.0
Ontario	87.3	1.2	9.3	2.2
Manitoba	89.2	0.5	8.2	2.1
Saskatchewan	93.6	0.2	5.0	1.2
Alberta	93.7	0.2	5.0	1.1
British Columbia	94.1	0.1	4.6	1.2
Yukon	93.2	0.0	6.6	0.2
Northwest Territories	73.2	0.3	6.1	20.4

* Respondents were asked, "Can you speak English or French well enough to carry on a conversation?"

Source: Adapted from Advance Bulletin, 1971 Census of Canada, Statistics Canada, Cat. 92-759.

Nevertheless, barriers to societal interaction in terms of language can be less significant if, as the federal government has been telling us, people are bilingual. Table 1.8 illustrates that the linguistic barrier is hardly being broken: a significant portion of the population can speak both English and French only in Quebec, New Brunswick, and in border areas of Ontario. A higher percentage of the residents of Quebec can speak both languages (27.6%) than of the residents of Ontario (9.3%). Interestingly, there has been an increase in bilingualism of only about 2% since 1961 with the greater gain recorded in Quebec.[29] It is thus clear that ethnicity and language are important correlates in the fragmentation of Canadian society. It is not so much that these differences cannot coexist, as that they strain the interaction. The existence of considerable monolingualism and of lingusitic regional blocs reduces the possibility of social integration.

Another important variable of regional differentiation is religious affiliation. Religion is an important sociological indicator because it is often closely correlated with ethnicity and social class, as well as being representative of a particular world view. Census data on religion obviously are not indicative of commitment or participation, but they do give us some measurement of religious preference. It is precisely because religious preference often gives us additional descriptive data on the population that it is significant to note regional differences in religious affiliation. Table 1.9 illustrates this diversity in demonstrating that, while 86.7% of the Quebec population is Roman Catholic, only 18.7% of the population of British Columbia claims Catholic affiliation. Similarly, while Saskatchewan claims 29.6% of its population as United Church members, Quebec only claims 2.9% as United

Table 1.9   Percentage Composition of Population by Religious Denomination for Each Province, 1971

	Roman Catholic	United	Anglican	Presby- terian	Lutheran	Baptist	Others
Canada	46.2	17.5	11.8	4.0	3.3	3.1	14.0
Newfoundland	36.6	19.5	27.7	.6	.1	.2	15.4
Prince Edward Island	45.9	24.9	6.2	11.7	.1	5.7	5.5
Nova Scotia	36.3	20.6	17.2	5.1	1.5	12.7	6.6
New Brunswick	52.2	13.4	10.9	2.1	.3	14.0	7.1
Quebec	86.7	2.9	3.0	.9	.4	.6	5.5
Ontario	33.3	21.8	15.8	7.0	3.5	3.7	14.8
Manitoba	24.6	26.0	12.4	3.1	6.6	1.9	25.5
Saskatchewan	27.9	29.6	9.4	2.2	9.8	1.6	19.4
Alberta	24.0	28.1	10.5	3.5	8.2	3.1	22.7
British Columbia	18.7	24.6	17.7	4.6	5.5	3.0	25.9
Yukon	25.4	16.9	25.3	3.8	5.0	4.7	18.9
Northwest Territories	41.3	8.6	36.4	1.3	2.1	1.1	9.1

Source: Adapted from Advance Bulletin, 1971 Census of Canada, Statistics Canada, Cat. 92-763.

Church. Over one quarter of the population of Newfoundland and the Territories is in the Anglican Church, whereas in Prince Edward Island only 6.2% is Anglican. Presbyterians and Baptists also evidence considerable variation in regional strength with the Presbyterians showing a higher percentage of affiliates in Prince Edward Island, and the Baptists displaying greatest strength in Nova Scotia and New Brunswick.

Several conclusions can be drawn from these variations. The Roman Catholic Church, the largest religious body in Canada, is strongest in the French-speaking regions of Quebec and New Brunswick. The strongest challenge to dominance by any single denominational body is in the area west of Ontario where the United Church claims a slightly larger percentage of the population. The greater ethnic heterogeneity of the West has produced a greater religious diversity among all groups, but particularly among those included under "Other" in the table. The Maritime provinces show less religious variance as most of the population is either Catholic, United, Anglican, or Baptist. The large Roman Catholic contingent in every province is thus challenged by a plurality of Protestants in which each main-line denomination alternates in strength with the region, although United and Anglican groups muster the most consistent opposing allegiance. However, while Protestantism is closely tied to English-speaking groups, Catholicism is strong, not merely because it is linked with French-speaking groups, but because it is also a common religious preference among other European ethnic groups settled in other parts of Canada.

Variance in ethnicity, language, and religion among Canada's population gives us further evidence of the regional differences that are present within the society. These variations can be summarized in the following way:

1. Ethnicity, language, and religion show a close regional correlation. A British heritage, Protestantism, and the English language are most likely in the Maritimes, Ontario, and the West; a French heritage, Catholicism, and the French language are most likely in Quebec and in the immediate provincial border regions.
2. Older and British-settled areas such as the Maritimes, Ontario and British Columbia tend to be more ethnically homogeneous (British), but share their religious domination between two of either United, Anglican, Presbyterian or Baptist.
3. The more ethnically diverse Prairie provinces also evidence greatest linguistic and religious diversity, though the United Church, itself a union, reduces this heterogeneity to some extent.

POPULATION CHANGE

Canada has grown tremendously from a population of 3 million in 1867 to a population of more than 21 million in 1971. Not only has this growth taken place in irregular spurts, but it has a variety of sources. Coupled with large-scale growth has been a significant paradoxical drainage of population from within Canadian borders. The fact that both this growth and loss have taken place unevenly throughout the society has contributed to regional differentiation. However, the main problem is that the society as a whole has experienced such population turnover that it has been difficult to forge permanent bonds of social unity and tradition. Coping with both in-migrants and population loss at the same time puts the society in a position of continual change in which perpetual adaptation and adjustment detract from the stability and the maturing process of normal interaction patterns.

Population growth takes place in two major ways: natural increase and immigration. *Natural increase* is determined by computing the total number of births in an area and subtracting the total number of deaths. Societies experience significant growth rates if the rate of fertility is considerably higher than the death rate. Canada's dependence on natural increase for its growth has popularly been underestimated. In spite of the fact that immigration

Table 1.10   Average Annual Rates of Natural Increase and Net Migration by Decades for Provinces, Canada, 1921-1931, 1931-1941, 1941-1951, 1951-1961

Province	1921-1931 Nat. Inc.	1921-1931 Net Mig.	1931-1941 Nat. Inc.	1931-1941 Net Mig.	1941-1951 Nat. Inc.	1941-1951 Net Mig.	1951-1961 Nat. Inc.	1951-1961 Net Mig.
Newfoundland	—	—	—	—	—	—	26.7	- 3.4
Prince Edward Island	9.2	-10.3	9.7	- 2.2	17.0	13.8	18.1	-11.1
Nova Scotia	9.9	-12.0	10.5	+ 1.5	17.1	- 6.4	18.6	- 5.0
New Brunswick	14.4	- 9.3	13.6	- 2.3	20.9	- 8.6	21.4	- 6.7
Quebec	19.1	+ 0.6	14.8	- 0.0	20.3	- 0.3	21.6	+ 4.4
Ontario	10.9	+ 4.9	7.7	+ 2.2	12.3	+ 7.4	17.6	+12.7
Manitoba	15.5	- 1.4	11.0	- 6.8	14.8	- 8.5	17.6	- 0.5
Saskatchewan	18.6	+ 1.3	14.2	-17.0	16.2	-23.9	19.5	- 9.0
Alberta	17.1	+ 6.6	13.7	- 5.4	18.7	- 0.9	23.6	+11.4
British Columbia	7.9	+20.0	5.5	+11.1	11.6	+23.0	16.0	+17.2
Yukon and Northwest Territories	—	—	6.2	+18.8	12.5	+16.7	29.0	+ 9.7

Source: From THE DEMOGRAPHIC BASES OF CANADIAN SOCIETY by Kalbach and McVey. Reprinted by permission of McGraw-Hill Ryerson Limited.

has been a very visible form of population increase, high fertility levels have been primarily responsible for the addition to Canada's population.[30] Table 1.10 indicates that with a few exceptions, the rate of natural increase was considerably higher than the net migration (total immigration minus total emigration) throughout Canada for the forty year period. The table shows that the rate of natural increase tended to attain its highest levels in the 1951-61 period. However, while the Canadian rate of natural increase was 19.6 in the 1956-60 time span, it had dropped significantly to 10.3 by 1969.[31] Ironically, Quebec, which previously had the highest birth rate in Canada, had the lowest crude birth rate in the country by 1969, and the highest rates of natural increase were held by Newfoundland, Alberta, New Brunswick, and Saskatchewan.[32] The significant fact about Table 1.10 is not only that there is considerable regional and historical variance in the causes for growth but that, in general, natural increase was a far more important source of growth than a positive migration flow. In fact, the Atlantic provinces and Saskatchewan depend on natural increase to restore population levels lost by emigration. Ontario, Alberta, and British Columbia are able to show significant total population increases because they are the recipients of migration flows and evidence healthy rates of natural increase.

The second predominant means of Canada's population growth has been immigration. Between 1851 and 1961, more than eight million immigrants came to Canada, and in the twenty years from 1946 to 1965 alone, two and one half million immigrants entered Canada.[33] During roughly the same period, the United States admitted over three and one half million postwar immigrants.[34] However, because the United States has over ten times the population of Canada, it can readily be seen that this influx had a far greater effect on Canadian society. At no point has the percentage of foreign born ever exceeded 22.3% of the total population but, for the last fifty years, the percentage has hovered around 20%.[35] The injection of a steady stream of British immigrants and short bursts of central, eastern, and then southern Europeans into the Canadian population have created immense societal pressures in assimilation and citizenship.

Seldom has the immigration into Canada proceeded at an even rate of dispersal in order to allow for the absorption and supposed disappearance of the migrant into the host society. Table 1.11 demonstrates that Ontario contains 51.8% of Canada's living foreign born. British Columbia, Quebec, and Alberta, in that order, have much smaller percentages of Canada's foreign born,

Table 1.11 Percentage of Foreign Born by Period of Immigration, for Canada and the Provinces

	% of Canada's Foreign Born	% of Province's Foreign Born	
	1971	Immigrated Prior to 1946	Immigrated 1946-1971
Canada	100.00	28.9	71.1
Newfoundland	0.2	15.8	84.2
Prince Edward Island	0.1	36.0	64.0
Nova Scotia	1.1	34.4	65.6
New Brunswick	0.7	40.4	59.6
Quebec	14.2	20.8	79.2
Ontario	51.8	22.3	77.7
Manitoba	4.5	45.9	54.1
Saskatchewan	3.3	70.4	29.6
Alberta	8.5	41.6	58.4
British Columbia	15.0	37.1	62.9
Yukon	0.0	21.0	78.8
Northwest Territories	0.0	15.8	84.2

Source: Adapted and computed from Advance Bulletin, 1971 Census of Canada, Statistics Canada, Cat. 92-761.

and even all together do not possess as many as Ontario. The western provinces contain the greatest percentages of foreign born who are "old timers" in that they migrated prior to 1946. From Ontario eastward, there is a smaller percentage of the earlier immigrants present, indicating the significance of the influx of postwar population into these provinces. The minute percentage of Canada's foreign born in the Maritimes and the low percentage of resident pre-1946 migrants indicates either a small immigrant population in the first place or a heavy loss of immigrants from the region after first settlement. The dominance of Ontario as an immigrant reception center in this century is clear in spite of heavy immigration to the plains in the early years of the century. As a general rule, postwar immigration tended to be from European urban centers to Canadian cities, whereas immigration before World War II was largely from European rural locations to Canadian rural areas.

The general effect of a high rate of natural increase interspersed with lower fertility during the depression and in the late 60s and early 70s is an ageing of the population. In-migration of young employables and families skews the trend somewhat, but the general tendency is that the Canadian population is getting older. According to Table 1.12, there is a greater percentage of the population in 1971 in the 10-14 and 15-19 age brackets than in 1951. Similarly, the percentage of the population seventy years of age and over has slowly increased from 3.1% in 1901 to 5.2% by 1971.

Table 1.12 Percentage Distribution of the Population by Five-Year Age Groups at Ten-Year Intervals, 1901-1971

Age Group	1901	1911	1921	1931	1941	1951	1961	1971
0 — 4	12.0	12.3	12.0	10.4	9.2	12.3	12.4	8.4
5 — 9	11.5	10.9	12.0	10.9	9.2	10.0	11.4	10.4
10 — 14	10.8	9.7	10.4	10.4	9.7	8.1	10.2	10.7
15 — 19	10.4	9.5	9.2	10.0	9.9	7.6	7.9	9.8
20 — 24	9.5	9.8	8.0	8.8	9.0	7.8	6.5	8.8
25 — 29	7.9	9.1	7.8	7.6	8.4	8.1	6.6	7.3
30 — 34	6.8	7.7	7.4	6.8	7.3	7.4	7.0	6.1
35 — 39	6.2	6.5	7.2	6.6	6.6	7.1	7.0	5.9
40 — 44	5.4	5.4	6.0	6.2	5.9	6.2	6.1	5.9
45 — 49	4.5	4.6	5.0	5.6	5.5	5.3	5.6	5.7
50 — 54	3.8	4.0	4.1	4.7	5.1	4.7	4.7	4.9
55 — 59	3.0	3.0	3.2	3.5	4.4	4.1	3.9	4.4
60 — 64	2.6	2.5	2.7	2.8	3.4	3.6	3.2	3.6
65 — 69	2.0	1.8	2.0	2.2	2.6	3.1	2.7	2.9
70+	3.1	2.8	2.8	3.3	4.1	4.7	5.0	5.2

Source: Compiled from 1961 Census of Canada, Vol. 1, Part 2, Statistics Canada, Cat. 92-542; and 1971 Census of Canada, Vol. I, Part 2, Statistics Canada, Cat. 92-715.

However, the ageing process has been altered not only by immigration but by emigration or movement away from Canada. If it is the ageing process that contributes to a society's durability and identity, it is the continual in-migration and out-migration of population that distracts from the formation of a cohesive social system. An influx presents one adjustment problem but a loss of population compounds the problem. Even though eight million people entered Canada through immigration between 1851 and 1961, it is estimated that more than six million left the country.[36]

Figure 1.13   A Comparison of Levels of Immigration and Emigration by Decade, Canada, 1851-1861 to 1961-1971

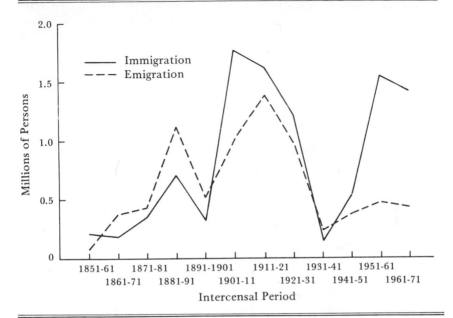

Source: Compiled from *Canada Yearbook 1957-58*, Statistics Canada, p. 160; Pierre Camu, E.P. Weeks, and Z.W. Sametz, *Economic Geography of Canada* (Toronto: Macmillan Co. of Canada, 1964), p. 58; *1971 Immigration Statistics*, Canada Manpower and Immigration, Table 2; and *Annual Report*, U.S. Immigration and Naturalization Service, 1966-1971. Emigration figures for 1961-1971 include only those who emigrated to the United States. Reprinted by permission of Information Canada and the Macmillan Company of Canada.

Figure 1.13 illustrates how close a shadow emigration has been to immigration through much of Canada's history. A large number of the emigrants were former immigrants who used Canada as a stop-off point for later migration into the United States. Others emigrated to the United States to take advantage of the employment possibilities in the burgeoning industrial enterprises of the northeastern states, particularly between 1867 and 1901. In spite of the opening of the West and increasing urbanization, emigration has been a continual drain on the Canadian population, though it has levelled off considerably in recent years.[37] Thus, from Confederation to 1967 Canada's growth was due largely to natural increase (14.5 million), whereas net migration produced only a 2.4

million increase.[38] This is not to minimize the effect of immigration on Canada, for it did infuse the society with new population to fill the gaps caused by emigration. It must also be acknowledged that the immigration of young couples and families from abroad contributed to the increased fertility within Canada.

The population making up Canada's national society has therefore been relatively unstable as the result of demographic changes caused primarily by immigration and emigration. Often the vacancy left by the emigrant was not filled by a person of similar ethnic background. Industrial societies are accustomed to adapting to geographical, occupation-related mobility; but international migration of the proportions of which Canada has been both recipient and donor, with consideration for the relatively small size of Canada's total population, has caused enormous difficulties in organizing the society around common goals and ends. Canadian society is thus a changing society which has experienced not merely rapid industrialization but also repeated accommodation to a changing population mix. Adaptation, accommodation, and adjustment to these demographic changes have understandably been dominant themes for Canadian society.

The reasons for population change within Canadian society can be expressed in the following observations:

1. A high rate of natural increase via high birth rates has produced most of Canada's population growth. It is most likely that social traditions and cohesiveness can develop when natural increase is the primary source of growth, and population ageing occurs naturally. The fact that Quebec and the Maritimes have evidenced greatest growth through natural increase has made it possible for traditions to form in a way not possible in regions of Canada where immigration levels have been higher.

2. The character of Canadian society has continually changed through the infusion of different ethnic groups at varying periods of history via immigration. For example, heavy pre-World War II immigration into the West brought one type of people and postwar immigration into Ontario brought migrants with different characteristics.

3. For many years, employment and other attractions within the society of Canada's southern neighbor have resulted in a perpetual drain of Canada's population. As a result, population instability has provided a weak base from which Canada could build her national society.

INTERNAL POPULATION SHIFTS

Regional cross-pressures have also been at work in the shifts and rearrangement of population within the nation. A redistribution of population for whatever reason changes the nature of a society's problems merely because it has altered previously existing social patterns. The growth of some regions or units within the region at the expense of other areas may have important repercussions: shifting the balance of power, creating gaping holes in local social organization (caused by out-migration), or arousing new problems produced by large-scale in-migration and higher population densities. There is generally an inequality in the way population shifts take place. Some areas lose more population than they gain and, as a result, lose their significance or bargaining role within the society; while other areas gain more than they previously possessed, thus increasing their power roles within a society. There are two major interrelated population shifts that have taken place within Canada that have had profound implications for the structure of the society: interprovincial migration and urbanization.

It could be argued that it is very difficult to organize socially a relatively new society that is experiencing repeated internal movements of its population. The historical variance in the settlement of the parts of Canada, the relationship of that settlement to different occupational pursuits, and the impact of increasing industrialization in changing the original settlement patterns have been largely responsible for the redistribution of the Canadian population.[39] The early settlement of coastal areas as trading and fishing centers in the tradition and order of colonial powers was considerably different from the more recent random settlement of the western plains by farmers of numerous ethnic groups who needed first to weld a basis for social interaction. The prior settlement of eastern agricultural land and its population saturation for that endeavor meant that the opening of the West would encourage a resettlement process. However, since most of Canada was really a vast hinterland, the society also needed centers of finance, administration, trade, and even manufacturing to foster the development of its primary industries. Thus as agricultural land was taken up, cities began to grow and develop.

Migration can be defined as any shift in population whereby a change in residence occurs. The movement of people within Canada has certainly not been a conscious resettlement policy but a type of migration known as *population drift*. Attracted by features of another area, individuals choose to move their residence to that new locale. Their migration may be prompted by a "push" such as the presence of a surplus population in relation to labor demands, or the "pull" of better opportunities elsewhere. The drift of people to new areas within Canada has been the result of both "push" and "pull" factors, and has changed the social landscape of the nation tremendously.

Kalbach and McVey suggest three reasons for population shifts both within regions and between regions in Canada.[40] Because Canada has experienced considerable immigration, it stands to reason that many people reached an initial destination in Canada that did not meet their expectations and thus sought an alternate location for residence at some later time. Secondly, many of the native born became disgruntled with the lack of opportunity where they lived and sought the more attractive possibilities in other parts of Canada. Thirdly, those areas experiencing the least economic growth possessed the highest rates of natural increase; higher fertility inevitably built tremendous population pressure in these areas, and thus out-migration was the most convenient means of reducing the pressure.

It is probable that internal migration would have been emigration if it had not been for the industrial boom in Canada. Particularly since World War II, urban centers have been the recipients of the major shift in residence among Canada's population.[41] The land had been overpopulated by agriculturalists and the mechanization of agriculture had released much of the labor that had previously been vital. All Canadian cities have demonstrated rapid growth, but cities with the biggest industrial base were ripe targets for the ensuing population shift. By 1971, Toronto, Montreal, and Vancouver were both retaining and increasing their dominant role within Canadian society by containing approximately 30% of Canada's total population and approximately 55% of Canada's population in cities of 100,000 and over. Therefore, with the unavailability of land for agriculture and the trend toward greater industrialization, interprovincial migration became almost synonymous with urbanization. Early population shifts may have been both to cities and rural areas, but since the 1930s the shift has been almost exclusively to urban centers.

Provinces that have evidenced the most out-migration have been those provinces without a large urban-industrial complex. The Maritime provinces as well as Saskatchewan have all lost population because of this shift. Table 1.14 shows that each of these provinces has only a small percentage of its population in census metropolitan areas (areas with a population of at least

Table 1.14   Percentage of Provincial Population in Census
Metropolitan Areas over 100,000, 1971

	CMA Population	Provincial Population	% of Provincial Population
Newfoundland			
St. John's	131,814	522,104	25.25
Nova Scotia			
Halifax	222,637	788,960	28.22
New Brunswick			
Saint John	106,744	634,557	16.82
Quebec			
Montreal	2,743,208		
Hull	149,230		
Quebec City	480,502		
Chicoutimi	133,703		
	3,506,643	6,027,764	58.17
Ontario			.
Toronto	2,628,043		
Ottawa	453,280		
Hamilton	498,523		
St. Catharines-Niagara	303,429		
London	286,011		
Windsor	258,643		
Kitchener	226,846		
Sudbury	155,424		
Thunder Bay	112,093		
	4,922,292	7,703,106	63.90
Manitoba			
Winnipeg	540,262	988,247	54.67
Saskatchewan			
Regina	140,734		
Saskatoon	126,449		
	267,183	926,242	28.85
Alberta			
Edmonton	495,702		
Calgary	403,319		
	899,021	1,627,874	55.23
British Columbia			
Vancouver	1,082,352		
Victoria	195,800		
	1,278,152	2,184,621	58.51
Total CMA Population	11,874,748	= 55.05%	
Canada's Population	21,568,311		

Source: Adapted from 1971 Census of Canada, Volume I, Part I, Statistics
Canada, Cat. 92-708.

100,000 people). This would indicate that they are seldom on the receiving end of population shifts and probably repeatedly lose population because of the trend toward metropolitan urbanization. In contrast, Quebec, Ontario, Manitoba, Alberta, and British Columbia each have census metropolitan areas that contain well over 50% of the province's population and usually possess at least one city that is overwhelmingly larger and is the major industrial center. It is these centers that are the recipients of our changing population distribution. This factor has led one author to claim that Canadians can now be understood only by looking to Canada's cities.[42]

While the shift from rural to urban has been a dominant theme within Canadian society for much of its history, there are some signs that internal population shifts of that nature have levelled off. Rural areas may have attained a population level that is conducive to large-scale farming and, as a result, we might expect that any further wholesale shifts of population from rural to urban are unlikely. What is increasing, however, is interurban migration. Even though all cities participate in this type of migration, Montreal, Toronto, and Vancouver receive the largest population gain. The extent of interurban migration was pointed out by a recent study in Western Canada. Roughly between 1948 and 1963, Saskatoon, Calgary, and Edmonton had shown a population increase of 116.3%, 143.2%, and 133.7% respectively.[43] Nevertheless, during approximately the same time period, 63%, 72%, and 66% respectively of the population resident in each of those cities in the initial year of that time span had migrated by the final year of the time period. One explanation for such rapid population turnover might be that smaller urban centers are merely intermediate residences for those moving from rural areas to the major centers of industrial activity. M.V. George's census study points out that 42.4% of the population of Canada aged five and over were internal migrants between 1956 and 1961.[44] The primary strength of regional urban migration was established in noting that 60% of these migrants were intramunicipal, 32% were intraprovincial, and 8% were interprovincial migrants.

In its short history, the face of Canada's society has changed markedly as industrialization has reconstructed rural and urban living. The fact that Quebec, Ontario, and British Columbia have been the destination of much of Canada's population shift has contributed to feelings of regional superiority and inferiority within the national society. Each part of the society thus enters into societal interaction with a relative position of advantage or disadvantage which often strains relationships among the regions as the result of what Schwartz describes as "institutionalized inequality".[45]

The movement of the population within Canada has also changed the character of the society. Since the most significant shift within the nation has been not only a movement from rural to urban but a movement to urban centers of over 100,000 population, we are speaking about a society with a specialized occupational structure, a complex corporate industrial base, and a whole set of social problems related to high concentrations of population. If Canadian society is now primarily a metropolitan society, it is obvious that the character of the society has changed substantially within its short history.

Our knowledge of the internal movement of population in Canada can be summarized in the following way:

1. The settlement of new territories within Canada fostered rural to rural migrations largely in a westerly direction until all agricultural land was occupied. Simultaneously, urban areas began to develop as financial, administrative, and trade centers, usually at port locations. Hinterland regions thus became intimately tied to these urban centers which developed a centripetal attraction.

2. Industrialization hastened a rural to urban shift as agriculture became mechanized and employment opportunities increased in the cities. Regional urban centers emerged and competed with urban industrial centers in attracting new population.

3. More recently, interurban migration has increased as a result of the relative industrial weakness of cities in some regions, which has created greater growth rates for a few cities in other regions.

From Regionalism to a National Society

It is clear that Canadian society does not consist of a homogeneous group of people with manifestly similar backgrounds who have lived together in the territory for a long period of time. In fact, just the opposite is true. The society has been constantly changing and has never attained a period of social stability and calm in which coherence and a common tradition could emerge naturally and throughout the society. The turnover of population through emigration and immigration; the fact that in-migration came in numerous waves and often each wave was of a different ethnic composition; the resultant variation in the degree of assimilation of the residents; the problems of creating patterns of social interaction between these diverse groups within the society; and the persistent shifting of population within the country due to urbanization and climatological factors — have all contributed to the lack of cohesion or "belonging together" within Canadian society. The national society is further divided by the fact that these continuous changes have taken place within a regional context. The uneven distribution and redistribution of population groups; the early settlement of some areas and the recent settlement of other regions; and the differential in population gains and losses so that some areas possess greater concentrations of the societies' members have produced numerous grounds for conflict within the societal unit. While it is these factors that produce problems for the national society, it is precisely these same qualities that give Canadian society her unique form and character.

Except for short recessions or depressions that are not particularly conducive to cementing a society, Canadian society as a whole has been in a perpetual state of development and growth. However, expansion and change are not notably good mechanisms for establishing social solidarity. It is understandable, then, that interaction within the society is often somewhat strained and that the parts of the society are not all attuned to what have been proclaimed as national goals. As a result, the society appears to possess a very diffuse national character because of its ethnic pluralism and population oscillation, and is very difficult to define as a unit,[46] to say nothing of the society's acting as a unit. Biculturalism or multiculturalism, for instance, may be politically useful policies but they reassert old loyalties and old traditions at the price of bypassing the Canadian loyalties and traditions necessary to give a society its peculiar character. As Porter has pointed out, cohesiveness and societal organization have been more likely to develop in Canada on the basis of regional or provincial loyalties.[47] It is at this level that ethnic, religious, or occupational understanding was more easily obtained. Part of the problem is that there are few mechanisms to socialize members of the society into the demands of the total society, and identification with the regional unit may come more naturally. A 1966 study demonstrated the tendency for residents of a region to prefer their own region to those of other provinces.[48] In a more recent study of first-year high school students, both French-Canadian and English-

Canadian students indicated a strong identification with their region.[49] It is interesting that only among some English-Canadian students was a strong national identification present as well.

But what is it that holds Canadian society together? Surely the diversity and regionalism that have been cited would have produced disorganization and societal breakdown if something did not provide the social cement to give the society at least minimal cohesion. Canada may lack sufficient permanence and durability, and may possess little self-identification, but is Canada nothing more than a political unit containing a collection of people living in scattered regions? To what extent does Canada form a society?

In a sense it is true that the political structure holds Canadian society together. By common agreement all regions send their representatives to Ottawa where, through the political process, rules are enacted that govern social interaction within national borders. The poorer regions need the goods produced by the industrial centers, and the industrial centers need the hinterlands for their resources and market. Thus political and economic necessity have created and maintain the society and produce the penchant for order that has crushed rebellious regional activity. The judical declaration "ultra vires" and the Emergency Measures Act have been utilized as political tools to contain regional demands in order to hold the society together forcibly.

It is not surprising, then, that Canada's political obsession is said to be the quest for national unity.[50] If Canada is merely a loose federation of regions and does not possess a social homogeneity or sufficient social links to bind those regions, then a society held together only by political and economic agreement is frail indeed. It might be argued that the fragmentation of Canada was assured by the fact that Ontario and Quebec, the two dominant provinces in population size and resources, were of two different cultures and thus ruled out any idea of a joint conspiracy at the expense of the weaker provinces.[51] However, in spite of regional differences and disparities, there does persist an ephemeral ideal of societal unity as a significant ultimate goal. If Canadian society does tend to exhibit a cautiousness or conservative orientation,[52] it has been molded from this desire to preserve the national unit intact.

Amidst population flux and diversity, there is undoubtedly emerging a more durable and stable population from the core of those who have lived in Canada for several generations. As emigration and immigration are reduced by tighter migration restrictions, and as industrialization and urbanization reach their apex, social solidarity and identification with the societal whole will become more likely. The loss of regional identities might be a great national loss, but what can be hoped for is better understanding and a clearer concern for the mutual well-being of all the parts that make up the national society.

If regions are the parts of the Canadian social organism, then it is clear that significant differences between regions have the potential of serving as barriers for free and equal interaction. One important way of viewing Canadian society is in terms of these regional population differences. The further determination of regional economic, historical, political, or geographic differences in addition to these population differences would also be instructive in illuminating the nature of this issue in Canada. Yet, the question whether regions are the basis for national divisions or merely complementary to each other requires attention to other factors that we will consider.

QUESTIONS FOR FURTHER EXPLORATION

1. *Does Canada need all her constituent parts to function as a society? Could parts of the society exist just as well independently?*
2. *Is some type of national crisis needed to weld the residents of Canada into a societal unit?*
3. *Should the urbanization of our best agricultural land with its preferable climate be restricted, and only land more unsuitable for agriculture be allotted for urbanization?*
4. *Have immigrant groups been encouraged to maintain their ethnicity because no one knows what is "Canadian"?*
5. *Do you think that it is appropriate to speak of the population within Canada's national borders as a society?*

NOTES

[1] T.B. Bottomore, *Sociology: A Guide to Problems and Literature*, rev. ed. (London: George Allen & Unwin, 1971), p. 116.

[2] Statistics Canada, *1971 Census of Canada*, Vol. I, Part 1, Cat. nos. 92-708 and 92-709.

[3] Don Martindale, "The Sociology of National Character", *The Annals of the American Academy of Political and Social Science*, Vol. 370 (March 1967), pp. 30-35.

[4] Auguste Comte, *The Positive Philosophy,* trans. and ed. by H. Martineau (London: Kegan Paul, Trench & Trubner, 1893).

[5] Herbert Spencer, *The Principles of Sociology* (New York: D. Appleton and Co., 1893).

[6] For an example of this approach, see Walter Buckley, *Sociology and Modern Systems Theory* (Englewood Cliffs, New Jersey: Prentice-Hall, Inc., 1967).

[7] For a discussion of this role of the RCMP, see Lorne and Caroline Brown, *An Unauthorized History of the RCMP* (Toronto: James Lewis & Samuel, 1973).

[8] Compare with Rupert Vance who argues that regionalism is essentially the study of the relation of parts to wholes, i.e. the relation of the region to the total national structure. "The Regional Concept as a Tool for Social Research" in Merrill Jensen, ed., *Regionalism in America* (Madison: University of Wisconsin Press, 1952), p. 119.

[9] See D.F. Putnam and R.G. Putnam, *Canada: A Regional Analysis* (Toronto: J.M. Dent & Sons Canada, 1970), and John Warkentin, *Canada: A Geographical Interpretation* (Toronto: Methuen, 1968).

[10] For example, N.H. Lithwick and Gilles Paquet, "Urban Growth and Regional Contagion", *Urban Studies: A Canadian Perspective* (Toronto: Methuen, 1968), pp. 18-39.

[11] For a discussion of the characteristics of a region see N.L. Nicholson and Z.W. Sametz, "Regions of Canada and the Regional Concept" in R.R. Krueger, F.O. Sargent, A. DeVos, N. Pearson, eds., *Regional and Resource Planning in Canada* (Toronto: Holt, Rinehart & Winston of Canada, 1963), pp. 6-23.

[12] Harold B. Barclay, "On Culture Areas and Regions in Anthropology", in B.Y. Card, ed., *Perspectives on Regions and Regionalism* (Edmonton: University of Alberta Press, 1969), pp. 3-9.

[13] B.Y. Card, *Trends and Change in Canadian Society* (Toronto: Macmillan Co. of Canada, 1968), p.9.

[14] H.W. Odum and H.E. Moore, *American Regionalism* (Gloucester, Mass.: Peter Smith, 1966), p. 413.

[15] Carl F. Kraenzel, "Great Plains Regionalism Reconsidered", in B.Y. Card, ed., *Perspectives on Regions and Regionalism* (Edmonton: University of Alberta Press, 1969), pp. 77-90.

[16] For a discussion of regionalism in a political context see M.A. Schwartz, *Public Opinion and Canadian Identity* (Berkeley: University of California Press, 1967), pp. 146-158.

[17] Gordon Merrill, "Regionalism and Nationalism", in J. Warkentin, *Canada: A Geographical Interpretation* (Toronto: Methuen, 1968), p. 559.

[18] Louis Wirth, "The Limitations of Regionalism", in Merrill Jensen, ed., *Regionalism in America* (Madison: University of Wisconsin Press, 1952), p. 392. For a Canadian regional study, see Richard Allen, ed., *A Region of the Mind: Interpreting the Western Canadian Plains* (Regina: Canadian Plains Study Center, 1973).

[19] P.W. Fox, "Regionalism and Confederation", in Mason Wade, ed., *Regionalism in the Canadian Community, 1867-1967* (Toronto:

University of Toronto Press, 1969), pp. 5, 28. For a good discussion on the dimensions and meanings of regionalism in Canada see Mildred A. Schwartz, *Politics and Territory: The Sociology of Regional Persistence in Canada* (Montreal: McGill-Queen's University Press, 1974), Chapter I.

[20] Frank G. Vallee, "Regionalism and Ethnicity: The French Canadian Case", in B.Y. Card, ed., *Perspectives on Regions and Regionalism* (Edmonton: University of Alberta Press, 1969), pp. 19-25.

[21] *Canada Yearbook, 1972* (Ottawa: Statistics Canada), p. 27. Comparative figures that follow are also based on this source, p. 27.

[22] See Table 1.3.

[23] R.T. Gajda, "The Canadian Ecumene — Inhabited and Uninhabited Areas", *Geographical Bulletin*, 15 (1960), p. 6.

[24] *Canada Yearbook, 1972*, p. 27.

[25] The 1971 Census of Canada defines as urban all incorporated or un-incorporated cities, towns, and villages with a population of 1,000 or over, or built-up fringes with a density of at least 1,000 persons per square mile. Rural farm population must live in dwellings located on farms of at least one acre, with sales of agricultural products of at least $50. Rural non-farm population refers to all persons not included in either of the above categories.

[26] The Census defines mother tongue as "the language first spoken in childhood and still understood". For example, 7.3% of the population of Manitoba claimed Ukrainian as their mother tongue, and 8.3% claimed German. However, only 3.4% and 4.0% respectively said that Ukrainian or German was the language most often spoken at home. Manitoba had the highest percentage of its total population claiming a language spoken most often at home that was neither English nor French.

[27] Except for the Northwest Territories where only 58.2% claimed English as the language most often spoken at home, and the French-speaking populations of Quebec and New Brunswick, the provincial population with the lowest percentage of persons using English as the language of the home was Manitoba with 82.6% and the highest was Newfoundland with 99.1%. See Table 1, Advance Bulletin, 1971 Census of Canada, Cat. 92-759.

[28] All statistics on language most often used in the home are taken from Table 1, Advance Bulletin, 1971 Census of Canada, Cat. 92-759.

[29] Comparative data available in Table 2, Advance Bulletin, 1971 Census of Canada, Cat 92-759. For a discussion of the "Bilingual Belt Thesis", see Richard Joy, *Languages in Conflict* (Toronto: McClelland & Stewart, 1972) and Chapter 4 in this book.

[30] For a historical review of fertility patterns in Canada, see W.E. Kalbach and W.W. McVey, *The Demographic Bases of Canadian Society* (Toronto: McGraw-Hill Ryerson, 1971), pp. 55-67.

[31] *Canada Yearbook, 1972*, p. 242.

[32] *Canada Yearbook, 1972*, pp. 249, 272.

[33] Anthony H. Richmond, *Post-War Immigrants in Canada* (Toronto: University of Toronto Press, 1967), p. 4.

[34] Warren Kalbach, *The Impact of Immigration on Canada's Population* (Ottawa, Statistics Canada, 1970), p. 338.

[35] *The Impact of Immigration on Canada's Population,* p. 25.

[36] Leroy Stone, *Migration in Canada: Regional Aspects* (Ottawa: Statistics Canada, 1969), pp. 22-26. For an excellent general discussion on population change in Canada see Pierre Camu, E.P. Weeks, and Z.W. Sametz, *Economic Geography of Canada* (Toronto: Macmillan Co. of Canada, 1964), Chapter 3.

[37] The significance and size of this out-migration is debated in K.V. Pankhurst, "Migration between Canada and the United States", *The Annals of the American Academy of Political and Social Science,* Vol. 367 (September 1966), pp. 53-62.

[38] T.R. Weir, "Population Changes in Canada, 1867-1967", *The Canadian Geographer,* Vol. 2, No. 4 (1967), p. 198.

[39] For a discussion of the history and nature of interprovincial migration in Canada see Leroy Stone, *Migration in Canada: Regional Aspects,* pp. 26-47; also M.V. George, *Internal Migration in Canada: Demographic Analyses* (Ottawa: Statistics Canada, 1970).

[40] W.E. Kalbach and W.W. McVey, *The Demographic Bases of Canadian Society,* pp. 74-75.

[41] See Leroy O. Stone, *Urban Development in Canada* (Ottawa: Statistics Canada, 1967), particularly pp. 17-24.

[42] James and Robert Simmons, *Urban Canada* (Toronto: Copp Clark, 1969), p. 163.

[43] R.E. DuWors, "Prevailing Life Perspectives and Population Shifts in the Canadian Prairie Provinces", in Carle C. Zimmerman and Seth Russell, eds., *Symposium on the Great Plains of North America* (Fargo: North Dakota Institute for Regional Studies, 1967), p. 75. See also R.E. DuWors, J. Beaman and A. Olmsted, *Studies in the Dynamics of the Residential Populations of Thirteen Canadian Cities* (Winnipeg: Center for Settlement Studies, University of Manitoba, 1972).

[44] M.V. George, *Internal Migration in Canada: Demographic Analyses,* p. 119.

[45] Mildred Schwartz, *Politics and Territory: The Sociology of Regional Persistence in Canada,* p. 336.

[46] See John Porter, "Canadian Character in the Twentieth Century", *The Annals of the American Academy of Political and Social Science,* Vol. 370 (March 1967), p. 49.

[47] John Porter, *The Vertical Mosaic* (Toronto: University of Toronto Press, 1965), p. 370.

[48] Mildred Schwartz, "Attachments to Province and Region in the Prairie Provinces", in D.K. Elton, ed., *One Prairie Province? A Question for Canada* (Lethbridge: Lethbridge Herald, 1970), pp. 101-105.

[49] Donald M. Taylor, Lise M. Simard, and Frances E. Aboud, "Ethnic Identification in Canada: A Cross-Cultural Investigation", *Canadian Journal of Behavioral Science,* Vol. 4 (January 1972), pp. 13-20.

[50] John Porter, *The Vertical Mosaic*, p. 369.

[51] James Ross Hurley, "Federalism, Coordinate Status, and the Canadian Situation", *Queen's Quarterly*, Vol. 73 (1966), pp. 147-166.

[52] See Frank G. Vallee and Donald R. Whyte, "Canadian Society: Trends and Perspectives", in B.R. Blishen, F.E. Jones, K.D. Naegele, J. Porter, eds., *Canadian Society: Sociological Perspectives* (Toronto: Macmillan Co. of Canada, 1971), p. 559; and John Porter, "Canadian Character in the Twentieth Century".

2
Stratification and Internal Power Model

Chapter 1 attempted to present clear evidence of the social and regional diversity that is characteristic of Canadian society. From a sociological perspective, this diversity is not primarily the result of individual differences among people but a consequence of their belonging to the larger social groupings with which we identify them. Sociologists use the term *social differentiation* to refer to the process by which persons are distinguished and classified according to the groups to which they belong. Social differentiation is a technical term that indicates that population aggregations sort themselves into smaller units based on common characteristics such as race, ethnicity, or religion. However, there is another aspect of social differentiation that this chapter will seek to explore, i.e. the tendency for members of a society to rank themselves on the basis of wealth, power, and prestige. *Ranking* is the status order that develops in a society. Its existence greatly affects the form and nature of interaction patterns within that society.

Social stratification, the result of the ranking which has occurred in a society, produces a hierarchical gradation of persons and clusters them according to similarity of rank. In our society, such a gradation is usually based on the degree of personal possession of scarce and desirable traits. For instance, if money is scarce and desirable, then it can be expected that those who are wealthy will be popularly assigned a higher rank. Just as a geologist notes how sedimentary deposits and upheavals of molten lava contribute to the production of strata or layers of rock that become relatively permanent, so a sociologist observes how movements and upheavals of societies ultimately result in relatively enduring social structures stratified according to criteria particularly valued in the society. A study of stratification is significant not merely because it establishes the existence of differences in rank among persons in a society, but because it shows how rank is closely correlated with power and therefore control over the rest of the society.

This chapter, then, is concerned both with discerning the nature of the ranking that is part of the structure of Canadian society and with the exercise of power or lack of power that ensues. For some readers this approach may be a bit unsettling at first because it exposes elements of the status quo that are preferably ignored. However, a social scientist describes and analyzes what is actually occurring, and stratification patterns are part of the description and reality of every society. Members of a society must be aware of the nature of the stratification system that exists and understand its effects on the society as a whole.

Deeply imbedded in the ideology of modern Western democracies is the notion of human equality. Whatever the principle of equality may mean in terms of equal rights and obligations, a concept of equality that insists that all people are the same does not conform to reality. Because every society possesses a ranking system of roles and statuses, authority and its consequent rewards become unequally distributed among the members of the society. Because some people possess capabilities that are scarce or engage in activity that requires greater responsibilities, a differential of rewards results in social inequality. While these inequalities are observed in individuals, the notion of stratification implies that all persons of a similar rank can be grouped on the basis of their similar status. Therefore, a study of rank and power is a study of the interactions among groups of people representing various strata. Social tensions resulting from differentials in social class and social power account for the color and explain much of the history of Canadian society.

Objective Indices of Rank

Our everyday vocabulary is replete with such terms as "upper crust", "underprivileged", "laborer", "haves and have-nots", and "wrong side of the tracks" that indicate our identification of various strata within the society. Popular designation often ties the concept of class directly to wealth and is usually not far wrong since money is highly correlated with other factors, such as lifestyle and world view. Even though sociologists do not always agree regarding the components and significance of social class in a society, social scientists most frequently combine measurements of income, education, and occupation as an adequate index for the ranking and clustering of individuals in social classes. The way a person thinks, where he lives, how he spends his time, and with whom he interacts is determined to a great extent by his income, level of education, and occupation. In other words, these three indices in the Canadian context are closely correlated with rank differentiations and together allow us to identify social strata. This is not to say that class boundaries can be sharply determined, although it is true that the highest and lowest levels are more easily demarcated. Furthermore, class lines are frequently blurred and there are many marginal cases in which a precise social class designation is inappropriate. Nevertheless, the persisting differences in income, education, and occupation in a society reveal a hierarchy among its citizens in which a clustering and stratifying process is observable.

Because rank is often difficult to determine objectively, income, education, and occupation are most frequently used as indicators of population stratification because they can be measured fairly precisely. The amount of income received and the years of education obtained permit relatively easy comparions between individuals on a statistical level, and together tell us something about the ranked value of occupation. Stratification studies in Canada have been increasing though they are somewhat fragmented in presenting a comprehensive and up-to-date picture of this phenomenon.[1] However, some data on each of these indices have been accumulated and they clearly evidence the existence of a stratified society.

INCOME

A study of the way in which a society distributes all earned income to its members most markedly demonstrates the presence of inequality and valuated differences among people. Because income is directly related to purchasing power, which in turn determines standard of living and life-style, a host of other characteristics can be predicted by noting a person's relative location in an income level.

One of the first sociologists to study systematically income differentials and distributions in Canada was John Porter. Using 1955 and 1957 data, Porter discovered that a surprisingly large proportion of people existed on low income. He pointed out that the lowest 20% of all taxpayers received less than one tenth of the total income obtained by all Canadians.[2] In the higher-income levels, one fiftieth of all taxpayers (i.e. those earning over $10,000) received more than one tenth of all income. The implication of his findings was that in Canada the very poor were a relatively large group and the very rich a relatively small group.

Basing her argument on 1961 census statistics, Jenny R. Podoluk has done an exhaustive study of income distribution in a book entitled *Incomes of Canadians*.[3] Podoluk was careful to point out that cash income may not necessarily be equivalent to real income, for items like agricultural products or non-monetary welfare benefits have monetary value though not in that form. Nevertheless, she argued that cash income still enables us to determine the nature of the inequality that does exist in the society. In the first place, her study evidenced glaring differences in income between men and women. Income of women was substantially

Table 2.1 Percentage Distribution of Income Recipients and
Aggregate Income by Income Group and by Sex, 1961

	Distribution of Income Recipients			Distribution of Aggregate Income		
	Male	Female	Total	Male	Female	Total
Under $999	9.0	17.1	26.1	1.4	2.5	3.9
1,000–1,999	7.3	7.7	15.0	3.4	3.5	6.9
2,000–2,999	8.6	6.1	14.7	6.8	4.7	11.5
3,000–3,999	11.7	3.6	15.4	13.0	3.9	16.9
4,000–4,999	10.2	1.2	11.5	14.6	1.7	16.3
5,000–5,999	6.6	0.5	7.1	11.3	0.9	12.2
6,000–9,999	7.1	0.5	7.6	16.6	1.2	17.7
10,000 and over	2.5	0.2	2.6	13.5	0.9	14.4
	63.0	36.9	100.0	80.6	19.3	100.0

Source: Computed and adapted from Jenny R. Podoluk, *Incomes of Canadians*,
Ottawa: Statistics Canada, 1968, Tables 3.4 and 3.5, p. 23.

lower than that of men. Table 2.1 shows that in the distribution of
income recipients, there were more women receiving income under
$2,000 than men (24.8% as opposed to 16.3% for men), although
they received a slightly higher percentage of the aggregate income
(6% for women and 4.8% for men). At all higher-income levels,
men received overwhelmingly higher percentages of the total
income. Although women constituted almost 37% of all income
recipients, they obtained only 19.3% of the aggregate income. This
tells us something about the role of men as primary wage earners
in our society, and perhaps suggests why social rank for families is
usually correlated with the male income.

Table 2.1 also demonstrates another stratification pattern
when a comparison is made between percentage totals of those
receiving an income in a category and the percentage of the aggregate income that that category received. For example, at the lowest level (under $1,000) 26.1% of all income recipients obtained
only 3.9% of the aggregate income distributed, whereas at the
highest level ($10,000 and over) 2.6% of all persons reporting
income obtained 14.4% of all income distributed. In 1961, 17.3%
of the population had income of $5,000 and over, but obtained
44.3% of the total reported income. The table is perhaps more
exactly significant at the higher levels because the lower levels are
partially inflated by family members who enter the labor force

only on a part-time or seasonal basis. However, this factor does not alter the essential point of the table.

Table 2.2 Percentage Distribution of Income by Quintiles, Non-Farm Families, 1951 and 1965

	1951	1965
First (lowest)	6.1	6.6
Second	12.9	13.3
Third	17.4	18.0
Fourth	22.4	23.5
Fifth (highest)	41.1	38.6
	100.0	100.0

Source: Adapted from Jenny R. Podoluk, "Some Comparisons of the Canadian-U.S. Income Distributions" (Ottawa: Statistics Canada, 1969), p. 14.

Table 2.2 shows the distribution of income in quintiles (20% groupings of the population). In 1965, the lowest 20% grouping of the population obtained only 6.6% of the total income, whereas the highest quintile received 38.6% of the income — considerably more than any other quintile. The figures gradually increase from the first to the fifth quintile indicating that a definite hierarchy of income exists.

It has been argued frequently in Canada that income inequalities should be reduced through the payment of government subsidies to those with low income. The postwar years saw a steady increase in the number of transfer payments made by the government. However, as Podoluk discovered, a substantial proportion of these government transfer payments has been received by families in the middle and upper income brackets, indicating that an expanded welfare system has not reduced inequality.[4] Table 2.2 gives some evidence that from 1951 to 1965 slight changes did occur, particularly in the growth of the fourth quintile, but that the basic inequality in income distribution remained. In spite of rising productivity and an attendant rise in the absolute standard of living, an inequality of income persists.[5] If level of income implies variability in purchasing power, then income will have socially visible effects which will make differences in rank more observable.

More recent data on the income of Canadian families continue to support the notion of an existing differential in financial resources. Table 2.3 reveals that in 1971 well over one half of the families of Canada had a combined family income of less than $9,000. Yet the considerable variation in family income can be noted by observing the spread from the low to the high range. Even though medium to low incomes predominate, the existence of some significantly high incomes makes the stratification pattern within Canadian society more noticeable.

Table 2.3   Income of Families,* Canada, 1971

Income Range	No. of Families	% of Total Families
Under $3,000	556,525	10.96
$3,000 – $5,999	936,885	18.46
$6,000 – $8,999	1,219,680	24.03
$9,000 – $11,999	1,032,695	20.34
$12,000 – $14,999	610,950	12.04
$15,000 – $19,999	423,130	8.34
$20,000 – $24,999	139,390	2.75
$25,000 and over	141,245	2.78

Total Families – 5,076,085
Average Income – $9,600
Median Income – $8,544

* Family excludes those non-family persons who live alone or who are not in a husband-wife or parent-unmarried child relationship. The total family income is computed by determining the sum of all incomes received by members of the family fifteen years of age and over.

Source: Compiled from Advance Bulletin, 1971 Census of Canada, Statistics Canada, Cat. 93-746, Table 1.

EDUCATION

In an industrial society, differences in the level and type of education obtained by its members are a significant factor in stratification. Because industrialization demands a high level of specialized training and job expertise, education becomes the key to success in the system. Therefore, better education leads to a better occupation which in turn generally results in a higher income. Education, then, is an important factor in the determination of rank order in Canada, for some persons are better prepared than others for participation in the industrial system. As we will see, it is a significant point in Porter's argument that education of the Canadian labor force did not keep pace with the demand for highly skilled personnel.[6]

Figure 2.4 Educational Attainment of the Population, 25 Years of Age and Over, 1965

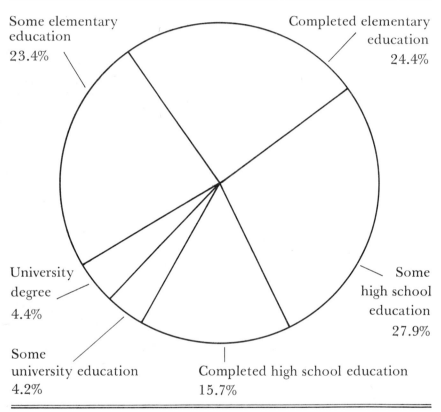

Some elementary education 23.4%

Completed elementary education 24.4%

University degree 4.4%

Some high school education 27.9%

Some university education 4.2%

Completed high school education 15.7%

Source: Adapted from Frank J. Whittingham, *Educational Attainment of the Canadian Population and Labour Force: 1960-1965*, Special Labour Force Studies, No. 1 (Statistics Canada, 1966), p.8.

Figure 2.4 provides evidence that there are vast differences in the level of education attained by the Canadian population as a whole. In 1965, 47.8% of the population 25 years of age and over had less than a Grade 9 education. As the highest level of their schooling, only 15.7% had a complete high school education, while 8.6% had at least some university training. It becomes clear that if education is a key factor in the establishment of rank in an industrial society, the bulk of Canada's population is poorly educated and inferior to a relatively small stratum of well-educated persons. However, one note of caution regarding these statistics is in order. The data refer to the total population over 25 years of age and are not restricted to the labor force, i.e. those under 65. If the statistical base is limited to this segment of the population, a slight improvement in educational level is noticeable.[7]

Table 2.5   Population 15 Years of Age and over Not Attending School Full Time, by Level of Schooling, 1971

Elementary (Less than Grade 9)	34.7%
Secondary (Grades 9–13)	38.0%
Vocational and Post-Secondary (regardless of level of public schooling attained)	17.4%
Some University	5.1%
University Degree	4.7%

Source: Adapted from 1971 Census of Canada, Vol. I, Part 5, Statistics Canada, Cat. 92-743.

In Table 2.5 the age spectrum is broadened to include those 15 years of age and up, excluding students. The percentage of those with less than a Grade 9 education drops from 47.8% to 34.7% in this 1971 census survey, and the percentage of those with a higher level of schooling increases. If vocational education is added to the secondary schooling percentages, 55.4% of the Canadian population had at least some secondary schooling as their highest level of education in comparison to 43.6% in the Whittingham study (though vocational schools are not singled out there). Similarly, the percentage of those with at least some university education has jumped from 4.2% to 5.1%, while the percentage of those with a university degree has shown only a slight increase from 4.4% to 4.7%. Thus, it is clear that a general improvement in the educational level of the Canadian population is taking place, particularly at the secondary and vocational levels.

Canadians often pride themselves on possessing a public educational system that makes higher education available to all members of the society. Intelligence and academic performance are considered to be the only criteria by which participation in higher education is determined. If that is so, it is somewhat surprising that so few obtain a university education. A number of Canadian studies have demonstrated that socioeconomic factors rather than intelligence are significant in determing the level of schooling attained. In a study in the Ontario community of Thunder Bay, Pavalko determined that entrance into Grade 13 (roughly equivalent to first-year university in other parts of Canada) was related to socioeconomic background rather than to high, measured intelligence.[8] 75% of those with high, measured intelligence and high socioeconomic background entered Grade 13, whereas only 52% of the students with high, measured intelligence and low socioeconomic background went on to Grade 13. Given a similar level of intelligence, location in the stratification system was a more important factor in determining the level of education attained.

Table 2.6 Distribution of Post-Secondary Students by Parents' Income, Academic Year 1968-1969

Family Income Group	% University Graduate	% University Undergraduate	% Community College
Less than $2,000	1.4	1.0	0.9
2,000–2,999	5.1	4.1	4.3
3,000–3,999	6.7	4.9	6.3
4,000–4,999	4.8	6.2	8.8
5,000–6,999	21.1	20.7	29.7
7,000–7,999	21.7	24.6	27.0
10,000 and over	39.2	38.5	23.0
	100.0	100.0	100.0

Source: Adapted from *Eighth Annual Review, Economic Council of Canada* (Ottawa, 1971), p. 220. Reprinted by permission of Information Canada.

Table 2.6 substantiates this fact by showing that well over one third of university graduates and undergraduates came from the highest-income category, and well under 20% of both university graduates and undergraduates came from homes with a yearly family income under $5,000. Conversely, less than a quarter of those enrolled in community colleges came from the high-income group. It appears that community colleges tend to be more accessible to those with lower income and are less preferred by those with high income. In spite of the fact that theoretically educational opportunity exists for everyone, it is largely those of higher income who take advantage of this opportunity. The existence of such a pattern, although difficult to explain,[9] does give us further evidence not only of stratification but of the perpetuation of that stratification through the educational system.

There is no doubt that until the end of the 1950s, students whose fathers were professionals were overrepresented and students whose fathers were semiskilled or unskilled were underrepresented in Canadian universities.[10] However, since that time a general increase in the enrollment of all post-secondary schools has occurred. The development of technical and vocational institutions and the expansion of universities in the 1960s provide ample evidence of this increase. If the average years of schooling in the male labor force increased by 38.6% between 1911 and 1961, we can expect to discover more significant increases in recent years.[11] School dropouts have been reduced considerably, so that the general level of educational attainment has increased. But, as Pike argues, class differentials in schooling attained persist, particularly at the lowest level where lack of education is undoubtedly perpetuating itself.[12]

In short, education is an integral means of social differentiation in Canada: It not only serves as a basis for ranking but it reinforces the system of rank that already exists.

OCCUPATION

The variation in responsibilities, skills, preparation, and rewards among occupations as perceived by a society also contributes to a hierarchy of rank. Because occupation often gives us a clue to a whole series of socioeconomic facts about an individual, it is an important means of locating him in the stratification system.

The pioneer study relating occupation to differences of rank in Canada was the work of Professor Bernard Blishen.[13] Utilizing data from the 1951 census, Blishen arranged all occupations reported in the census according to income and years of schooling in order to compute an average income and schooling level. Standard scores for each of these indices were determined and then combined in one score for each occupation. This made possible the construction of a hierarchical ranking of occupations based on that score. Then, making somewhat arbitrary decisions about cutoff points that reflected his own awareness of the prestige of occupations, Blishen divided the 343 occupations into seven classes. Table 2.7 selects a few of the listed occupations for each class.

It is interesting to observe which occupations predominate at

Table 2.7   Selected Occupations in Blishen's Class Divisions by Ranked Scores

Class 1 — Professional
Judges
Physicians
Lawyers
Architects
   Total = 10
Class 2 — White Collar
Statisticians
Professors
Stockbrokers
Managers
Chemists
Armed forces officers
Librarians
Social welfare workers
Teachers
Accountants
Clergymen
   Total = 49
Class 3 — High Blue Collar
Commercial travellers
Laboratory technicians
Railway conductors
Music teachers
Nurses
Stenographers
   Total = 33
Class 4 — Low Blue Collar
Bookkeepers
Foremen
Photographers
Office clerks
   Total = 24

Class 5 — Skilled
Policemen
Mechanics
Firemen
Telephone operators
Electricians
Machinists
Barbers
Postmen
Salesclerks
Butchers
   Total = 113

Class 6 — Semi-skilled
Beverage workers
Construction machine operators
Service station attendants
Painters
Tailors
Chauffeurs
Sailors
   Total = 84
Class 7 — Unskilled
Janitors
Longshoremen
Waitresses
Messengers
Laborers
Fishermen
   Total = 90

Source: Adapted from Bernard R. Blishen, "The Construction and Use of an Occupational Class Scale", *Canadian Journal of Economics and Political Science*, Vol. 24 (1958), pp. 526-530, Table I. Published by the University of Toronto Press and reprinted by permission of Bernard R. Blishen and the Canadian Political Science Association.

Table 2.8   Percentage Distribution of Labor Force by
Occupational Class, 1951

Class 1 — Professional	.9
Class 2 — White Collar	10.7
Class 3 — High Blue Collar	6.3
Class 4 — Low Blue Collar	7.0
Class 5 — Skilled	34.2
Class 6 — Semi-skilled	19.6
Class 7 — Unskilled	21.3

Source: Adapted from Bernard Blishen, "The Construction and Use
of an Occupational Class Scale", *Canadian Journal of Economics and
Political Science*, Vol. 24 (1958), p. 531. Published by the University
of Toronto Press and reprinted by permission of Bernard R. Blishen and
the Canadian Political Science Association.

the varying levels of the Canadian class structure. Table 2.8 points
out the percentage distribution of these occupations in the population. Note that the largest class by far is Class 5 (skilled) with
34.2% of the Canadian labor force. Industrialization always requires skilled labor and tradesmen. Nevertheless, it is clear that
there are fewer persons at the top end of the occupational ranking
than at the bottom where the labor force is largest. Some slight
changes in the class distribution of the labor force have probably
taken place since 1951 but, as we will see, Blishen's updating of
this study introduced a new dimension to the ranking method and
ignored his former class designations, so that a direct comparison
is impossible.

We have established that concrete measurements can be used
to determine the nature of the stratification system found in
Canadian society. Income, education, and occupation are all
mutually reinforcing indices of rank that perpetuate differences
within the society. A high income increases the possibilities of obtaining higher education, which in turn makes a higher-ranked occupation possible. Or, a good education leads to a better occupation usually with a more favorable income. The considerable differences in educational attainment and income within the population
indicate that occupations vary in rank and importance. Individuals
within the society are frequently differentiated by belonging to
groups made up of those who have similar ranking levels.

Subjective Indices of Rank

Karl Marx drew our attention to the fact that ranking is not merely the result of objective conditions, but that these objective conditions (e.g. income, education) have a subjective effect on the consciousness of the individual in the social system.[14] Stratification is perpetuated because individuals make comparative self-evaluations about their own level of social standing. Sociologists use these subjective evaluations of perceived social ranking by asking respondents to rank themselves among other persons or to make personal evaluations of the prestige rank of others.

In a representative sample of 793 Canadians, Pineo and Goyder discovered a typical North American pattern of subjective social class identification.[15] Canadians possessed a definite tendency, quite similar to that of Americans, to identify themselves as middle-class, or perhaps working-class, in spite of the fact that one or more objective factors indicated the possibility of a more accurate designation. The predilection for identification with the middle class is undoubtedly tied to what Porter calls North America's dominant mythology about equality and opportunity.[16] There is no question that a subjective self-evaluation as middle class by the majority in reality only masks more refined strata distinctions. When pressed to make a more precise class identification, Canadians tended to refer to objective socioeconomic criteria, though Protestants displayed a greater tendency to do this than Catholics. Again, it could be argued that prestige is determined by the demands and rewards of the industrial system which emphasizes income, education, and occupation.

Max Weber went somewhat beyond Marx to make a distinction between class and status.[17] Whereas class tended to be directly related to economics and other objective indices, Weber added another dimension, namely status, in which specific reference was made to the degree of prestige or honor assigned to persons in a society. Because those of similar status also possess a similar lifestyle, the prevailing system of rank is again reinforced. Sociologists have devised techniques which can help us to determine the degree of prestige assigned to members of a society.

Pineo and Porter[18] in 1965, asked their respondents to rank occupations in Canada on a ladder with nine boxes into which they were to arrange a series of cards labelled with the name of an occupation in a hierarchy of prestige. Professional occupations ranked highest and, interestingly, both French- and English-speaking people ranked artistic occupations low. However, French

Canadians displayed a tendency *not* to rank occupations into the very lowest and the very highest divisions to the same extent that English Canadians did. Also, they tended to rank more prestigious white-collar jobs lower and many blue-collar clerical jobs higher than in the ranking by English Canadians. Given the fact that French Canadians have been most frequently found in this lower middle-class category, such a pattern can be referred to as an *aggrandizement effect*. Those jobs that are held or appear attainable are upgraded, while those occupations which appear out of reach are downgraded. Pineo and Porter contend that this is a "self-enhancing manner of ranking". Self-perceptions of status thus are extremely valuable tools in determining the existence of a hierarchy of strata within Canadian society.

Using 1961 census data instead of 1951 data, Blishen updated his index of occupational rank by combining education and income factors with the added dimension of prestige-scale scores from Pineo and Porter's study to obtain a more comprehensive status hierarchy of all Canadian occupations. Table 2.9 again uses an arbitrary grouping measure to cluster the occupations into categories according to their score on the socioeconomic index. Six groups of occupations are identified and the percentage of the total labor force in each group is given. Blishen is less interested in identifying classes, groups, or categories than he is in providing a more accurate ranking scale of all occupations in Canada. Nevertheless, I have included the clustering as an aid to students, though we must be mindful that the index scale itself is extremely valuable as a research tool for other kinds of studies.

Ethnic Stratification

One of the most significant things to note about social stratification in Canada is that it is not random; i.e., some groups of people tend to have a proportionately larger share of their members in one particular class than in another class. When ethnicity is selected as the primary variable and the stratification system is held constant, it becomes clear that many ethnic groups are over-represented or underrepresented in particular strata. In short, I am suggesting that the members of some ethnic groups generally have a more favorable position than those of other ethnic groups in the society as a whole.

When the British and French first settled in Canada, there was a tendency to recreate a stratified society similar to that of the homeland.[19] For example, factory workers from the northern and

Table 2.9   Percentage Distribution of the Canadian Labor Force
by Socio-Economic Intervals, 1961

Group*	Socio-Economic Index Scores	No. of Occupations in Group	Selected Examples of Occupations	Percentage of Total Labor Force
1	70+	24	Dentists, Engineers, Professors, Lawyers, Physicians, Scientists	4
2	60–69	26	Managers, Owners, Pilots, Editors	4
3	50–59	36	Salesmen, Clergymen, Musicians, Welfare Workers	9
4	40–49	52	Bookkeepers, Foremen, Agents, Nurses, Photographers	20
5	30–39	103	Inspectors, Operators, Factory Workers, Machinists, Drivers, Butchers	32
6	Below 30	79	Laborers, Attendants, Janitors, Fishermen, Lumbermen, Shoemakers	31

* Since Blishen refrains from the designation of these groups as classes in this more recent study, we refer to them as groups to avoid other connotations that class might have.

Source: Adapted from Table I and Table III of B.R. Blishen, "A Socio-Economic Index for Occupations in Canada". Reprinted from *The Canadian Review of Sociology and Anthropology*, Vol. 4, No. 1, by permission of the author and the publisher.

central parts of England became the blue-collar workers in Canada, while the learned, the merchants, and the property owners became the administrators and professionals. Similarly, the clergy and professionals from France became the leaders in Quebec for the farmers and laborers. Stratification, then, was to a great extent patterned after the former society of residence.

The two dominant culture groups existed side by side with their own individual structure of social organization even after the British had defeated the French and attempted to control ultimate policy in Quebec. Significantly, French social structure remained relatively intact. Doctors, lawyers, and clergy occupied the highest levels of social standing. Outside trade and necessary internal manufacturing, though usually under British control, were more or less distant from everyday French society. In spite of the fact that British North America contained these two societies, it became clear quite early that most capitalist activity, whether it took place in Quebec or elsewhere in Canada, would be directed by those of British descent. The matter was not interpreted as problematic, however, as long as the societies were relatively rural and traditional in character.

The onset of serious industrialization produced marked changes in both societies. The predominance of English-speaking people in industrial and capitalist activity, in addition to the general shrinking of the farm population and its corollary of rapid urbanization, meant that the entrenched English-Canadian upper class were in an excellent position to spread their influence in relatively commanding fashion over all of Canada. Thus it was natural that the English should become the industrial leaders of Quebec and easily utilize French manpower as lower-class workers. Because the Quebec educational system emphasized classical studies and was not designed to prepare its students for technological occupations,[20] a professional manpower void was created into which English Canadians eagerly entered, especially since they had easy access to leadership roles anyway. As a result, the British were considerably overrepresented at the professional and financial levels in the Quebec labor force — meaning, of course, that the French were underrepresented at that level. Similarly, the French were overrepresented in agricultural, primary, and unskilled occupations, while the British were underrepresented in these occupations. Blishen's study documented this tendency for those of British heritage in Canada to be overrepresented in the higher classes and underrepresented in the two lowest classes.[21] Fully 66.3% of the highest class was of British origin. In contrast, the French were overrepresented in the two lowest classes and underrepresented above that point. The unskilled or semiskilled factory orientation of the rapidly urbanizing French thus produced what Porter called an "industrial proletariat". In comparison with English Canadians within Quebec, they have also been called the "oppressed majority".[22] It could be argued that such an exploitative trend is somewhat explainable in the early stages of industrialization; in more recent years, a better prepared French-Canadian population has attempted to overcome its sense of oppression and class fixation in a way which we will discuss later. However, this does not change the fact that, traditionally, people of British heritage in Canada have always held a proportionately higher percentage of the upper-class positions.[23]

I have suggested that French-English differences in status roles may have a historical explanation within the society as a whole; but is there any other reason why stratification differences are so noticeable? Could it be that each ethnic group has a different set of goals and standards which it transmits to its members? A study of a large Canadian business organization indicated that it was not an inherent differential of aspirations or values that produced cleavages in status between the two ethnic groups, but that status was based on the expectations of each ethnic group which served as the primary *reference group* for its members.[24] On the average, the French were more likely to be satisfied with lower occupational status because they compared themselves with members of their own ethnic group in a relatively segregated environment rather than comparing themselves with members of the other ethnic group. Ethnicity as a basis for stratification was thereby maintained because each ethnic group served as its own reference group, and as a result there was little dissatisfaction. Needless to say, when the reference group changed to the competing ethnic group, then, of course, the existing stratification patterns were challenged. We will return to this idea in Chapter 4.

The addition of other ethnic groups to the society through immigration contributed to the complexity of ethnic stratification patterns. Obviously, the reference to Canada as a "vertical mosaic" is meant to indicate that the ethnic groups found within Canada can be differentiated not only culturally but also vertically according to usual location in the class structure. It is important to note that it is federal government policy that determines which ethnic groups are preferable immigrants, and a change in qualifications required for admittance can significantly affect the nature of ethnic representation.[25] The government perception of the society's needs determines the class level at which immigrants will be admitted. For example, when East Europeans entered the country in the 1920s, they were largely rural peasants encouraged to settle western farmland, whereas the immigration of Asians in the postwar period was mostly of skilled and professional persons destined for urban centers. Sociologists use the term *entrance status* to refer to the class level at which immigrants enter a society. An examination of immigration since World War II reveals, for example, that Italians had a relatively low entrance status, whereas the British had a relatively high entrance status. It is debatable whether immigration officials deliberately discouraged the immigration of British with no skills, but encouraged that of Europeans with a low level of skills. Nevertheless, the result was that British immigrants were overrepresented in middle-class levels and above, in contrast to the more proletarian representation of European immigrants.[26]

In matching occupation with ethnicity, Germans, Dutch, Scandinavians, and East Europeans have been overrepresented in agricultural occupations, while the British composition has declined considerably. The French and Italians have been overrepresented in the unskilled category and conversely underrepresented in the professional and financial class where the British and Jewish ethnic groups maintained a significant overrepresentation. In any case, analysis reveals that the postwar immigration into Canada merely reinforced class differences previously existent among ethnic groups in which the British maintained their relatively high class standing as an ethnic group.

Social Mobility

Industrialization produces significant shocks to traditional patterns of social organization. The development of new skills, the acquisition of new knowledge, and geographical movements to meet new labor demands foster a significant reorganization of the taken-for-granted social order. As the industrialization process gains momentum, those who are prepared to meet its demands usually can anticipate a higher status role in the changed society. The social class system no longer appears ironclad and caste-like. Genuine improvements in social position are likely to take place.

Social mobility is the term used to designate movements or shifts by persons in the stratification system. In a society where the boundaries separating social strata or occupational groups are not permanently hardened, any change in social position produces what is known as social mobility. While mobility may be either upward or downward, it is most common in our society to speak of upward mobility. If it occurs in one person's lifetime, it is known as *intragenerational mobility*; if it occurs between parent and child, it is known as *intergenerational mobility*.

It is significant to note that for many immigrants the challenge of settlement in Canada was linked to the anticipation of upward mobility. The opportunity for landless European peasants to become landowners and to manage their own agricultural enterprise was an attraction for many of the early settlers, and no doubt represented a significant improvement in social position in itself. However, mobility by migration tells us less about the class system than mobility within the same society. For example, when agriculture became industrialized and was no longer viable as a small enterprise, a high level of urban expertise was needed within the society to meet the new labor demands. The difficulty of meeting this need was pointed out by the Royal Commission on Bilingualism and Biculturalism when it noted that the majority of Canadians in 1961 lacked sufficient education to meet the challenge which could have produced notable social mobility.[27] In the male labor force of French origin, 53.5% had not finished elementary schooling, while only 30.6% of the British population had not passed beyond that level. The implication was clear that within Canadian society the mobility potential produced by industrialization could not be exercised at that time. Vertical social mobility depended on adequate training, which meant that a large share of the population had no real opportunity to change their social position.

The major theme of Porter's lucid argument is that there has been less upgrading of the Canadian labor force and therefore less social mobility than might be expected in an industrializing society because of failure in education.[28] When Canada needed skilled and professional people, it was much easier to import them through preferred immigration regulations than to insist on educational reform. Additional complications appeared when opportunities in the United States produced a "brain drain" and a general labor drain from Canada among those who perceived that their life chances were better south of the border.[29] The vacancies that ensued in the labor force meant that the recruitment of unskilled and skilled professional persons through immigration ("brain gain") was an immediate means of resolving the problem. Thus

Canada has been both donor and recipient in what has been aptly labelled the "brain trade". [30] The out-migration of some of the most highly skilled, coupled with the additional demands for new skilled and professional persons, should have meant greater opportunities (i.e. greater social mobility) than it did for the working population already resident in Canada; but because of large-scale immigration, social mobility was greatly reduced. Porter conservatively estimates that between 1950 and 1960, immigrants filled 50% to 60% of the new, skilled jobs which were the result of the nation's industrial development. Because the democratization of education had not proceeded apace, the social structure remained relatively fixed as the result of mobility deprivation. There was more movement in and out of the stratification system than movement within it. Instead of immigrants entering Canada at the lower social-class levels and pushing the resident working class up in the social strata, skilled immigrants were more likely to meet the need because of the lack of preparation for mobility by the resident population. Certainly, the observable large-scale shift from manual to nonmanual occupations (i.e. from farmer to office worker) in the Canadian labor force is not vertical mobility in itself.

It is important to note that Porter was *not* saying that no upward mobility occurred or that immigrants (particularly skilled immigrants) were detrimental to Canadian society. Obviously, some mobility within the labor force took place when the necessary skills were acquired, and a skilled immigrant body both hastened and encouraged Canadian industrial development. What rankled Porter was that immigration was a convenient substitute for educational reform and retarded both the demand for better education and the development of fuller educational participation. In addition, a potentially dynamic social structure remained relatively static because Canada was not a "mobility-oriented society".

Porter analyzed his evidence in the early sixties before the effects of educational change really began to occur in Canada. University attendance increased dramatically in the 1960s and postsecondary schools of technology emerged, boasting excellent facilities and large enrollments. By 1970, enrollment in postsecondary educational institutions had almost tripled: Full-time enrollment in universities jumped from 115,000 in 1960 to 355,000 in 1970. [31] With community colleges making education more accessible, mobility possibilities have become more real. Even the financial requisites that controlled access to higher education show definite signs of improvement. [32] Immigration regulations still give priority to skilled and professional persons, and rightly so, but now the Canadian labor force is in a better position to meet the nation's technological needs and to make social mobility within the society a greater likelihood. However, the extent of the mobility that has occurred since Porter's study has yet to be documented.

It is a basic sociological observation that migration is usually prompted by the perception that a geographical move will result in a chance for improvement in life conditions and perhaps ultimately in social status. Using the Blishen scale in a study of postwar immigrants, [33] Anthony Richmond found that there was a greater tendency for non-British immigrants to fall in status in comparison with their status in the country of previous residence. When British immigrants did fall in status, their downward mobility was much less than that of other immigrants. Sociologists refer to any change in social position produced by migration as *status dislocation*, and it appears that most immigrants to Canada do experience some of this change. However, the longer a British immigrant remained in Canada, the greater was the chance that he would not only recover lost status but also experience some social mobility. In contrast, non-English-speaking immigrants demonstrated both the largest initial decline in social status as well as considerable difficulty in recovering their original status in their lifetime. Migration, then, tended to be a means of social mobility more likely for British immigrants than for other immigrants, though in many cases, a rise in the standard of living minimized any significant effect of status dislocation.

An interesting study of social mobility among the Portuguese of Toronto has recently been published. [34] It is Anderson's major finding that the Portuguese immigrant operates in a complex network of contacts among his kinfolk. It is not particular individuals or the ethnic group as a whole, rather a network of friendships that provides job information to the recent migrant. Therefore the particular social network into which the individual is taken in Canada determines the type of job opportunities and resulting mobility that will ensue, for some networks have fewer contacts and less mobility potential than others.

The possibilities for upward social mobility in Canada vary with educational level, occupation, social network contacts, and plain personal initiative. It is doubtful, however, whether upward social mobility takes place as frequently as we would like to believe, for social mobility is usually confused with rises in the standard of living.

Social Power

If Canadian society is a stratified society, then it is clear that some persons have greater accessibility to the mechanisms for decision making than others. We have established that Anglophones have traditionally possessed decidedly higher income and schooling levels and more important occupational roles within Canadian society. What is now to be established is that there is a further concentration of control among Anglophones in leadership and administrative roles.

Power implies control over the decisions that affect other people. Somehow the idea of inequality in wealth or prestige is far more acceptable in our society than the idea of inequality in decision making. It is not so much that some individuals are constrained from making decisions (though that may be the case), but that some persons are in a position to make decisions that reach considerably beyond their own personal lives, affecting vast numbers in a population. Thus, while the idea of a "ruling class" may appear reprehensible, it is a fact of Canadian life that power roles tend to be concentrated in a relatively small group of people. Decisions are made on behalf of the collectivity by an *elite*, simply defined as people in power roles.

Once again we return to John Porter's incisive work for a description of those at the highest level of the stratification system, the power elite. The second half of *The Vertical Mosaic* is devoted to this purpose and reflects many concerns similar to those of the American sociologist C. Wright Mills in his influential book *The Power Elite*.[35] Porter's intent is not only to establish that elitism in Canada exists but to demonstrate that these elites possess a consierable degree of social homogeneity; i.e., they possess similar social characteristics. The social interrelationships that emerge among the elites of each institutional system in the society make them more than a statistical grouping: They become an interwoven unit with significantly similar traits. After demonstrating that a disproportionate share of economic activity in Canada is concentrated in a small group of firms, Porter determined that in the early 1950s there were 985 men holding directorships in 170 dominant corporations, banks, and insurance companies, and he designated these individuals as the economic elite.[36] He observed that it was largely this same group which held most of the common stock and thus received most of the dividend income, meaning that ownership and management was concentrated in the hands of a few individuals rather than dispersed in general shareholding throughout the society. Furthermore, the economic elite was characterized by interlocking directorships in that they recruited internally from among themselves to serve on each other's boards. Biographical sketches of 760 of the 985 members of the economic elite were constructed, and it became apparent that family continuity and the absence of independent entrepreneurs were striking features of this stratum of persons. Many of them had obtained a university education and a surprising number had also attended private schools. Only 6.7% of the economic elite were French-Canadian, substantiating my earlier point about the dominance of British-Canadians at the highest class level of Canadian society. Similarly, only about 10% were Catholic, indicating that Protestants were considerably overrepresented. The economic elite extended its influence in decision making by holding numerous other board positions in charitable organizations, educational institutions, and trade associations.

While economic institutions and the people who control them are highly significant, there are other institutions in the society which also possess elites with important decision-making roles. Analysis of the economic elite was joined with similar social profiles of the political elite, bureaucratic elite, labor elite, and ideological elite. In contrast to other elites, the elite of organized labor had the highest proportion of foreign born of all elites, the lowest level of education, and tended to come from working-class backgrounds. The political elite, on the other hand, was mostly native-born, possessed the highest percentage with university education, frequently stressed private schools, and tended to be of British, Protestant, and professional (particularly legal) background. The federal bureaucratic elite was very similar because its requirement for higher education made internal bureaucratic recruitment less likely. [37] Ontario as a region was well overrepresented in the higher echelons of this elite. The mass media elite was a smaller group than the other elites; ownership was shared by only a few families, often as the result of inheritance. The media in French Canada were an exception because they were independent of syndicates or chains. Porter also identifies intellectual and religious elites, though he concludes that they are not as homogeneous.

More recently, Robert Presthus has spoken of three groups in Canada which he has labelled the "political elite": [38] legislators (particularly cabinet ministers), senior civil servants, and directors of the many financial, educational, professional, and labor-interest groups in the nation. Their mutual interaction of bargaining and accommodation maintains the survival of the social system and centralizes decision making in national policy formation. While such a situation has its positive features, it does raise a question about the minimal role of democratic participation in the life of Canadian society.

In bringing Porter's line of inquiry up to date, Wallace Clement, a student of Porter's at Carleton University, observed that since Porter's study there had been a growing concentration of capital into large firms, and that direct U.S. investment had increased markedly.[39] Clement identified three major elites: the *indigenous elite* of Canadian-controlled corporations, particularly in transportation, finance, and utilities; the *comprador elite* of directors and management personnel of foreign-controlled corporations operating in Canada, particularly in resources and manufacturing; and the *parasite elite* largely outside of Canada, controlling the multinational corporations operating in Canada. He identified 113 dominant corporations which, with their subsidiaries, investments, and interlocking directorships, concentrated at the top a small number of persons with similar characteristics. Clement noted that 41 of the dominant corporations Porter identified had since been reduced to 17 companies through mergers and purchases. Interlocking directorships were again a dominant feature, and of the 113 dominant corporations, there were 1,848 directorships interconnected, with the Canadian Imperial Bank of Commerce, the Bank of Montreal, the Royal Bank, the Canadian Pacific Railway, and Sun Life most closely interlocked. Significantly, 29% of this total elite of the 113 corporations held 54% of all directorship positions. Clement concluded that there had certainly been an additional concentration of power in Canada among the indigenous elite since Porter's study, in addition to the strengthened hand of the parasite elite and the comprador elite.

The Royal Commission on Bilingualism and Biculturalism, also concerned about power roles, subsidized a research team to determine who holds the important positions in the federal public service.[40] Beattie, Désy, and Longstaff found that Francophones were considerably less successful than Anglophones in pursuing federal administrative careers, because Francophones were handicapped by being forced to use English — a language in which they were clearly less competent. They also experienced conscious and unconscious discrimination that tended to block their advancement to the higher levels of an Anglophone-dominated civil service. More important, Francophones felt cultural pressures to Anglicize their thinking and acting in order to obtain promotions and rewards. Under personal strain, many Francophone adminis-

trators "gave up", and by doing so only entrenched the Anglophone control. As a result of this study, the Royal Commission
made significant proposals that would open governmental positions of control to greater French participation.

What is important about these studies of elites is not just that
every sphere of Canadian society possesses a small group of people
with power jurisdiction over that sphere of society, but that
numerous connections can be found among these elite groups on
both formal and informal levels. [41] For example, Porter points out
that intermarriage has been very high among children of the
economic elite, and that friendship and kinship links are frequent
among the non-economic elite because relationships are often
begun at private schools and universities. The labor elite is the
most separate and distinct from the other elites, but even it learns
to participate according to informal ground rules established
among elites. In spite of the fact that elites each have their own
areas of jurisdiction, a considerable degree of coordination among
elites gives stability to the social system and thereby reinforces
their individual power roles. Porter is concerned that, if decision
making must be concentrated among elites, then mobility or recruitment from all classes should take place so that the elite will
be more representative of the society at large.

COMPONENTS OF ELITISM

Exclusivism.   Robert Michels, a European sociologist, argued that
there is a universal tendency for a small elite to dominate the
masses. [42] He called this tendency *the iron law of oligarchy* and
claimed that it was not so much that some individuals possessed a
lust for power as that their elitist position was virtually given to
them by the people — even in democracies. People tend to accept
passively the flow of power to a few persons at the top.

Even though Michels was speaking in a more political context,
there is a sociological sense in which his observation that elites
become small self-perpetuating groups is true. However, it is this
notion of elites as an exclusivist group that believers in democracy
find a bitter pill to swallow, for, as the evidence cited has suggested, much of Canadian elitism appears to be perpetuated on a
long-term basis. If Michels is right in claiming the tendency to
elitism, then there should be at least some mobility to open the
elite group to other people in succeeding generations. In a democracy, elitism should not be so intergenerationally exclusivist that
it can never be penetrated by outsiders, and thereby enlarge its
base of participation to all members of the society.

A study by Merrijoy Kelner in Toronto attempted to determine whether it was possible for outsiders to penetrate into that city's elite. [43] A basic distinction was made between the *strategic elite* and the *core elite*. The strategic elite, the lower level of the elite structure, contained persons such as labor leaders and corporation executives who had *achieved* key functional roles in the society. The core elite, on the other hand, was a smaller though somewhat more homogeneous group at the upper level of the elite structure, usually with *inherited* wealth, class position, and power. The strategic elite tended to achieve their status, while the core elite inherited theirs. Kelner discovered that some mobility had taken place, but that it was definitely into the strategic rather than into the core elite. Access to the strategic elite was obtained by sharpened skills and competency in developing fields. But this sort of mobility encouraged the core elite to circumscribe further their interaction among themselves in organizations such as private clubs. Nevertheless, this apparent penetration of the elite structure from below, particularly by non-Anglo-Saxons, never increased proportionately to their total representation in the general population.

In spite of the fact that it has been argued that upward mobility into the elite structure is possible for a few, it is clear that such a position of social power is beyond the reach of most members of the society. At this point, however, it is merely important to recognize that Canada does possess an elite and that it is at least relatively exclusivist in nature.

Social Control.   Elitism can be viewed as a mechanism of social control by which an entire society's destiny is shaped. The concentration of power in the hands of a few produces a sense of powerlessness among the majority. It has become almost axiomatic to note that many of the tensions within Canadian society are the direct result of the unequal distribution of power throughout the society. When people feel that they are deprived of power, which someone else possesses, and that the exercise of that power is affecting them adversely, social protest or an attempt to break the hold of power and social control can be expected.

One of the dominant themes of Canadian social history has been that elitist power and decision making have been geographically biased. Regions within Canada have felt that they have no control over what is happening to them because the center of power is elsewhere in Canada. [44]

While the paradigm is not really original with him, sociologist Arthur Davis has elaborated on the significance and effects of the regional differential of elite power and control as previously noted by Canadian historians.[45] He argues that the centers of political, financial, and industrial power in the society are found in *the metropolis*. The rest of the nation serves as *the hinterland* which merely exports raw materials and labor at the behest of the centers of power. Decision making and ultimate control rest with the elites who reside in the metropolis. In addition, the hinterland is organized around the metropolis in order to maintain the latter's high industrial momentum. The relationship between the metropolis and hinterland is *symbiotic*; i.e., one needs the other, though in an unbalanced relationship. The metropolis tends to *dominate* and to *exploit* the hinterland for its own benefit. Davis also argues for the existence of a hierarchy of metropolis-hinterlands in that, for example, northern Manitoba may be a hinterland to Winnipeg, and all of Manitoba in turn may be a hinterland to the "industrial east". As a result, there has frequently been a feeling that some sinister metropolitan power is controlling the hinterland region.

There is indeed a basis in fact for the sense of regional inferiority and exploitation by metropolitan elites. While the society supposedly consists of equals in interaction, it is clear that some parts of the society are in a more favorable position than others. Thus a perceived differential in power develops. For example, the level of earned income per person in the Atlantic region is more than 40% less than that of Ontario and British Columbia which are considerably above the regional average in Canada.[46] Quebec and the Prairie region are also below the Canadian average-income level (the latter only slightly). Of great significance for Canadian society is the fact that these regional differences have retained their relative position for a long time and continue to persist in spite of other changes. When one region compares itself to another and sees little ability to effect change, feelings of powerlessness result.

If one region feels disadvantaged in relation to another, it usually blames not the other region but the elites who wield the power. Thus former Premier William Aberhart of Alberta gathered widespread regional support with his attack on the "Fifty Big Shots" and the "Bay Street Barons" in Toronto whose financial decisions were perceived as exploitations of their region.[47] Similarly, Pierre Vallières argued that the people of Quebec were the "white niggers" of America because they were being exploited by the industrialists of the ruling class.[48]

Numerous political attempts have been made within the society to redress this perceived misuse of power.[49] Parties such as the Parti Québecois, the Social Credit Party, and the Cooperative

Commonwealth Federation have all had a strong regional base that protested external control and sought to retain power within that region — often via populist endeavor. Not all struggles have centered on attempts to become unshackled from a national elite; for, as Ossenberg has argued, not only have French Canadians frequently been on the lower rungs of the Canadian class system, but the presence of a strong elitist tradition within their regional society has produced enduring class differences among themselves.[50] From this perspective, the FLQ Crisis of October 1970 can be interpreted as a signal of the attempt that was taking place within Quebec to redistribute power.[51]

The metropolis-hinterland paradigm is a very important interpretive framework for understanding many issues facing Canadian society. Perceptions of elite control with a regional bias have certainly been the source of regional politics and conflict that perpetuate considerable tension within the society. But parallel to the tensions of regional politics are the tensions of class politics in which elite control is being resisted by those at lower-class levels. In some instances, regional politics has displaced class politics for a time, as on the prairies or in Quebec when the majority of persons in the area have attempted to overcome a sense of external elite exploitation. In other instances, class politics has begun to crystallize in response to elite control. One account of the 1972 situation in Quebec argues for the increasing struggle of the working class against elite control.[52]

It is clear, then, that elitism carries within itself the idea of control by the few of the many. When elitism is seen as a means of social control it provokes vigorous reaction whereby people try to regain a measure of their own control. As a result, Canada has had a fairly active socialist movement which has challenged the arbitrary decision-making powers of the elite.[53] In spite of the fact that this movement has introduced many innovative ideas into the society, the concentration of power tends to persist.

Poverty

While it might be argued that in Canada the majority of the population exists considerably above the subsistence level, mere subsistence cannot be accepted as adequate. The poor in Canada may fare considerably better than the poor in Asia. However, since the lowest stratum in Canadian society does not have any experience with Asian societies, its members compare themselves with members of their own society who define them as poor. Thus it is clear that what we define as poverty in Canada is at least partially a *relative* matter. *Relative poverty* refers to poverty based on comparisons to a chosen standard. On the other hand, *absolute poverty* indicates physical privation in which the sustenance of life is questionable. Agencies have been established to eliminate absolute poverty, but we are also concerned with relative poverty, for it is comparative to the average standard of living. Since the definition of relative poverty varies through time,[54] poverty is not always defined in dollars and cents because it is easily identified as the lowest standard of living in a society. For example, possession of a car may be a luxury in some cultures, but may be a real necessity in our society for employment, or merely because the lack of a car deprives a family of experiences available to most Canadians. Because of the relativity of poverty, debates rage over its extent and precise desig-nations of its range are difficult to determine.

One specification of poverty refers to any family unit that must spend more than 70% of its total income on the subsistence items of food, shelter, and clothing.[55] If the average Canadian family allocates about one half of its income for these three essen-tials, a 70% allocation would be considerably above the average and leave little "discretionary income" for items that are part of normal living. Since changes in the cost and standard of living rendered the 70% figure obsolete by 1971, the Senate Committee on Poverty computed a new poverty line somewhat higher than Podoluk's but concluded that a similar percentage of one in four Canadians was below the poverty line.[56] The incidence of poverty was lowest among families with three or four members and highest among families with five or more members, two-member families, and unattached individuals; and included the working poor, the rural poor, the welfare poor, and minorities. Urban poverty tended to be highest among specific groups such as the aged, families with female heads, large families, and the handicapped; whereas rural poverty was a more general and pervasive phenomenon (four times as high as urban poverty) not restricted to any specific group.[57] The circle of poverty is reinforced, as a Canadian study tells us, by the socialization of behavior that perpetuates poverty which is learned early in life and from which it is hard to extricate one-self.[58]

An interesting document that advocates sweeping changes to the socioeconomic system of corporate capitalism which perpetu-ates poverty is the book entitled *The Real Poverty Report.*[59] Written by four men who were members of the staff of the Senate

Committee on Poverty until their resignation in anger, the book attempts to explain why inequality persists. The unwillingness to change the status quo by those who are privileged, it is argued, produces numerous programs that tinker with the problem but do not advocate the necessary structural reform. Interestingly, however, both reports suggest the introduction of a guaranteed annual income as a means of closing the poverty gap.[60]

The Implications of a Stratified Society

There are two basic theoretical approaches to understanding the significance or purpose of a stratified society.[61] One is that inequality derives from a society's necessity to survive as the result of a differential of tasks and rewards. Such a system is supposedly just because the class level attained is the result of individual merit.[62] The second approach holds that inequality is not necessary and that its existence eventually produces a struggle for control between those who possess the wealth and power and those who lack wealth and power. This position is best represented by Karl Marx who argues that the maldistribution of wealth and power in the hands of a few produces a populist desire to overcome this concentration of control.

There is no doubt that Canada is a stratified society. Whether that inequality is necessary or unnecessary is a matter of considerable ideological debate. To believe in equality at the ballot boxes is certainly not the same as to believe in equality in economic matters. The search for a just society appears to be an unending one. Canadian society has apparently modified both of these approaches and accepted relatively peaceful class confrontations in which some measure of parity is sought at the same time that a stratification system based on a differential of rewards and responsibilities is accepted.[63]

What then are the consequences of a stratification analysis? There is a pessimism inherent in Porter's argument about the strength of elite control that may be due to an assumption that control by elites has rendered and will continue to render the masses powerless. However, as I have pointed out, there are certainly occasions when decision making takes place in the crucible of interaction and confrontation between the public and the elites. Ultimate power may be held by a small group, but they may be forced to consider general societal pressures. It is also significant to note that there are differences in the kind of power wielded by elites. For example, labor and political elites are much more susceptible to public pressures than are economic elites, and this fact in itself might engender more conflict between elites than Porter assumes. One reviewer of *The Vertical Mosaic* objects to the picture Porter paints of most Canadians as "politically impotent and submissive" and "undisturbed" by the inequalities that exist in their society. [64] This view, it is argued, does not give Canadian society much hope for the future because of its stress on passivity and inevitability. Another reviewer points out that conceptual and theoretical problems in Porter's use of the terms "class" and "power" give evidence of his "strategy of respectability" whereby the radical implications of his research have been muted by his shift to a liberal value position. [65] There have been numerous changes in the society since Porter made his analysis. [66] The level of education has shown considerable improvement; but, no doubt more importantly, a general upgrading in the standard of living (or perhaps pay increases due to inflation that give illusions of improvement) has subverted any wholesale desire for the rearrangement of the existing organization of Canadian society. Furthermore, a 1974 study[67] has shown that the income differential between the British and the French in Canada has undergone a considerable levelling process in the last decade and this has undoubtedly had a cooling effect on ethnic class conflict. Nevertheless, the voicing of demands for a more equitable arrangement of society continues — particularly as differences in social starting points reflect badly on our vaunted ideal of the equality of opportunity.

The perspective on Canadian society presented in this chapter has enabled us to document the existence of inequalities in the society and also to specify some of the effects of these inequalities on the society. We must be aware that the stratification of Canadian society is a fact of life. This awareness opens a whole range of sociological inquiries into differing social life-styles and world views that emerge from the existence of social strata. [68] Whatever your personal conclusions regarding the legitimacy of stratification, it is clear that its existence has contributed to the character of Canadian society.

QUESTIONS FOR FURTHER EXPLORATION

1. *Why is poverty a problem in Canada and by what means can it be reduced?*

2. *Compare stratified Canadian society with a society where class differences are not so varied. What differences do you observe?*

3. *How do differentials in power roles affect your regional area? Give some examples of the metropolis-hinterland conflict in Canada.*

NOTES

[1] John Porter, a sociologist at Carleton University, has done the most thorough stratification study in Canada, as documented by his book *The Vertical Mosaic* (Toronto: University of Toronto Press, 1965). On the basis of its comprehensiveness, insight, and originality, Porter won the MacIver Award of the American Sociological Association in 1966.

[2] John Porter, *The Vertical Mosaic*, p. 112. See Chapter 4 for an excellent discussion of the difficulties in utilizing census data and income tax form statistics as a true picture of financial position.

[3] Jenny R. Podoluk, *Incomes of Canadians* (Ottawa: Statistics Canada, 1968).

[4] Jenny R. Podoluk, "Some Comparisons of the Canadian-U.S. Income Distributions", unpublished paper (Ottawa: Statistics Canada, 1969), p. 17.

[5] For a discussion of the persistence of an income differential see Podoluk, *Incomes of Canadians*, Chapter 2 and D.W. Rossides, *Society as a Functional Process: An Introduction to Sociology* (Toronto: McGraw-Hill Co. of Canada, 1968), p. 250.

[6] John Porter, *The Vertical Mosaic*, Chapter 6.

[7] See Frank J. Whittingham, *Educational Attainment of the Canadian Population and Labour Force: 1960-1965*, Special Labour Force Studies No. 1 (Ottawa: Statistics Canada, 1966), pp. 10-11.

[8] Ronald M. Pavalko, "Socio-Economic Background, Ability, and the Allocation of Students", *Canadian Review of Sociology and Anthropology*, Vol. 4 (1967), pp. 250-259.

[9] For a detailed examination of this issue see Robert M. Pike, *Who Doesn't Get to University — and Why* (Ottawa: Runge Press, 1970); Marion R. Porter, John Porter, and Bernard Blishen, *Does Money Matter? Prospects for Higher Education* (Toronto: York University Institute for Behavioral Research, 1974); and Raymond Breton, *Social and Academic Factors in the Career Decisions of Canadian Youth* (Ottawa: Department of Manpower and Immigration, 1972). Breton looks at the educational plans of youth, considering factors such as the father's occupation, education of parents, size of community of residence, size of family, birth order, and linguistic affiliation.

[10] See John Porter, *The Vertical Mosaic*, p. 186, Table XXIII.

[11] *Second Annual Review, Economic Council of Canada* (Ottawa: 1965), p. 76, Table 4-2.

[12] R.M. Pike, *Who Doesn't Get to University — and Why*, pp. 61-63. Another discussion on educational inequalities in Canada can be found in R. Manzer, *Canada: A Sociopolitical Report* (Toronto: McGraw-Hill Ryerson, 1974), pp. 188-206.

[13] Bernard Blishen, *"The Construction and Use of an Occupational Class Scale"*, *Canadian Journal of Economics and Political Science*, Vol. 24 (1958), pp. 519-531.

[14] Karl Marx, *Early Writings*, trans. and ed. by T.B. Bottomore (Toronto: McGraw-Hill Co. of Canada, 1963), pp. 120-134.

[15] Peter C. Pineo and John C. Goyder, "Social Class Identification of National Sub-groups" in James E. Curtis and William G. Scott, *Social Stratification: Canada* (Scarborough: Prentice-Hall of Canada, 1973), pp. 187-195.

[16] John Porter, *The Vertical Mosaic*, pp. 3-6.

[17] "Class, Status, and Party" in H.H. Gerth and C.W. Mills, *From Max Weber: Essays in Sociology* (New York: Oxford University Press, 1958).

[18] Peter C. Pineo and John Porter, "Occupational Prestige in Canada", *Canadian Review of Sociology and Anthropology*, Vol. 4 (1967), pp. 24-40. This was not the first such study on prestige ranking in Canada, but it contained the largest and most representative list of occupations. Compare with J. Tuckman, "Social Status of Occupations in Canada", *Canadian Journal of Psychology*, Vol. I (1947).

[19] Detailed specifications of the following discussion can be found in John Porter, *The Vertical Mosaic*, pp. 73-103 on which many of my observations are based.

[20] For additional evidence see Everett Hughes, *French Canada in Transition* (Chicago: University of Chicago Press, 1943) and his study of factory workers in a French-Canadian community called Cantonville in the late 1930s.

[21] B.R. Blishen, "The Construction and Use of an Occupational Class Scale", p. 524.

[22] S. H. Milner and H. Milner, *The Decolonization of Quebec* (Toronto: McClelland and Stewart, 1973), Chapter 3.

[23] For this reason, Oswald Hall suggests that the study of occupations in Canada has been fundamentally a study in ethnic relations. "The Canadian Division of Labour Revisited" in R. Ossenberg, *Canadian Society: Pluralism, Change, and Conflict* (Scarborough: Prentice-Hall of Canada, 1971), pp. 89-99. See also *Report of the Royal Commission on Bilingualism and Biculturalism*, Book 3, Part 1 (Ottawa: Queen's Printer, 1969).

[24] Raymond Breton and Howard Roseborough, "Ethnic Differences in Status" in B.R. Blishen et al., *Canadian Society: Sociological Perspectives*, 3rd ed. (Toronto: Macmillan Co. of Canada, 1971), pp. 450-468.

[25] See Anthony Richmond, *Post-War Immigrants in Canada* (Toronto: University of Toronto Press, 1970), pp. 3-26 for a brief sketch on immigration policy.

[26] For details on the class representations of various ethnic groups see A.H. Richmond, "Social Mobility of Immigrants", *Population Studies*,

Vol. 17 (July 1964); Porter, *The Vertical Mosaic*, pp. 73-91; Blishen, "The Construction and Use of an Occupational Class Scale", p. 531; and Blishen, "Social Class and Opportunity in Canada", *Canadian Review of Sociology and Anthropology*, Vol. 2 (May, 1970), pp. 124-125.

[27] *Report of the Royal Commission on Bilingualism and Biculturalism*, Book 3, Part 1, p. 26.

[28] John Porter, *The Vertical Mosaic*, pp. 38-59.

[29] For an excellent discussion of the nature and significance of the brain drain, see Walter Adams, ed., *The Brain Drain* (Toronto: Macmillan Co. of Canada, 1968); also K.V. Pankhurst, "Migration between Canada and the United States" in *The Annals of the American Academy of Political and Social Science*, 367 (September 1966), pp. 53-62.

[30] T. J. Samuel, "The Migration of Canadian-Born between Canada and the United States of America, 1955-1968" in C.F. Grindstaff, C.L. Boydell, and P.C. Whitehead, eds., *Population Issues in Canada* (Montreal: Holt, Rinehart, and Winston of Canada, 1974), p. 96.

[31] Economic Council of Canada, *Seventh Annual Review: Patterns of Growth* (Ottawa: Queen's Printer, 1970), pp. 56-60.

[32] E.A.S. Fisher, "Financial Accessibility to Higher Education in Canada during the 1960s", *CAUT Bulletin*, Vol. 18 (Summer 1970), pp. 92-106.

[33] Anthony H. Richmond, *Post-War Immigrants in Canada*, Chapter 5.

[34] Grace M. Anderson, *Networks of Contact: The Portuguese in Toronto* (Waterloo: Wilfred Laurier University Press, 1974).

[35] C. Wright Mills, *The Power Elite* (New York: Oxford University Press, 1959). For an interesting biographical statement by Porter on influences on his work see "Research Biography of a Macro-Sociological Study: The Vertical Mosaic", in J.S. Coleman, A. Etzioni, and J. Porter, *Macrosociology: Research and Theory* (Boston: Allyn and Bacon, 1970), pp. 149-182. Porter compares his approach with that of Mills in this account.

[36] After a review of other evidence of corporate dominance, Porter says that his report of the nature of the economic concentration he discovered was likely to be an understatement. See also G. Rosenbluth, "Concentration and Monopoly in the Canadian Economy" in Michael Oliver, ed., *Social Purpose for Canada* (Toronto: University of Toronto Press, 1961), pp. 198-248.

[37] John Porter, *The Vertical Mosaic*, p. 418 and pp. 451-456. Porter notes that the civil service was too dependent on patronage until fairly recently (particularly at its highest ranks) and that this only compounded the influence of elites. Porter points out that in the years following 1957, achieved characteristics replaced patronage and thus produced a federal bureaucracy with greater independence.

[38] Robert Presthus, *Elite Accommodation in Canadian Politics* (Cambridge: Cambridge University Press, 1973).

[39] Wallace Clement, "The Changing Structure of the Canadian Economy", *Aspects of Canadian Society*, special publication of the *Canadian Review of Sociology and Anthropology* (1974), pp. 3-27. See Clement's *The Canadian Corporate Elite: An Analysis of Economic Power* (Toronto:

McClelland and Stewart, 1975) for a more detailed account. Clement also provides a good historical perspective on the evolution of elitism in Canada (particularly in Chapter 2). Dave Smith and Lorne Tepperman provide the framework for an excellent comparative analysis of the Canadian legal and business elite in the eighteenth and nineteenth century and the changes that have taken place through time. "Changes in the Canadian Business and Legal Elites, 1870-1970", *Canadian Review of Sociology and Anthropology*, Vol. 11 (May 1974), pp. 97-109. For an early account of the centralization of control in Canada see Gustavus Meyers, *History of Canadian Wealth* (Chicago: Charles Kerr, 1914) who argues that at the time of his writing, 50 men controlled more than one third of Canada's material wealth.

[40] Christopher Beattie, Jacques Désy, and Stephen Longstaff, *Bureaucratic Careers: Anglophones and Francophones in the Canadian Public Service* (Ottawa: Information Canada, 1972). Beattie has since published his own study of 300 middle-level members of the federal civil service in which he pinpoints the problems of Francophones in an English-controlled institution. *Minority Men in a Majority Setting* (Toronto: McClelland and Stewart, 1975).

[41] John Porter, *The Vertical Mosaic*, Chapter 17.

[42] Robert Michels, *Political Parties: A Sociological Study of the Oligarchical Tendencies of Modern Democracy* (New York: Free Press, 1966).

[43] "Ethnic Penetration into Toronto's Elite Structure", *Canadian Review of Sociology and Anthropology*, Vol. 7 (May, 1970), pp. 128-137.

[44] An excellent book which brings out this theme in a number of articles is Richard J. Ossenberg, ed., *Canadian Society: Pluralism, Change, and Conflict* (Scarborough: Prentice Hall of Canada, 1971). See, for example, the articles by McCrorie on the exploitation felt by Saskatchewan farmers, by Carstens on the powerless and dependent Canadian Indian, and by Vallee on the powerless native people of the Canadian North.

[45] Arthur Davis, "Canadian Society and History as Hinterland and Metropolis" in Ossenberg, *Canadian Society: Pluralism, Change, and Conflict*, pp. 6-32. Davis modifies the Hegelian-Marxian dialectic of thesis/antithesis/synthesis and argues that society evolves through a series of oppositions (reformative, however, rather than revolutionary), in this case between the metropolis and hinterland.

[46] F.T. Denton, *An Analysis of Interregional Differences in Manpower Utilization and Earnings*, Staff Study No. 15 (Ottawa: Queen's Printer, 1966), p. 2.

[47] For a good account of this sense of alienation in a historical framework, see C.B. Macpherson, *Democracy in Alberta: Social Credit and the Party System*, 2nd ed. (Toronto: University of Toronto Press, 1962).

[48] Pierre Vallières, *White Niggers of America* (Toronto: McClelland and Stewart, 1971).

[49] For a description of the role of the regional variable in Canadian politics, see F.C. Engelmann and M.A. Schwartz, *Political Parties and the Canadian Social Structure*.

[50] R.J. Ossenberg, "Social Pluralism in Quebec: Continuity, Change,

and Conflict" in R.J. Ossenberg, *Canadian Society: Pluralism, Change and Conflict*, pp. 103-123.

[51] This is essentially the interpretation of Raymond Breton, "The Socio-Political Dynamics of the October Events" *Canadian Review of Sociology and Anthropology*, Vol. 9 (1972), pp. 33-56.

[52] Daniel Drache, ed., *Quebec — Only the Beginning: The Manifestoes of the Common Front* (Toronto: New Press, 1972).

[53] For an analysis of a range of issues in the Canadian context from a socialist perspective see Laurier La Pierre et al., *Essays on the Left: Essays in Honour of T.C. Douglas* (Toronto: McClelland and Stewart, 1971). It must be pointed out that socialist parties are not necessarily the means to overcome elitism. Such parties would perhaps only have the effect of strengthening the hand of the political elite in relation to the corporate elite.

[54] A short discussion on the definition of poverty in Canada is available in *Poverty in Canada: Report of the Special Senate Committee on Poverty* (Ottawa: Information Canada, 1971), pp. 1-8. This Report is often referred to in relation to its committee chairman David A. Croll. Benjamin Schlesinger's study of poverty in Canada defines poverty as the condition of having seriously fewer resources than those commanded by the average person or family in a society. *What about Poverty in Canada?* (Toronto: University of Toronto Guidance Centre, 1972), p. 5.

[55] Jenny R. Podoluk, *Incomes of Canadians*, p. 185. A very readable account of the real-life implications of poverty in Canada is found in Ian Adams, *The Poverty Wall* (Toronto: McClelland and Stewart, 1970).

[56] *Poverty in Canada: Report of the Special Senate Committee on Poverty*, p. 11.

[57] N.H. Lithwick, "Poverty in Canada: Some Recent Empirical Findings", *Journal of Canadian Studies*, Vol. 6 (May 1970), pp. 27-41.

[58] T.J. Ryan, *Poverty and the Child: A Canadian Study* (Toronto: McGraw-Hill Ryerson, 1972).

[59] Ian Adams, William Cameron, Brian Hill, Peter Penz, *The Real Poverty Report* (Edmonton: M.G. Hurtig, 1971).

[60] For a good analysis and critique of both *The Poverty Report* and *The Real Poverty Report*, see Thelma McCormack, "Poverty in Canada: The Croll Report and Its Critics", *Canadian Review of Sociology and Anthropology*, Vol. 9 (November 1972), pp. 366-372. For a book of readings on poverty in Canada, see John Harp and John Hofley, eds., *Poverty in Canada* (Scarborough: Prentice-Hall of Canada, 1971).

[61] For a critique of these approaches as they relate to the Canadian context, see John Porter, *The Vertical Mosaic*, pp. 15-28.

[62] This idea has been soundly discussed in the well-known Davis-Moore-Tumin debate: Kingsley Davis, *Human Society* (New York: Macmillan, 1949); Wilbert Moore, "But Some Are More Equal Than Others", *American Sociological Review*, Vol. 28 (February 1963), pp. 13-18; Melvin Tumin, "On Inequality", *American Sociological Review*, Vol. 28 (February 1963), pp. 19-26.

[63] An alternative to my stratification perspective can be found in D.J. Goodspeed, "The Canadian Revolution: The Bourgeoisie Versus Marx", *Queen's Quarterly*, Vol. 64 (1957), pp. 521-530. Goodspeed asserts that Canada has already achieved a classless society in abolishing an aristocracy and in elevating the lower class without the bloodshed of revolution.

[64] Menno Boldt, "Images of Canada's Future in John Porter's *The Vertical Mosaic*", in Wendell Bell and James A. Mau, *The Sociology of the Future* (New York: Russell Sage Foundation, 1971), pp. 190-191.

[65] James L. Heap, ed., *Everybody's Canada: The Vertical Mosaic Reviewed and Re-examined* (Toronto: Burns and MacEachern, 1974), pp. 89-163. The first part of the book reprints a rather selective number of reviews of *The Vertical Mosaic* which had already been published in professional journals; thus Heap's work can serve as a convenient sourcebook of critiques on Porter.

[66] The most stirring and recent critique of Porter is contained in Harvey Rich, "The Vertical Mosaic Revisited: Toward a Macro-Analysis of Canadian Society", *Journal of Canadian Studies* (November 1975). Rich refutes the comparative implications of Porter's argument for which he says there are no comparative data, and says that Porter ignores changes that were taking place during his research, such as the industrialization of Quebec and evidence of significant upward mobility in Canada.

[67] C.M. Lanphier and R.N. Morris, "Structural Aspects of Differences in Income between Anglophones and Francophones", *Canadian Review of Sociology and Anthropology*, Vol. II (February 1974), pp. 53-66.

[68] For example, compare the sociological analysis of a Canadian upper-class residential area by Seeley et al. with W.E. Mann's analysis of a working-class district: J.R. Seeley, R.A. Simm, E.W. Loosely, *Crestwood Heights* (Toronto: University of Toronto Press, 1956); W.E. Mann, "The Social System of a Slum: The Lower Ward, Toronto" in S.D. Clark, ed., *Urbanization and the Changing Canadian Society* (Toronto: University of Toronto Press, 1961).

3
External Power and Domination Model

Another perspective that tells us something about the nature of Canadian society can be obtained by analyzing the effect that other societies have had on the development of Canadian society. It is frequently argued that Canadian society is merely the reflection of older or more dominant societies that tend to mold Canada in their own image. If the influence has really been of such magnitude, then the means whereby these external pressures are exerted must be described and their implications for the society must be determined.

The Notion of Colonialism

Historically, Canadian society has always lived in the shadow of more powerful societies. These societies derived their power and international stature from military might, industrial strength, larger populations, economic concentrations, prestigious educational centers, and technological expertise. While a peripheral role is not unique to Canada, Canadian society actually emerged as a direct response to the power and influence of these world powers, for they furnished people, goods, capital, and protection to assist in Canada's development. As a result, the early Anglo-Saxon inhabitants perceived that Canadian society was in some unique way an extension of the more dominant society that sponsored and fostered the establishment of the new colony. Consequently, Canadian native peoples could easily be pushed aside.

The expansion of French and British power beyond their own national borders and around the world enabled both of these societies to participate in the molding of Canadian society. For many residents of Canada, France and Britain served as the primary external referents by which the growth of the new society was measured. Thus a paternalistic relationship between the more dominant societies and Canada was established early, with an intricate set of *dependencies*. The "mother country" or the "fatherland" created a pattern of interaction in which Canadian society was continuously the *recipient* of a culture that had an external source. Whether these influences were economic, political, or generally cultural, the new society saw itself as dependent.

It is significant to note that the orientation of Canada's subordinate colonial position has shifted from one empire to another. French dominance of Canada was succeeded by British influence, only to be followed by that of the United States around the time of the First World War. The United States has curiously perpetuated the colonial status of Canadian society despite Canada's political independence and maintenance of loose traditional ties with the British Commonwealth. The notion of colonialism has therefore shifted from its old sense of direct formal control to its modern sense of indirect, informal control.

Colonial powers may view the colony primarily as an extension of their power and influence in the world, or as a hinterland for the supply of resources necessary to maintain their dominant role. In the first case, the colony serves as a symbol of prestige for the more dominant power, and numerous mechanisms are established to maintain supervisory control over the colony. In the second instance, control over the colonial society is unnecessary except to ensure the extraction of raw materials or the staples which the colonial power lacks. Prestige and the exploitation of resources have seldom been mutually exclusive goals of colonial powers. Under the French and the British, Canadian society was subject to both the formal and informal controls that link the colonized and the colonizers. However, with the attainment of nationhood, Canada was less amenable to direct political colonial controls; yet, at the same time, the door was held open to the more indirect controls of the economic exploitation of her hinterland potential by the American industrial complex. In either case, Canadian society was on the receiving end of a diffusion process and retained the sense of dependency even after attaining political autonomy. As a result, Canadian society has remained a colonial society because it has developed in the shadow and often under the sponsorship of foreign powers rather than in response to indigenous forces.

From a sociological point of view, the significance of colonial status is that the colony is the recipient of a continuous transferring process known as cultural diffusion. *Cultural diffusion* is the transmission of knowledge, institutions, customs, or technology from one society to another. The originating society shares elements of its culture with the receiving society, so that the two societies become increasingly similar. Institutional and organizational linkages (e.g. service and social clubs, unions, business franchises, and professional associations) serve as cultural pipelines from one society to another. Theoretically, diffusion is not a one-way process; through interaction with each other, societies share cultural traits. Cultural distinctiveness is thus reduced in interacting societies and a growing *homogenization* of culture takes place. But the colony invariably has less to offer the more advanced colonial power (at least as the colonial power sees it) and thus the colony is repeatedly merely the recipient in the diffusion process. Because of the thrust and direction of this process, *cultural penetration* may be a more accurate term than "cultural diffusion" to describe what has taken place.

The Nature of the External Societal Pressures

The autonomous development of Canadian society has been thwarted by pressures at several levels because Canada has lived so closely under the influence of more dominant societies as a shadow society.[1] A *shadow society* is a society whose sense of independence and uniqueness is obscured by the cast of continuous alien influences. I will list and discuss briefly some of the external pressures which Canadian society has felt and suggest reasons for the existence of these dependencies. I will outline the following types of formal and informal domination: economic, political, educational, athletic, cultural, technological, and resource.

Economic. It is often assumed that economic control is at the root of the subordinate status which Canadians have experienced.[2] Consequently, foreign ownership has become a major issue, and organizations like the *Committee for an Independent Canada* have been formed to resist the intrusion of foreign capital and to encourage the development of homeowned enterprises. Because Canada generally lacked sufficient capital to industrialize rapidly,[3] capital for immediate economic expansion has been freely imported. At the same time, considerable consternation has been expressed over the degree of foreign ownership in Canada, which is substantially higher than that of any other industrialized country.[4]

Foreign investment in Canada dates from the country's colonial beginnings. Prior to World War I, three quarters of the foreign investment in Canada was British.[5] By the early 1920s, the United States had supplanted Britain as Canada's largest supplier of capital and has continued in this role.[6] Inherent in this change was another shift that had far-reaching significance though it attained its peak somewhat later. The earlier investment of capital in Canada was known as *foreign portfolio investment;*[7] that is, the capital injected into the Canadian economy was in the form of bonds or loans with fixed returns on investment and with little legal control over their use. However, by World War II, the influx of capital changed to *foreign direct investment* which had a variable rate of return and in which the investor could participate through shareholder vote. This raises the question of decision making: If most capital invested in Canada is directly invested by outsiders with voting control over their stock, then significant decisions may be made by those who do not have the interests of Canadian society at heart. The real fear arose that the destiny of the society was dependent on the whims and personal preferences of those who lived outside the society. Putting issues like employment security, the most basic of individual concerns, in the hands of foreigners understandably produced a general nervousness in the society. Admittedly foreign capital is needed to ensure rapid development, but foreign control of that capital has become increasingly problematic.

Political. If Canada is a shadow society, it will no doubt be directly affected by what happens in the society that casts the shadow. Prime Minister Pierre Trudeau's metaphor of sleeping next to an elephant that affects all the little creatures around him was an apt description for the present effect of the United States on Canada. Because of the spillover effect, U.S. policy changes in Washington are often just as significant to Canadian society as decisions made in Ottawa. It is not surprising that many Canadians seem to be more aware of American politicans than of their Canadian counterparts. Federal government legislation is often provoked by the desire to protect this society, or to counteract the legislative influence of more dominant countries.

Educational. Because universities developed more slowly in Canada and had less prestige than those of Great Britain or the United States, Canadian scholars often chose to complete their education in these countries. Since major research breakthroughs usually took place in these foreign schools, Canadian institutions automatically regarded them as their standard point of reference. Even when the maturation of Canadian educational institutions lessened the need to look to foreign educational institutions, Canadians found that the staffing of their own universities was to a large degree dependent on persons recruited from the more dominant world-societies. Faculty could be found most quickly by bringing in skilled persons from other countries (usually from the United States and the United Kingdom), so that Canadian faculty were a minority in Canadian universities. Mathews and Steele estimate that 58% of the new appointments in 1963-65, 72% of the appointments in 1965-67, and up to 86% of the appointments in 1968 went to non-Canadians.[8] Thus the "brain drain" through emigration was followed by the "brain swamp" through immigration. To reverse the trend, Canadian schools began graduate programs, but for lack of planning overproduced potential faculty in some areas such as the physical sciences, and trained an insufficient number of persons in other areas such as the social sciences. Nevertheless, the impact of foreign educational experiences, training, and foreign-born personnel continues to be a dominant feature of Canadian educational institutions.

Athletic. Athletics has not been immune to foreign controls and pressures. The professionalization and commercialization of sport has called the whole notion of a Canadian national sport into question.[9] Hockey, for example, orientates its most successful athletes to participation in international leagues, with most teams playing in U.S. cities. Canadian hometown heroes play for Boston or Chicago and their hometown fans cheer for them in games televised back to Canada. Recently, the defense of the Canadian Football League has become an issue of national unity. Although Canada has revised the rules to make Canadian football a Canadian game, American players and coaches are the major participants in the sport. In addition, the attractiveness of the athletic scholarship programs at American universities and the deliberate policy of deleting athletic scholarships from Canadian schools have drained away many of Canada's best athletes. In sum, even athletics is not immune to the pressures of sports events and personalities originating in more dominant societies — particularly the United States.

Cultural. Much cultural activity that originates outside the country has become part of Canadian society.[10] The underdeveloped nature of the visual media in Canada, the lack of variety of printed media, and the resultant flooding of the Canadian market with foreign films and magazines have created a dependency on foreign culture and its media. Because geographical proximity permits reception of American radio and television signals, Canadian broadcasters must compete for the attention of their own national population. Depending on broadcasting choice, many Canadians may be more attuned to events occurring in the United States than to activity in their own society. Because Canadian broadcasters have often found it easier and perhaps cheaper to buy successful American programs, the Canadian Radio-Television Commission began to formulate Canadian content regulations, insisting that stipulated percentages of broadcast time must be devoted to Canadian programming. While this demand has helped to develop enterprises like the Canadian record industry, it does not necessarily ensure a loyal audience that refuses to select a program from the American cable alternatives. The media are an important means for the diffusion of foreign culture; the similarity of advertising in Canada and the United States points out how it has created cross-cultural wants and tastes. Tax concessions given to *Time* and *Reader's Digest*, with merely the inclusion of a small Canadian supplement, made these American-oriented magazines readily available to Canadians. And it is not even clear whether the majority of Canadians are fully supportive of government attempts to resist and control this influence.

If newscasts are important vehicles not only for imparting information but also for interpreting its significance, Canada again depends on larger countries for their edition of news reports. The Canadian Press relies on the same international news services (e.g. Associated Press) as does the United States, and frequently uses reports from the B.B.C. International news, then, may not be filtered through Canadian eyes and is often determined in the first place by another society. Furthermore, newsworthy events are more likely to be those which happen in the dominant society. Newscaster Lloyd Robertson of the C.B.C. has pointed out that Canadian news is not just news of Canada, but news that affects Canada. Such a rationale sanctions the incorporation of considerable foreign news that supplants the "less important" news of a Canadian event.

In the field of entertainment, the "big time" is often defined as Hollywood, Nashville, New York, or perhaps London or Paris. Canadian entertainers who want to succeed may find it difficult to compete by remaining in the society in which their popularity emerged. Singer Anne Murray, commenting on this dilemma, has said she ultimately may be forced to establish a residence outside of Canada to advance her career. Conversely, the big-name entertainers that are desired by audiences in Canadian cities often come from another country.

Technological. The slow growth of Canada's research industry and scientific complex has meant that the country has depended on others to make the significant discoveries and inventions. A Standing Committee of the House of Commons in 1970 reported that in 1964, 96% of Canada's patents were issued to nonresidents; whereas in the United States nonresidents obtained only 20% of the patents, in Germany 39%, and in Japan 36%.[11] The Gray Report acknowledged that Canada imported more of its technology than any other industrial country.[12] In this way, another set of dependencies is established: The society becomes accustomed to the short-term benefits of foreign importations as solutions to its own needs.

Resource. It is characteristic of hinterlands or colonies to serve as necessary appendages to a dominant power when they provide required resources. In the contemporary world, industrialization makes new demands for resources which are absolutely necessary for the maintenance of the strong industrial complex. With her rich variety and abundance of natural resources, Canada is a natural hinterland to more highly industrialized countries which require her coal, iron ore, gas, and oil. The difficulty is that Canada has become an important source of these resources but not a location for their use in the actual manufacturing process. Perhaps it is not altogether surprising that heavy U.S. investment in Canada in resource extraction meant that Canada would be developed in a fashion complementary to rather than competitive with the manufacturing giants of U.S. industries; but such action has perpetuated a continued Canadian colonial posture.

From a societal point of view, there is a significant difference between extraction and manufacturing. In the former activity, relatively few people are being employed, often impermanently. In the second instance, large-scale, more permanent employment results in a higher general standard of living and in the growth of a variety of tertiary industries. Canadians have been concerned that much of the resource exploitation has led to only extractive employment. As a result, the insatiable external pressures for release of these resources have produced numerous counter-demands for the growth of secondary manufacturing industries. Only as the trend toward the domestication of industry continues will it be possible for Canadian society to become more than a hinterland or a shadow of a dominant society.

Primary Factors Responsible for Canada's Subordinate Role

I have suggested that Canadian society revolves around the needs, demands, and activity of stronger societies. The fact of colonialism is that the subordinate society is merely a satellite in the gravitational pull of a larger body rather than being the center of its own universe. Rocher points out that such satellitic status makes a society peripheral, unbalanced, and inhibited.[13] The society is peripheral because it is far from the decision-making center and yet dependent on that center. It is often unbalanced because some sectors of the society are extensively developed while others are not. It is inhibited because the more dominant society produces feelings of inferiority or perhaps of unwarranted modesty in the satellite society. Canadian society has faced all three of these issues as the result of the dominant influence of other societies.

The dependencies which Canadian society has experienced are the result of four factors: the presence of the American empire, the growth of multinational corporations, the relatively small Canadian population, and the pressures of continentalism.

THE PRESENCE OF THE AMERICAN EMPIRE

The concept of empire is nothing new in the history of mankind. In various time periods, the world has known the Roman Empire, the French Empire, and the British Empire, to name just a few; now we have the American Empire.[14] Earlier empires usually maintained direct control through military strength, whereas the contemporary American empire maintains control not as much through government as through cultural and economic ties. All empires have as their center a dominant society which gives the empire its name, and usually has overwhelming military, economic, and in modern times industrial strength. Its language becomes the major vehicle of communication among all societies within its influence. It attracts outstanding persons from other societies to serve in its institutions, and to be educated in its schools. The level of technology of this dominant society is usually superior, and its culture is often emulated by the upper class in the constituent societies.

There is no doubt that the United States is presently such a society; It is a military, industrial, and technological tower of strength. It attracts top scientists and entertainers from other countries, frequently because it promises prestige and handsome financial rewards, and thereby can become the center of activity within that field. Its economic advantage automatically relegates other societies to an inferior position. American educational institutions have trained large numbers of promising individuals from other societies; these students who become important decision makers in their own society frequently take American culture back with them. American manufactured products are available in many countries — a process known as "Cocacolonization".[15] Economic decisions made in the United States affect other societies drastically. In sum, there is a perpetual diffusion of culture and power to all societies under the influence of American society, and the activities of these subordinate societies, in turn, usually support the strength of the empire — whether they are aware of it or not. This colossal power is a factor in contemporary Canadian existence. Dismissing its influence as immoral does not diminish it. Any society which cannot compete with the overwhelming might of the United States must struggle with its influence.

The high standard of living in the United States is an enviable trait which others eagerly have sought to attain; but the price usually has been tighter enmeshment in the empire itself. Canadian society has become part of the American Empire through a complex pattern of interaction. The United States is Canada's best export customer, while in turn the bulk of Canada's imports are from the United States.[16] In financial matters, Canadians have preferred making secure and reliable investments in U.S. industry to speculating on new, unpredictable, and innovative industry in Canada.[17] The historical in-empire loyalties of Canadian society are clearly reflected in the nationality of imported capital. In 1900, 85% of the foreign capital in the country was provided by the United Kingdom and about 14% came from the United States; however, by 1950 the percentages were almost reversed.[18] As fundamental economic ties draw Canadian society into the Empire, the development of relationships at other levels is facilitated. George Grant has argued that because Canadians have succumbed to the belief in progress through technology they have been amenable to the yoke of the American empire.[19] As long as the United States retains its position of dominance in the world, it will be difficult to repel its influence on Canadian society.

THE MULTINATIONAL CORPORATION

One of the unique features of the present period in history has been the emergence of huge multinational corporations in what is referred to as the "New Mercantilism". No doubt the international corporation has contributed more than any other agency to the integration of national economies, for after the United States and Russia, it forms the third largest unit economy in the world.[20] The Gray Report has predicted that such large-scale corporations with their conglomerates and holding companies could eventually supplant the nation-state as the type of social organization most characteristic of the post-industrial world.[21] Committed to profit and to their own expansion, they cross national boundaries, promoting a common culture and making decisions that affect the economy of countries and the standard of living of individuals.

In its political sense, the term "multinational" really conveys a meaning of supranational, i.e. operating outside the jurisdiction of any single national government.[22] However, as the Gray Report explains, it is not the ownership of these corporations that is international; it is only the extent of the corporation's operations that tends to be international. Sixty-two of the largest 100 American corporations are multinational.[23] Since 1965, Harvard University has studied multinational corporations through its Multi-National Enterprise Project. In its first study, it determined that 187 American international corporations tended to dominate, and that the greatest number of American subsidiaries was in Canada.[24] Clearly, for Canada the multinational corporation is an operation with international scope but with a national label. Since the American economic empire is currently flourishing, these corporations are largely American in composition and direction.

What are the implications of the multinational corporation for Canadian society? One concern has been that international enterprises are unlikely to be tuned to national priorities.[25] Will profits be used internally or be taken out of the country? Will decisions be made by officers of the parent firm or by local managers? Will they abide by government regulation or will they use the threat of shifting their operation to another country to impose their own way on the host government? While an international corporation may have no single national allegiance, it may be forced to abide by regulations of the country of its home operating base. Therefore, it is possible that few decisions will be made in the interests of the host country. The constraints put on subsidiaries of multinational corporations by the government of the home office are known as *extraterritoriality*. For example, the Trading with the Enemy Act in the United States prevented Ford of Canada from selling trucks to China.[26] Or, more recently, the sale to Cuba of Canadian locomotives manufactured by M.L.W.-Worthington of Montreal was threatened by the fact that 59% of its stock was owned by Studebaker-Worthington of New Jersey whose actions were circumscribed by the U.S. law.[27] Jobs and general industrial expansion in Canada can be regulated, then, by an extension of the laws of foreign countries, which undermines national sovereignty.

However, at this point, a more penetrating question ought to be asked: Does any corporation ever act on the basis of national loyalties? John Porter argues that it is the very nature of corporations to make decisions according to the norms of capitalism and their desire for profit; national sentiments are rarely able to change these basic norms.[28] No corporation will sustain financial losses over long periods just because its operation is "good for the country". Whether the financier is in Canada, Chicago, or Calcutta, his primary aim is to maximize profits.[29] Thus a critique of the multinational corporation by nationalists is often a critique of the capitalist system itself.[30]

Walter Gordon, Liberal cabinet minister in the Pearson administration, argues that capital does have a nationality.[31] A solely Canadian-owned enterprise will act differently from a foreign-owned branch plant or subsidiary because the latter must always reckon with the interests of the parent company in issues like the location of plants, production plans, and the timing of investments. Yet Canadian economist A.E. Safarian claims that the suggestion that foreign ownership in itself is detrimental to Canadian society is "at variance with the facts".[32] In his study of 280 direct investment firms in the commodity-producing sector, Safarian concluded that it is the larger rather than the smaller firms that have the most decentralization of decision making. He argues that even though a corporation will choose to operate in Canada only if it is profitable to do so, it will always have to reconcile the interests of the national society with the corporation's economic concerns.

Another problem with the multinational corporation is its tendency toward *truncation*; i.e. a subsidiary seldom performs all the major functions which a major corporation requires for its operation.[33] For example, scientific research or marketing are operations that are vital to the existence of the subsidiary but that are often centralized in the offices of the parent firm and therefore performed outside the country. While the branch plant may provide employment for residents of Canada, truncation contributes to the technology gap and professional gap by minimizing the demand for such trained personnel within this country. If such a trend continues, Canadian society will always be comparatively underrepresented in the development of these professions because the industry does not support their employment here. Truncation may have been an advantage initially in that it provided expertise when little was available in Canada. But in the long run it tends to retard the development of research and the growth of certain occupations.

A corollary to this difficulty is that multinational corporations almost become a state in themselves. Primary loyalties of personnel are to the corporation, for this is where the rewards can be obtained. Nationals are frequently promoted out of their country to serve where they are needed, so that one almost becomes a citizen of the corporation's empire. Levitt insists that it is this aspect of corporation organizations which has given Canada the appearance of possessing a shortage of high-level expertise.[34] For instance, he notes that Procter and Gamble had promoted several Canadians through their ranks to managerial positions in subsidiaries around the world. Thus, large corporations that operate internationally have a complex organization that minimizes national concerns and societal goals and creates new loyalties. Since it is advantageous (raises, promotions) to be committed to the corporation rather than to the country, personnel move in and out of Canada according to company need.[35]

A further implication of the multinational corporation for Canadian society follows from the standardization of personnel, products, policies, and procedures. The Gray Report speaks of the foreign-controlled company or subsidiary as a "continuous transmission belt" of culture in general.[36] Examining the new values, beliefs, and other influences that impinged on the city of Galt, Ontario through its U.S. manufacturing subsidiaries, Robert L. Perry writes of the "subculture of subsidiaries".[37] There is no doubt that the similarities between Canada and the United States have encouraged the duplication of products and commercials, for example, which contributes to the erosion of particularisms in each culture and encouraged the development of these similarities in the first place. The U.S.-oriented multinational corporation has contributed to the homogenization of culture and is a factor with which an independent Canadian society must come to grips.

Whatever negative effects the multinational corporation may have, it cannot be wished out of existence. Therefore repeated efforts have been made to bring these corporations under control. Some view such corporations as the newest form of imperialism, while others see them as the most practical solution for world order because of the present plurality of world states.[38] While their fate is yet to be determined, the present existence of corporations has profound implications for Canadian society and, given Canada's proximity to the center of dominant world power, presents unique problems which will not be easily solved. As one step toward a solution, the Canada Development Corporation was established in 1971 to assist in the establishment and growth of Canadian firms. However, the problem of strengthening indigenous industry leads us to the major factor, in my estimation, that has produced external dependencies.

RELATIVELY SMALL POPULATION

The relatively small Canadian population and its resulting small domestic market have made purely Canadian enterprises less feasible economically. In an attempt to increase employment, national income, and industry in Canada in general, the federal government established a tariff policy of taxing imported goods to protect Canadian manufacturers from foreign competition. Canada was to develop and strengthen its own industry and not to remain merely a hinterland that imports all of its manufactured products which were mass produced elsewhere. The result of this tariff policy was what is known as the *miniature replica effect*. Foreign corporations were encouraged by the tariff to establish subsidiaries in Canada to turn out almost identical product lines as in other countries, only on a smaller scale. Thus the protective tariff had the effect of segregating the Canadian market from the rest of the world market, but in doing so encouraged the creation of branch plants which were largely truncated enterprises.

The industry that is replicated in Canada on a small scale in comparison to the larger enterprise in the foreign country has unfortunately raised product costs significantly. The tariff gives domestic producers an additional margin of the tariff charge by which their product's price can be increased and still be competitive. It follows that the protected Canadian manufacturer produces at costs above world costs and because of this situation finds it difficult to export.[39] Therefore, the standard of living is lower than it might be as Canadian consumers pay the price individually for the protection of their own industry. If the Canadian population were large enough to support a more efficient industrial structure, or if Canadian industries could compete on the world markets, the Gross National Product and thus the standard of living would be higher. As it is, the transference of products, technology, and research from other countries to our small-scale replicated industries of multinational corporations has enabled the manufacture of a greater variety and choice of products but at a higher cost.[40] From a cultural perspective, such a process not only contributes to the homogenization of culture but also perpetuates the *branch plant mentality*[41] so characteristic of Canadian society.

CONTINENTALISM

Geography had decreed that it was often more natural to communicate north and south across the border, rather than east and west within Canada; therefore, in order to thwart the development of a continentalism, specific efforts were needed to unite the population north of the 49th parallel. In addition to geographic factors, there is no doubt that the Cold War and its communist threat also carried Canada into a continental policy with the United States in such cooperative efforts as the Distant Early Warning (DEW line) System.[42] Thus Canadian defense policy has contributed to continentalism. Furthermore, the prior growth of American industry and the retarded development of Canadian industry also fostered Canada's inclusion into a continentalist dependency.

Canadian society's answer to this continentalist tendency has been government involvement in activity that might foster greater independence. Public ownership of internal communication facilities such as broadcasting (C.B.C.), railroads (C.N.R.), or airlines (Air Canada) has been deemed vital to the forging of east-west relationships and, interestingly, has reinforced *internal* colonial or hinterland relationships. Generally, the government has taken a "key sector" approach to foreign control.[43] Financial institutions, transportation, and communication are considered the keystones to internal unity; therefore foreign ownership of private-enterprise broadcasting, newspaper facilities, and banks has been largely prevented. In addition, public agencies have been set up to regulate industries not only in terms of their ownership but in terms of their ultimate function (e.g. the Canadian Radio-Television Commission and the National Energy Board). However, pressure is mounting for internal control of other aspects of the society as well. [44] In each instance, the goal is to thwart or at least to contain continentalist pressures and to ensure the independence of Canadian society.

Effects of External Pressures on Canadian Society

Canada has looked abroad for direction throughout its history. Consequently it was not unnatural for the society to move from colonial status in one empire to colonial status in another. The conflicting goals of a higher standard of living and of national independence have produced enduring tension. The rate at which our standard of living has risen would probably have been impossible without some foreign assistance. However, if independence is a cherished national goal, to move from colonialism to economic independence and still retain a high standard of living might be impossible without long-term social change. Perhaps in the modern world economic independence is a myth and cultural independence an impossibility. Yet Canadian society continues to resist external control and to repudiate the loss of cultural distinctiveness.

There is no question that Canada's ascribed "little boy" status and the paternalistic attitude of more dominant societies have affected Canadian society. What effect have these external powers had, and what has been our reaction to them?

First, external dependencies have produced a general *inferiority complex* because the center of significant decision making or activity is so frequently outside Canadian borders. The relatively greater importance of other societies as centers of finance, marketing, and entertainment, for example, produces conflicting feelings. On the one hand, the power and importance of the more dominant society evoke admiration, envy, and the desire to identify with it; on the other hand, hostility and hate emerge because of the inferior role that Canada is forced to take. These ambivalent feelings coexist. Inferiority is also fostered by Canada's position of marginality[45] in which the society does not really aim to identify with the dominant society nor does it really succeed in detaching itself from that more powerful society. Because of Canada's comparative weakness and frequent dependence on the more dominant society, a sense of inferiority persists.

Second, a *hostile reactionism* sets in to repudiate the society's secondary role. An attempt is made to reduce the superiority of the dominant society by ridiculing it, belittling its virtues, and exploiting its liabilities (racism, crime, and urban problems). This reaction of hostility to external domination can be characterized as the "anti-spirit". It is not so much what the Canadian society stands for that is important but what the society stands against. S.D. Clark has pointed out that anti-Americanism has also been a useful means of playing down internal disaffections and divisions within Canadian society by providing a new focus for opposition.[46]

It is from the combination of the inferiority complex and the hostile reactionism that the spirit of nationalism emerges. (This approach stresses the negative origins of nationalism; we will turn to the more positive aspects of the concept later.) The type of nationalism that emerges from this source is somewhat paranoic. The sense of persecution and the persuasion of one's own greatness in spite of that persecution have fathered the "pro-spirit". As a defensive reaction, a pro-Canadian attitude develops in which one forms loyalties opposite to those of other societies. The struggle to survive independently has been perhaps the predominant factor welding Canadian society together.[47] Much of the nationalism that has emerged has been of this nature. "Buy Canadian", for example, is advocated not because it is necessarily better to do so, but because it is a way of protesting external influence and control.

The position of a shadow society can change only when the more dominant society or societies begin to weaken or disintegrate, or when the shadow society comes into a position of power itself. Perhaps more than anything else, Canadian society seeks, not comparative power in the world arena, but greater control over her own destiny.

This approach to the study of Canadian society has revealed how external forces have made it difficult for Canada to establish her own unique character. Above all, we have seen the complexity of the matter, for in the modern world the choice can no longer be either foreign influence or no foreign influence. No doubt this problem will continue to plague Canadian society while it searches for solutions.

QUESTIONS FOR FURTHER EXPLORATION

1. *What are the advantages and disadvantages for Canada of being a society subordinate to more powerful societies?*
2. *Is it realistic for a modern society to attempt to isolate itself from the influence of other societies? To what extent should Canada attempt to assert her independence of other societies?*
3. *Find examples in your local newspaper of how other societies affect Canadian society. Discuss the significance, and analyze the consequences of this influence.*

NOTES

[1] D. Michael Ray speaks of the "economic shadow" of U.S. parent companies felt in southern Ontario. "The Location of United States Subsidiaries in Southern Ontario" in R.L. Gentilcore, ed., *Geographical Approaches to Canadian Problems* (Scarborough: Prentice-Hall of Canada, 1970), pp. 69-82.

[2] For a good example of a book that emphasizes this type of assumption see Abraham Rotstein and Gary Lax, *Independence: The Canadian*

Challenge (Toronto: The Committee for an Independent Canada, 1972).

3 The Science Council of Canada observed that Canadians had one of the highest rates of savings (e.g. pensions, bank deposits, life insurance) of any country in the world, indicating that they would rather save than invest capital in a Canadian innovative industry. Science Council of Canada, "Innovation in a Cold Climate: Impediments to Innovation" in Rotstein and Lax, p. 123.

4 M.H. Watkins, *Foreign Ownership and the Structure of Canadian Industry* (Report of the Task Force on the Structure of Canadian Industry) (Ottawa: Privy Council, 1968), p. 300. Government of Canada, *Foreign Direct Investment in Canada* (Gray Report) (Ottawa: Information Canada, 1972), p. 5.

5 J.J. Deutsch, "Recent American Influence in Canada", in H.G.J. Aitken et al., *The American Economic Impact on Canada* (Durham, N.C.: Duke University Press, 1959), p. 36.

6 H.G.J. Aitken, "The Changing Structure of the Canadian Economy" in H.G.J. Aitken et al., p. 7. For a recent review of Canadian—United States economic relations and their implications, see the Autumn 1972 issue of the *Journal of Contemporary Business*, particularly Glazier's article on Canadian investment in the United States.

7 A.E. Safarian, *Foreign Ownership of Canadian Industry* (Toronto: McGraw-Hill Co. of Canada, 1966), p. 2.

8 Robin Mathews and James Steele, *The Struggle for Canadian Universities* (Toronto: New Press, 1969), p. 1.

9 See Bruce Kidd, "Canada's 'National' Sport" in Ian Lumsden, ed., *Close the 49th Parallel: The Americanization of Canada* (Toronto: University of Toronto Press, 1970), pp. 258-273.

10 See Rotstein and Lax, pp. 196-226 and Lumsden, pp. 117-134, and pp. 157-168.

11 House of Commons Standing Committee on External Affairs and National Defence, *Proceedings* No. 33, "Special Committee Respecting Canada-U.S. Relations", July 1970, pp. 33-58.

12 *Foreign Direct Investment in Canada*, p. 130.

13 Guy Rocher, *A General Introduction to Sociology* (Toronto: Macmillan Co. of Canada, 1972), pp. 513-514.

14 George Grant is the Canadian who has most frequently used this designation in application to the United States. See his *Lament for a Nation* (Toronto: McClelland and Stewart, 1965), p. 8 and *Technology and Empire: Perspectives on North America* (Toronto: House of Anansi, 1969). An American sociology text that also uses the term is Thomas F. Hoult's, *Sociology for a New Day* (New York: Random House, 1974), pp. 232-233.

15 Kari Levitt, *Silent Surrender: The Multi-National Corporation in Canada* (Toronto: Macmillan Co. of Canada, 1971), p. 112.

16 H.G.J. Aitken, "The Changing Structure of the Canadian Economy", p. 8.

17 M.H. Watkins, *Foreign Ownership and the Structure of Canadian Industry*, pp. 12-13.

[18] I.A. Litvak, C.J. Maule, and R.O. Robinson, *Dual Loyalty: Canadian-U.S. Business Arrangements* (Toronto: McGraw-Hill Ryerson, 1971), p. 2.

[19] George Grant, *Technology and Empire: Perspectives on North America*, p. 64.

[20] Abraham Rotstein, "Development and Dependence" in Rotstein and Lax, p. 29.

[21] *Foreign Direct Investment in Canada*, p. 60.

[22] Jack N. Behrman, *National Interests and the Multi-National Enterprise*, (Englewood Cliffs, New Jersey: Prentice-Hall, 1970), p. 4. This is a study done from within the U.S. and very much aware of the implications of multi-national enterprises.

[23] *Foreign Direct Investment in Canada*, pp. 55-56.

[24] Raymond Vernon, *Sovereignty at Bay: The Multi-National Spread of U.S. Enterprises* (New York: Basic Books, 1971), pp. 11, 20.

[25] A study of seven multinational corporations in Canada (e.g. Imperial Oil, Ford, Reader's Digest) explores this issue: I.A. Litvak, C.J. Maule, and R.D. Robinson, *Dual Loyalty: Canadian-U.S. Business Arrangements*.

[26] A.A. Fatouros, "Multi-National Enterprise and Extra-territoriality", *Journal of Contemporary Business*, Vol. 1 (Autumn 1972), p. 36.

[27] *Calgary Herald* (March 19, 1974), p. 48.

[28] John Porter, *The Vertical Mosaic*, p. 269.

[29] L.C. Park and F.W. Park, *Anatomy of Big Business* (Toronto: Progress Books, 1962), p. 159.

[30] For example, see Gary Teeple, ed., *Capitalism and the National Question in Canada* (Toronto: University of Toronto Press, 1972) and Robert Laxer, ed., *Canada Ltd.: The Political Economy of Dependency* (Toronto: McClelland and Stewart, 1973).

[31] Walter L. Gordon, "Foreign Control of Canadian Industry", *Queen's Quarterly*, Vol. 73 (1966), p. 6. See also his *Troubled Canada* (Toronto: McClelland and Stewart, 1961), and *A Choice for Canada* (Toronto: McClelland and Stewart, 1966). Gordon's crusade was more in the direction of an independent capitalist Canada, whereas Mel Watkins opts for an independent socialist Canada.

[32] A.E. Safarian, *Foreign Ownership of Canadian Industry* (Toronto: McGraw-Hill Co. of Canada, 1966). See also "Some Myths about Foreign Business Investment in Canada", *Journal of Canadian Studies*, Vol. 6 (August 1971), pp. 3-21. Safarian wants to get behind the usual stereotyped accusations and to analyze the actual situation — particularly well summarized in the latter article.

[33] *Foreign Direct Investment in Canada*, p. 405.

[34] Kari Levitt, *Silent Surrender: The Multi-National Corporation in Canada*, p. 108.

[35] The only limitation to this movement is immigration regulations which recently have become more of a problem.

[36] *Foreign Direct Investment in Canada*, p. 297. See particularly Chapter

17, "The Impact of Foreign Control of Canadian Business on Canadian Culture and Society".

[37] Robert L. Perry, *Galt U.S.A.: The American Presence in a Canadian City* (Toronto: Maclean-Hunter, 1971), p. 36.

[38] C.S. Burchill, "The Multi-National Corporation: An Unsolved Problem in International Relations", *Queen's Quarterly*, Vol. 77 (1970), pp. 3-18.

[39] For an excellent study of the role of the tariff in Canada see J.H. Dales, *The Protective Tariff in Canada's Development* (Toronto: University of Toronto Press, 1966), particularly Chapter 6. Dales notes that while the tariff was to protect "infant" industries in Canada, their continued dependence on the tariff indicates that Canadian manufacturers "are not expected to grow up" (p. 143).

[40] Safarian argues that the protective tariff meant that Canadians would be better off economically with the direct investment of international corporations than without it. Restricting imports at world prices and disallowing the transference of technology by multinational corporations would have further depressed the standard of living. However, this is not to ignore the disadvantages. *Foreign Ownership of Canadian Industry*, p. 305.

[41] Rex A. Lucas, *Minetown, Milltown, Railtown: Life in Canadian Communities of a Single Industry* (Toronto: University of Toronto Press, 1971), p. 338.

[42] See Philip Resnick, "Canadian Defense Policy and the American Empire" in Ian Lumsden, ed., *Close the 49th Parallel*, pp. 93-115.

[43] House of Commons Special Committee Respecting Canada-U.S. Relations, Vol. 33-24.

[44] Philip Mathias has reported how, in an attempt to promote local industry under Canadian control, federal or provincial governments have invested huge amounts of public money into projects that have become financial disasters, e.g. Manitoba's forest products plant at The Pas and Nova Scotia's heavy water plant. Mathias details a number of interesting case studies: *Forced Growth* (Toronto: James Lewis and Samuel, 1971).

[45] Rocher uses concepts of both marginality and ambivalence to describe the relationship and feelings of the colonized for the colonizers: *A General Introduction to Sociology*, Chapter 14.

[46] S.D. Clark, "Canada and Her Great Neighbor", *Canadian Review of Sociology and Anthropology*, Vol. 1 (November 1964), p. 197.

[47] See Glen Frankfurter, *Baneful Domination* (Toronto: Longman Canada Ltd., 1971). Frankfurter argues that English speaking Canadians created an imaginary, ideal Britain to which they could be loyal as a means of distinguishing themselves from the United States.

4
Ethnic Group Conflict Model

The diversity of groups to which people belong and the priority of group loyalties over general societal concerns make it difficult to speak of one set of norms, values, or roles characteristic of the Canadian social system. Instead, we have numerous social systems, subcultures, and counter-cultures. Individuals interact in the wider society with the values and attitudes they have learned within their smaller groups. Since Canadian society consists of a plurality of groups, this chapter will examine the dynamics of inter-group relations and their impact on the society as a whole.

The Human Group

The sociologist's basic unit of analysis is the human group. Because man is a social being, he associates with others in groups that are formed on the basis of shared characteristics. These common qualities can be *ascribed* (assigned or inherited) as the result of attributes such as skin color or language, or they can be *achieved* through factors such as occupation or education. Such criteria determine whether a person will become a member of one group rather than another. Groups are formed and maintained by the interaction of persons with traits in common. As a collective unit, the group both reflects and molds the thinking and behavior of all its participants. In exchange for their participation, the group provides its members with a sense of belonging and identity that locates them within the wider society.

In some ways, national societies are a poor unit for sociological analysis because at the macro-level significant differences among persons are obscured. Furthermore, individuals tend to interact with those who are similar to themselves in smaller, manageable units rather than as isolated individuals in a mass society. Social groups join like-minded persons together, provide a sense of community, and help the individual to distinguish himself from those with different characteristics.

Every society is subdivided into numerous social groups and Canadian society is no exception. However, much of the group diversity within Canadian society is based on the rigid, ascribed characteristics of race, language, and ethnic tradition rather than on achieved characteristics. Every member of the society brings his group identity and background with him into any interaction, so that bonds of sociality must be constructed before meaningful relationships can develop. The frequent use of the hyphenated-Canadian nomenclature shows that Canadians tend to see each other in terms of their group origins.

Although Canadian society lacks one national consciousness, it possesses a number of group consciousnesses. Continuous population turnover produced by repeated waves of immigration and emigration could only strengthen the importance of shared group characteristics for social interaction and friendship formation. If tensions were to develop within the society, inter-group conflict based on heritage would be a more likely basis than conflict between economic classes. For example, the French resentment of Anglo dominance and exploitation has usually not been couched in bourgeois-proletariat economic terms but has been promulgated as the right to ethnic sovereignty by Quebecers of French extraction.

THE CONCEPT OF ETHNIC GROUP

We distinguish between those who are of a different race from us and those who are of the same race but of different culture. Thus, the *racial group* is physically identifiable and the *ethnic group* is culturally identifiable. However, since a racial group is seldom only physically distinguishable but is also culturally distinguishable, sociologists have used the concept *ethnic group* to refer to any group whose culture sets them apart. So an ethnic group may be characterized by a unique language or dialect, religion, nationality, or peculiar customs or habits that may include or transcend inherited biological traits. It may be somewhat inaccurate to speak of native peoples as just another ethnic group in Canada, for the legal constraints of the Indian Act do give them totally different status. Nevertheless, having acknowledged this limitation, I propose to use the term "ethnic group" in this broad sense to refer to any group sharing a distinct culture.

Table 4.1 indicates the percentage distribution of the population by ethnic origin in 1971. The data were obtained by the census in response to a question asking what ethnic or cultural group the person or his ancestors on the male side were from on coming to this continent. This table tells us nothing about the degree to which the ethnic tradition is embraced, the number of generations that have been resident in Canada, or the nature of the assimiliation that has taken place. What the table does tell us is that those of British and French origin are the largest component of the population and that other groups have sizeable numbers even though their percentage of the total population is considerably smaller.

Table 4.1 Absolute Numbers and Percentage Distribution of the Population by Ethnic Groups, 1971

	Absolute Number	Percentage
British	9,624,115	44.62
French	6,180,120	28.65
German	1,317,200	6.10
Italian	730,820	3.38
Ukrainian	580,660	2.69
Netherlands	425,945	1.97
Scandinavian	384,795	1.78
Polish	316,430	1.46
Jewish	296,945	1.37
Hungarian	131,890	0.61
Greek	124,475	0.57
Yugoslavian	104,955	0.48
Czech and Slovak	81,870	0.37
Russian	64,475	0.29
Finnish	59,215	0.27
Belgian	51,135	0.23
Austrian	42,120	0.19
Romanian	27,375	0.12
Lithuanian	24,535	0.11
Indian and Eskimo	312,760	1.45
Other Asian (e.g. Indian, Pakistani, Filipino)	129,460	0.60
Chinese	118,815	0.55
Japanese	37,260	0.17
Negro	34,445	0.15

Source: Compiled and computed from 1971 Census of Canada, Statistics Canada, Vol. I, Part 3, Cat. 92-723.

IS ETHNICITY REALLY IMPORTANT?

There are a number of reasons why this ethnic diversity is more significant than is readily apparent from statistical data. First, the fact that the British and French were the first ethnic groups to migrate to Canada from abroad meant that they were in a power position to formulate policies that would give preference to the addition of other residents of the same ethnic origin. John Porter has coined the term *charter group* to refer to the ethnic group that first settles a "previously unpopulated territory" and who then controls which other groups can come in.[1] While it is true that Porter's definition ignores the existence of native peoples already resident in the territory, the idea that a charter group is itself a foreign people who merely happen to be the first of a diverse stream of migration to enter the country and, as a result, are in a position of power makes the concept a good one. These charter members of Canadian society, however, were not of equal strength. The British were the *higher* charter group and the French the *lower* charter group, for ultimate control of the immigration process always seemed to favor the British because the political apparatus was in their hands. The nature of this power role was to make the native ethnic groups, as well as the ethnic groups permitted entry from other nations, very much aware of their subordinate status and power. In some cases, discrimination reinforced the dominant position of the charter group in the mind of the member of the smaller ethnic group. The feeling of apparent insignificance forced the numerous ethnic groups into a defensive position where group consciousness was further strengthened.

Second, since the culture of the majority group is the dominant culture of the society, smaller groups must continually fight to retain their culture — if it is to be retained at all. Because of the overwhelming strength of the charter groups in enforcing their will and in propagating their culture in Canada, other ethnic groups were forced to distinguish themselves in some way. On arrival in the new society, immigrants often attempt to recreate the social patterns of the old country; in this case, minority groups such as the Ukrainians easily perpetuated their culture as a reaction to their socialized sense of inferiority in Canadian society. Since the charter group's policy allowed entry, additional waves of immigrants of the same ethnic group (e.g. the Germans) or the constant trickle of new immigrants (e.g. the Chinese) fostered the perpetuation of ethnic traditions. By serving as a receiving community these ethnic groups were reinvigorated.

A third reason why ethnicity has been more important in Canada than the statistical data indicate is that the ethnic counterforce of the charter groups sets the pattern among other ethnic groups for the necessity of maintaining strong ethnic loyalties and identities.[2] If one group had dominated, there would have been more accord about the specific nature of the dominant culture; but since the British and French were in conflict themselves, the society had a greater built-in tolerance for the perpetuation of ethnic identities. Canada's claim to be a multicultural society reflects this tolerance and support for numerous ethnic components within the society.[3]

The dominance of the British and French ethnic groups in Canada has focused attention on the bicultural and bilingual nature of the society. However, in a speech in the Canadian Senate in 1964, Senator Paul Yuzyk spoke of a "third force" in Canadian society consisting of those of non-English and non-French origin.[4] Yuzyk argued that it was the minority status of the "third force" that welded these groups together to the point where they could hold the balance of power in any struggle between the French and the English. Clearly, a wide diversity of ethnic groups could be mechanically added together to demonstrate the strength of the non-English and non-French element in Canadian society. However, there is no proof that there is any actual unanimity among these groups except in a general awareness of their subordinate status, or that every ethnic group actually does serve as a pressure group.

Table 4.1 reveals that in 1971, 26.73% of the total population was of neither English nor French descent.[5] While most of these persons have found the customs and language of the British charter group quite congenial, the many ethnic backgrounds and loyalties outside the two charter groups are a variable that complicates interaction in the society. Thus the society that is polarized into French and English is further divided by multi-ethnic allegiances. The regional variation in ethnic strengths provides the fourth reason why ethnicity takes on additional meaning in Canadian society. Italians and Ukrainians may be minor ethnic groups in Nova Scotia and British Columbia, but in Ontario and Saskatchewan it is a different matter. The French may be almost non-existent in British Columbia, but certainly not in New Brunswick. Each region in Canada experiences its own ethnic tensions due to the unique composition of its population.

Inter-group Relations

From a sociological perspective, groups form because of *consciousness of kind* (individuals identify with those who are similar to themselves) and *consciousness of difference* (they recognize those who are unlike themselves).[6] It is the nature of groups to distinguish between "we" and "they", the "in-group" and "outgroup", on the basis of their identifying characteristics. For example, the kinship and neighborhood relationships of the Italian community in Montreal reinforce the distinctions of language, religion, and culture that set them apart from other ethnic groups and from the urban society as a whole.[7] These unique attributes are needed to *legitimize* the independent existence of the group. Members need to know not only *what* distinguishes their group from others but *why* the distinction is being made. Montreal Italians know that if they did not emphasize their differences, their value system, social controls, and web of social organizations would collapse.

OUT-GROUP CONFLICT

Since in every society a variety of groups coexists, the threat of absorption by stronger groups is always a fear of the minority group. Such is the case with all groups whether religious, racial, or national. Often the continued existence of the in-group is dependent on the perceived threat of the out-group, so that even if it is not acutely felt, out-group conflict must be exaggerated in order to produce in-group solidarity. Out-group conflict, then, is functional to the group by reestablishing and reaffirming its identity and its boundaries.[8] Thus, through conflict Indians remind each other as well as the white man of their differences, and the French can more easily distinguish themselves from the English.

Obviously, out-group conflict need not be physical. In fact, the revolutionary language and tactics of the FLQ in Quebec almost had the unintended effect of reducing group boundaries between French and English in the events of October 1970. The appeal to the shared values of unity and freedom in Canada legitimated the invocation of the War Measures Act to which Canadians gave overwhelming support.[9] The physical conflict did, however, make English-speaking Canadians aware of the seriousness of French demands for an alteration in their relationships with the English, and in particular assisted in the redistribution of power taking place within the society.[10] Since the conflict was not a collective act by all members of the ethnic group, group hostilities and boundaries did not harden.

Even the more sophisticated and less violent forms of conflict can be powerful weapons in assisting groups to be more cognizant of each other, to win new rights, and to obtain different status. John Jackson's study of a small town in southwestern Ontario illustrates how conflict between ethnic groups can even be institutionalized.[11] Tecumseh, Ontario possessed three factions: French Catholics, English Catholics and English Protestants. Since tax support for Catholic schools and linguistic educational rights were crucial issues, conflict between the contending groups frequently focused on education. Although the conflict appeared to be continuous, it had been regularized in agencies such as a dual school inspectorate whereby the contending parties made compromises with one another at a formal level. Jackson points out that such institutionalization strengthens the structural position of each party in conflict but reduces the visibility of the conflict, with the result that in-group solidarity is more difficult to engender.

Conflict can also teach the majority greater respect for minorities. The embittered stand taken by the Cree Indians of Northern Quebec on the James Bay Project has made all Canadians aware of the rights of this ethnic group.[12] The series of dams and the new flooding that will take place as the project proceeds could wreak havoc with the traditional Indian means of subsistence and way of life. The legal conflict that ensued was an attempt by these Indians to protect the cultural life and property of their ethnic group. Whether the cash settlement which the Indians won was really a victory is a moot question.

Collective resistance to a common foe enables all members of a group to become more aware of the qualities which differentiate them from others. The organization that emerges to deal with the out-group becomes an important mechanism to arouse identification with the group. For example, provincial Indian organizations such as the Union of Ontario Indians or the Manitoba Indian Brotherhood have an important role to play in unifying Indians, making them aware of their common identity, and representing them to the wider society. So the Indian reminds himself and others of who "we" are and who "they" are. The pressure that the organization can bring to bear on the society, even just by verbal conflict, improves its bargaining role by establishing the legitimacy of its case and by making it familiar to most Canadians.

Instead of weakening the societal unit, group conflict has just the opposite effect in the long run. As long as minority groups allow the dominant group to bully them and as long as they remain reclusive, there will be little conflict, but also little equality and little independence.[13] Only when protest and conflict develop will minority groups tend to communicate with and participate in the society as a whole.

REQUIREMENTS FOR GROUP CONFLICT

In Canadian society there are numerous minorities which engage in minimal conflict. We hear little from persons of Finnish or Japanese descent, for example, partially because their culture is not transmitted by the dominant socializing agencies of the society.[14] Thus the presence of minority groups does not in itself mean that societal tension or inter-group conflict will result. Furthermore, the possession of ascribed characteristics such as race or language that differentiate persons in a highly visible manner from the dominant society is also not sufficient to provoke group conflict. The minority group will accept its subordinate status quite passively unless two factors are present: a feeling of deprivation and a sense of group awareness.

Relative deprivation is the disadvantage a person feels when comparing his own status or opportunities with those of someone else. Whether one feels deprived or not is a relative matter since it obviously depends on the standard of comparison.[15] As long as Francophone Quebecers compared themselves with other French Quebecers there was little conflict, but as soon as they began comparing themselves with Anglophone Quebecers they felt they were being deprived, and sought measures by which such inequalities could be overcome.

Group awareness is the sharpening of the distinctions between the in-group and the out-group so that the in-group becomes aware of itself as a collective unit. Not only does the group member become aware of similarities which all members of the group share, but the group becomes aware of its cohesiveness. Furthermore, the group is not just a collection of those with similar aggregate characteristics; rather the group comes to view itself as a unit of power because of these similarities. When group members recognize themselves as comrades in opposition to the out-group, a militancy is injected that concentrates on the collective unit and its defense. For example, when native Canadian Indians began to view themselves collectively as a source of power rather than merely as an aggregation of people with similar characteristics, group conflict could arise.

The Inuit (Eskimos) provide a good example of a group that has engendered little conflict in Canadian society to this point. Their flexibility, adaptability, and increasing dependence on the trading post have brought them into frequent contact with Euro-Canadians.[16] However, a sense of deprivation has been slow to develop since comparison has been based on a different set of values. Showing a weak sense of group awareness, most Eskimo cooperatives allow themselves to be sustained by white initiative rather than asserting a Pan-Eskimo solidarity.[17] As a result, out-group conflict has developed more slowly among Eskimos than among Indians in spite of the recent self-designation of their people as Inuit rather than Eskimo. Thus, if an ethnic group possesses little sense of relative deprivation and little group awareness, conflict will not be expressed even though the ingredients for such conflict may be implicitly there. Significantly, when the majority group serves as both the standard for comparison and the enemy against which one must defend, conflict will become acute.

THE ETHNIC GROUP AS REFERENCE GROUP

The ethnic group can also foster tensions in Canadian society on the personal level. The ethnic group often succeeds in demanding conformity from its members because it is an important source of personal identity in an ethnically diverse society. In an unfamiliar social world, the recent migrant or native minority member maintains the ethnic traditions as a meaningful activity and participates in the ethnic society. Because his prestige in the ethnic group is not necessarily tied to his rank in the wider society,[18] the individual finds in the minority group an alternate society with norms, customs, and values which he gladly maintains.

Canadian social history is replete with data supporting these generalizations. A study of Jews in Halifax has shown that although they live in different parts of the city, they have developed a strong "we-group" feeling because of frequent socialization through both informal and formal Jewish organizations.[19] Italians in Toronto tend to congregate in one section of the city and to restrict their primary-group interaction to those of their own ethnic background with the result that there is little intermarriage.[20] Francophones in St. Boniface, Manitoba, maintain their geographical ethnic strength by providing a full set of activities within their community and by emphasizing the maintenance of kinship bonds.[21]

According to Raymond Breton, when ethnic communities possess a formal structure of organizations to perform most of the services required by their members, they have a high degree of *institutional completeness.*[22] Churches, welfare organizations, and periodicals contribute to the cohesiveness of an ethnic group; the more services available to the individual from members of his ethnic group, the greater the likelihood that social interaction with the rest of the society will be limited. Relatively high institutional completeness was registered by Greek, German, Hungarian, Italian, Lithuanian, Polish, and Ukrainian groups, while low institutional completeness was indicated by Austrian, Belgian, Spanish and Swedish ethnic groups.

╀ There are many groups to which an individual may belong simultaneously that do not engender conflicting loyalties. The Steelworkers' Union and the Italian-Canadian Club, for example, tend to supplement rather than compete with each other. In other instances, the demands of one group may run counter to the demands of another group to which one has established an allegiance. Participation in a university community and active membership in a native Indian association may produce personal conflict because of the strain of wanting to succeed in a white man's institution while remaining loyal to the native culture. A Ukrainian boy who has been schooled in the culture and customs of his ethnic group may later feel the tensions of attempting to identify with both Canadian and Ukrainian culture. The determining factor, however, is which group the individual chooses as his reference group. A *reference group* is any group whose values and world view become the basis for a person's own values and world view. When circumstances create pressure to choose between alternative groups, the reference group that is chosen will determine the individual's behavior.

The greater the difference between the ethnic group and the predominant culture in an area, the greater the likelihood that the ethnic group will serve as the reference group. As a result, there is a difference in the institutional completeness various ethnic groups will demonstrate. Sociologists use the term *social distance* to indicate the degree of affinity persons have for each other on the basis of cultural and social similarities. A British immigrant is not nearly as socially distant from Canadian society in culture and customs as an Italian or an Asian Indian; hence the ethnic group as a reference group is of less importance to the Briton.

The significance of the ethnic group as a reference group will usually alter with time. When children of ethnic parents are educated in public schools, ethnic particularisms are endangered. As a result, there is considerable tension between generations when children are torn between conformity to parental ethnic demands and the demands of their peer group and the dominant culture.[23] If the claims of Canadian society are strong enough, ethnic ties may be an embarrassment to the insecure and torn second generation which is apprehensive about accepting its minority position. It has been suggested that it is the more secure, native-born third generation which shows renewed interest in the ethnic group.[24] While this phenomenon has not been documented in Canada, experience has indicated that in spite of the ethnic tolerance supposedly present in the society, an ethnic identity might be shunned in order to reduce the dissonance when alternative reference groups make competing demands on the individual. Later, when the individual feels more secure in his adopted society, he identifies with his ethnic tradition more freely.

THREE IMPORTANT ETHNIC VARIABLES

Race, language, and religion are important indices of ethnicity. All three of the variables have been a significant means of social differentiation in Canadian society.

Race is a highly visible distinction among persons. It is something that no amount of cultural adaptation can completely eradicate. Color of skin identifies people to each other and leads to *stereotypes* or generalizations. *Prejudice* as an attitude and *discrimination* as behavior resulting from that attitude easily follow when people are so immediately confronted with differences between "us" and "them". The Japanese were easily discriminated against during World War II in Canadian society and were interned as a racial group in camps in the interior of British Columbia for several years. Persons of Chinese descent tend to cluster near downtown areas and to form ethnic associations in which race is an important factor. In Nova Scotia, race has also contributed to prejudice and discrimination against blacks and to their areal segregation.[25] Davis and Krauter's study of all these minorities has indicated that Canadian society has been quite discriminatory and racist toward them in the past but that persistent efforts to change the situation appear to be succeeding, at least on the legislative level.[26]

Language is also an important means of differentiation, for it insulates the ethnic group from the pressures of the dominant culture. Language radically distinguishes the in-group from the out-group because, by erecting barriers to communication, it gives the in-group a common bond and lets the out-group know that they are on the outside. The maintenance of the ethnic language is, then, an important indicator of the degree to which ethnic groups are sustaining themselves as entities.[27] Conversely, it can be seen why ethnic groups fight for the retention of their language in the Canadian environment as the chief means to resist absorption. Language is the key to maintaining culture, and the one depends on the other. Thus in Western Canada, Ukrainians have fought for the teaching of their language in the public school system, and the French throughout Canada have felt strongly about maintaining their language. Even the scattered Moslem community in Canada uses the shortwave radio to receive news and entertainment in their native language as a means of participation in their ethnic tradition.[28]

Religion is the third major area of ethnic identity. It has been suggested that when immigrants came to the United States, social pressures forced them to adapt in all spheres of life except religion.[29] Your new employer might make you give up your ethnic holidays, your classmates might ridicule your style of dress, but there was one area which the society accepted as being your own private world and that was religion. As a result, ethnic customs, traditions, and even language were deposited in the ethnic church. While Canadian society has been far more tolerant than the United States of secular ethnic associations (the government has provided official and financial support), it is still true that one meaningful way to express ethnicity in Canada has been through religion. Some ethnic churches hold language schools and celebrate ethnic holidays with religious services. Nagata's study of Greek immigrants in Toronto indicated a fairly sharp compartmentalization between the public and private spheres of Greek life in Canada.[30] For instance, while economic and educational activities were accommodated to Canadian society, intense efforts were made to retain Greek language and culture in religion and family life. On the other hand, among the Lebanese in an Alberta community the lack of an *imam* or minister and a weak religious organization reduced the strength of their ethnic community considerably.[31] Lee has also demonstrated the nature of the relationship between religion and ethnicity in a French-Canadian community within a largely English-Canadian city.[32] The pressures toward assimilation were so great that the ethnic dilemma was reduced to a matter of religion. Rather than emphasizing their ethnic difference, French Canadians distinguished themselves by being Catholic in a Protestant area. The rumbling among some Indians to reject Christianity has also been an attempt to reassert the native culture with which it is thought the white man's religion is incompatible.[33]

Ethnic language and religion are important elements in reinforcing the ethnic identity. When these factors are weakened or destroyed, the ethnic group becomes a vulnerable social unit in the face of pressures toward Anglo-conformity. Racial factors introduce a less adaptable variable which is not susceptible to the same type of pressures. The ethnic group may choose to separate itself from the wider society or may be forced to seek refuge in each other's company because of the hostility of the society. The drawing of group boundaries as well as their relaxation must be a free choice made by the persons involved.

The French-English Conflict

There are two group conflicts which tend to preoccupy Canadian society and which ought to be discussed more specifically: the French-English conflict and the white - native Indian conflict.

The notion of conflict between the French and English as two ethnic groups is not new in Canada.[34] The British conquest of the French on the Plains of Abraham in 1759 stirred resentments and antagonisms that were only submerged rather than obliterated during the ensuing years. Jones speaks of this conquest as a *primordial event* which made an indelible mark on French Canadians for years to come and produced in them a minority complex which they are now seeking to overcome.[35] In spite of being conquered, the traditional society continued under the guidance of the parish clergy who filled the leadership void left by the removal of the French entrepreneurs and administrators. Rural French-Canadian society thus remained relatively intact even though aware of being under the watchful eye of English Canadians.

Given this sort of détente between the two ethnic groups, an explanation is needed for the more recent conflict in Canadian society. My explanation will stress the social changes that have taken place, particularly in French-Canadian society, which have brought out latent resentments and new hostilities.

The old way of looking at the French-English conflict pointed out the sharp contrasts that could be drawn between two fundamental societal styles. Quebec was familistic and Catholic in orientation, whereas English Canada was individualistic and Protestant. English Canada was supposedly progressive, industrial, and capitalistic, whereas French Canada was traditional, rural, and consisted of small subsistence farmers. According to this type of contrast, the French and English lived in two different, relatively self-contained social worlds. The language gap continued to reinforce the barriers between two markedly different societies.

Rossides sketches three stages in the development of French Canadian society.[36] The period from 1600 to 1760 he identifies as "the Frontier Trading Society" in which the authoritarianism of the state and church brought order to the diverse goals of explorers, administrators, traders, and missionaries. The second period from 1760 to the First World War is identified as "the Frontier Rural Society" in which the agricultural *habitant* family centered around the small-town parish. The elites of the society were doctors, lawyers, and priests rather than those engaged in business and economic activity, as in English-Canadian society. By the late 1800s, the overpopulation of rural Quebec had forced migration into the industrial towns of New England where employment was readily available. The third period from the First World War to the present is labelled "the Industrial-Urban Society" or "the New Quebec". During this period a marked change took place. Secular values, science, and rationality began to predominate, the birth rate declined, the family orientation was replaced by an emphasis on individualism, large-scale urbanization took place, and classical education began to make way for an education geared to technological and industrial occupations. Indeed, Rossides points out that Quebec had become quite similar to any other urban-industrial society; if this tendency is true, the whole notion of biculturalism must be questioned, for a "growing homogenization of Canadian culture"[37] is taking place.

One explanation for the French-English conflict, then, is that the tensions of rapid social change, in which the contradictory values of the old society are juxtaposed to the urban secular values of the new society, have produced a "displaced aggression" of hostility to outsiders. In this interpretation, it is the social changes within Quebec itself that have produced tensions which are vented on the previously agreed-upon enemy. Needless to say, this is only one part of the explanation.

The British conquest destroyed the French political and entrepreneurial class in what has been called the "social decapitation"[38] of Quebec. With the exception of the priests, the French leadership was replaced with the victors' own elite. Again, this situation did not become critical until Quebec began to industrialize and urbanize. Until that point, external control was not harshly felt and could be largely avoided. But as the society urbanized, the need for the expansion of bureaucratic institutions in areas such as education and health became obvious. A middle class of white-collar workers began to emerge in the public sector, creating new aspirations and channels for upward mobility.[39] Of course, urbanization was made possible in the first place by industrial employment which had opened up under the sponsorship of Anglophone capital, technology, and enterprise. Thus, industrialization meant the reassertion of English control — this time in an economic way.

French resentment against English economic domination finally reached its peak in 1960 when it emerged into what has been described as the *Quiet Revolution*.[40] The new middle class which consisted of young, educated, professional, and semi-professional white-collar workers particularly resented English control of federal bureaucracies and private corporations because it essentially blocked French participation at the upper levels.[41] Guindon argues that separatist discontent was a protest by the middle class against their restricted occupational mobility.[42] In essence, the Quiet Revolution represents an attempt by the Francophone middle class to modernize Quebec while overcoming its subordinate status. The reassertion of the French language and culture and the doctrine of *maîtres chez nous* ("masters of our own house") have been ways of seeking equality without giving in to pressures to Anglicize.[43]

But how important really is language distinctiveness for French Canadians? Can a distinct culture be maintained without the language which transmits and expresses this culture? French Canadians have largely answered this question with a firm no, and have made the language issue critical in the defense of their own society. The resistance to Anglo-conformity was shown by controversial Quebec Bill 22 which made French the official language of that province.

The federal government has made bilingualism its official policy in order to affirm French equality in Canadian society and to ensure French participation throughout the society. Two very interesting studies on the use of French and English in Canada have startling implications for the society. According to Richard J. Joy, historically there was more bilingualism in Canada than there is now. He uses census data to show that the only bilingual areas in Canada are a small zone in northern New Brunswick and east-northeastern Ontario — both extensions of Quebec.[44] This bilingual belt separates an increasingly French unilingual population from an increasingly English unilingual population. Since French minorities are disappearing in Anglo-Canada and the strength of Anglophones in Quebec is waning, language boundaries are becoming more, not less, defined.

Stanley Lieberson's highly technical sociological study points out that bilingualism in Canada is more likely to mean that a French-speaking Canadian has learned English than that an English-speaking Canadian has learned French.[45] He also observes that in most provinces a French Canadian who becomes bilingual is likely to raise his children in English. If bilingualism is really only an intermediate step in the final acquisition of English as the common language in the country, it is understandable why some Quebecers feel that the only way of saving their culture is to become independent.[46] If, on the other hand, bilingualism in the sense of a coexistence of two languages of equal strength and on an equal basis is both possible and probable, such action might be avoided. However, this utopian, long-term goal does not take into account factors such as the dominance of English in the world[47] and the present unilingualism of whole regions of Canada. Consequently, both parties in the conflict regard bilingualism with considerable pessimism.

The geographic segregation of French Canadians has helped to delay a solution. Both sides had coexisted fairly peacefully as long as there was no need for considerable interaction. However, interaction has increased because of the corporations operating in Quebec under English-speaking management. Moreover, both the French and the English have agreed to participate in a government that passes legislation affecting both ethnic groups. As long as an ethnic identity is important to each side, a just coexistence will always remain a struggle.

The Native Indian - White Conflict

Conquered, segregated on reservations, their old way of life destroyed, Canadian Indians remain subordinate to the dominant English-speaking culture.[48] They rightfully blame the white man for cracking the foundations of their culture and the white man in turn blames the Indian for not adjusting to white society.

The Indians' increasing conflict with white society raises the question of why the Red Power movement has recently emerged when white control was reluctantly accepted for so long. My explanation is based on a theory of status crystallization.[49] *Status crystallization* takes place when an individual possesses similar standing along several status variables such as income, education, and occupation, rather than high standing on some status variables and low standing on others. I would suggest that conflict results when the leadership of an oppressed minority such as the native Indians is recruited from those whose status has improved on some dimensions but who are not fully accepted by those of similar status in the white society. Because they lack a crystallization of status, they become the militant leaders of the minority. With the increase of education among Indians, articulate representatives develop who engender conflict.

For example, Harold Cardinal, the president of the Indian Association of Alberta, and a member of the board of the National

Indian Brotherhood, has been an active spokesman of the Indian people.[50] Cardinal's education in sociology (St. Patrick's College, Ottawa) has equipped him for leadership in the Indian-white conflict: He knows how to confront the white man on the white man's terms. He has participated successfully in white society; yet because he is an Indian and chooses to retain that identity, his status cannot fully crystallize in the white society. As more Indians attend Canadian universities and obtain the confidence to challenge the white society at vulnerable points, social conflict is likely to increase.

Canadian Indians are presently struggling with a marginal position. A *marginal man* is a person who accepts much of a new way of life while he retains many ways of the old life from which he came. Some Indians would like to restore the old way of life of hunting and gathering; yet the changed environment and economy of the modern world make that option appear hopeless. Another option would be to accept white society and to develop all the skills necessary to participate in it. Indian lawyer William Wuttunee represents this school of thought and speaks accusingly of the "treaty mentality" of dependence among most Indians.[51] Such a position appears to do violence to Indian culture and society. Cardinal struggles with a type of median position in which a few necessary compromises are made without capitulating to white control and a traditional society is maintained. Such a median position produces conflict not only with white society but also among Indians themselves.

Recovering a culture that has almost been wiped out is a difficult task; however, it is preferable to the pain of participating in the annihiliation of that culture. The Indian struggle to find the solution that will allow them to retain their identity will undoubtedly continue to create conflict with white society at critical moments.

Melting Pot or Mosaic?

In contrast to the United States, Canada has been called a mosaic rather than a melting pot. Supposedly, Canadian society has greater tolerance for ethnic identities and traditions — particularly since government policy actually encourages the maintenance of cultural differences. Perhaps such tolerance is due to the fact that there is no one "Canadian way of life" or culture into which the ethnic groups can melt. The notion of a melting pot has been rethought as it applies to the United States[52] and, at least officially, Canadians have rejected the melting pot image for themselves. The problem with both of the terms "melting pot" and "mosaic", however, is that they oversimplify a very complex process and perhaps are journalistic phrases that ought to be discarded.[53] Sociologists prefer to use the more precise conceptual alternatives: assimilation, segregation, and pluralism.

Assimilation is the breakdown of particularistic attributes, so that the individual participates in the common culture.[54] It implies that ethnic groups ought to lose their ethnicity and become like "everybody else". One of the reasons why this notion has been rejected in Canada is that no one knows exactly what the common culture is. Yet the British culture and tradition have priority in the society, and there are the "unofficial" pressures at school or at work to conform to cultural modes that have become an accepted part of Canadian society.

Segregation or the complete separation of an ethnic group from the society also appears to be unworkable. The pressures facing segregated groups like the Hutterites show that their survival is unsure. As an alternative to the two extremes of assimilation and segregation, *pluralism* is frequently suggested as a middle road. *Pluralism* means that cultural differences are allowed to exist on the basis of equality of opportunity.

Hughes and Kallen have taken a somewhat pessimistic view of multiculturalism or cultural pluralism in Canada.[55] They suggest that these terms only subtly mask an old form of majority group dominance. Encouraging the preservation of some aspects of an ancestral culture (e.g. arts and crafts), they argue, is certainly not the same as encouraging a living culture. Therefore, this type of cultural pluralism gives minority group members the illusion of preserving their ethnic identity, while at the same time it ensures Anglo-conformity.

Neverthless, what might we expect as a result of a policy of ethnic pluralism? If groups coexist in the same society over a period of years there is bound to be a blending of cultural traits as each ethnic group both gives and receives. This gradual process is *integration*.[56] While pluralism is the official policy, there is no doubt that assimilation is taking place at a rapid rate. And, as Jones has pointed out, the pressure is not so much to conform to the values and customs of the British majority as to conform to the values and customs which are becoming common to all industrial societies.[57] However, the tolerance which is part of pluralism will probably lead to a sifting and blending of the elements of a variety of ethnic traditions into a culture representative of Canadian society. On the other hand, ethnic group conflict also contributes to such a goal by forcing Canadian society to change, adapt, and innovate as a response to such conflict.

The Ethnic Group Conflict Model has illustrated how ascribed social characteristics have fragmented Canadian society into relatively enduring social units. Since interaction in Canadian society has frequently required an ethnically-labelled identity, it is clear that ethnicity has been an important means of social location within the society. Whether ethnicity will retain its overt societal significance in spite of the processes described above, or whether it will become only a vestige of a once vital personal heritage will undoubtedly affect the future character of Canadian society.

QUESTIONS FOR FURTHER EXPLORATION

1. *Do we really want people to retain their complete culture or to retain just interesting artifacts of that culture? Is multiculturalism a real goal or a psychologically reassuring ploy?*
2. *Outline a strategy whereby Canada can ensure that her ethnic mosaic is retained to counteract the idea that assimilation is inevitable.*
3. *Do members of ethnic groups in Canada really want to retain their ethnicity or is it just a "fad" or a goal of recent immigrants? Give evidence.*
4. *How have specific ethnic groups retained their identity and yet accommodated themselves to the Canadian environment? Give specific examples.*

NOTES

[1] John Porter, *The Vertical Mosaic*, p. 60.

[2] Porter argues that the desire of the French, Scottish, and Irish to distinguish themselves from the English sets the pattern for this tendency. *The Vertical Mosaic*, p. 71.

[3] Good bibliographies of various ethnic groups in Canada are: Andrew Gregorovich, ed., *Canadian Ethnic Groups Bibliography* (Toronto: Ontario Department of The Provincial Secretary and Citizenship, 1972); *Citizenship, Immigration and Ethnic Groups in Canada: A Bibliography of Research* (Ottawa: Department of Citizenship and Immigration, published at frequent intervals); and a journal entitled *Canadian Ethnic Studies*, Bulletin of the Research Centre for Canadian Ethnic Studies, University of Calgary.

[4] Cited in Elizabeth Wangenheim, "The Ukrainians: A Case Study of the 'Third Force' ", in Peter Russell, *Nationalism in Canada* (Toronto: McGraw Hill Co. of Canada, 1966), p. 72.

[5] For a discussion of the role of other ethnic groups in Canada in relation to the two dominant groups, see the Report of the Royal Commission on Bilingualism and Biculturalism, Book IV, *The Cultural Contribution of the Other Ethnic Groups* (Ottawa: Queen's Printer, 1970).

[6] Robert Bierstedt, *The Social Order*, 4th ed. (Toronto: McGraw Hill Ryerson, 1974), p. 481.

[7] See Jeremy Boissevain, "The Italians of Montreal" in W.E. Mann, ed., *Canada: A Sociological Profile* (Toronto: Copp Clark, 1971), pp. 150-165.

[8] Lewis Coser, *The Functions of Social Conflict* (Glencoe: Free Press, 1956), p. 38.

[9] Jill Armstrong, "Canadians in Crisis: The Nature and Source of Support for Leadership in a National Emergency", *Canadian Review of Sociology and Anthropology*, Vol. 9 (November 1972), pp. 299-324. Armstrong cites a poll in November 1970 that indicated 89% of the sample of Canadians approved the use of the War Measures Act. For a largely negative view of the government action see Abraham Rotstein, ed., *Power Corrupted: The October Crisis and the Repression of Quebec* (Toronto: New Press, 1971).

[10] Raymond Breton, "The Socio-Political Dynamics of the October Events", *Canadian Review of Sociology and Anthropology*, Vol. 9 (February 1972), pp. 33-56. Breton argues that the kidnappings developed into a major political event because they were used to justify the goals and ideas of numerous groups confronting each other in the society, e.g. federalists, provincial autonomists, separatists, police power advocates, and intellectuals.

[11] John D. Jackson, "Institutionalized Conflict: The Franco-Ontarian Case", in Gerald L. Gold and Marc-Adélard Tremblay, *Communities and Culture in French Canada* (Toronto: Holt, Rinehart and Winston of Canada, 1973), pp. 218-242. See also an earlier account: John D. Jackson, "A Study of French-English Relations in an Ontario Community: Toward a Conflict Model for the Analysis of Ethnic Relations", *Canadian Review of Sociology and Anthropology*, Vol. 3 (1966), pp. 117-131.

[12] See Boyce Richardson, *James Bay: The Plot to Drown the North Woods* (Toronto: Clarke, Irwin and Co., 1972), particularly Chapter 4.

[13] The eight techniques of discrimination that have been used by the majority to contain minorities in Canada are discussed in David R. Hughes and Evelyn Kallen, *The Anatomy of Racism: Canadian Dimensions* (Montreal: Harvest House, 1974), pp. 136-146. They have included denial of franchise, control of land ownership and use, control of numbers through limiting migration, separate and unequal educational opportunities, employment discrimination and low wages, substandard housing, media stereotyping, and persecution. Hughes and Kallen's book is the best comprehensive account presently available on group conflict in Canada.

[14] Jean L. Elliott, ed., "Minority Groups: A Canadian Perspective", in Elliott, *Minority Canadians 2: Immigrant Groups* (Scarborough: Prentice-Hall of Canada, 1971), p. 2.

[15] For a theoretical examination of the choice of comparison groups as an explanation for feelings of deprivation, see R.K. Merton and A.S. Kitt, "Contributions to the Theory of Reference Group Behavior", in Merton and Lazarfeld, *Continuities of Social Research*, pp. 40-105.

[16] W.E. Willmott, "The Flexibility of Eskimo Social Organization", in V.F. Valentine and F.G. Vallee, *Eskimo of the Canadian Arctic* (Toronto: McClelland and Stewart, 1968), pp. 149-159.

[17] Such organization, however, may be a possibility for the future. Frank G. Vallee, "Notes on the Cooperative Movement and Community Organization in the Canadian Arctic", in V.F. Valentine and F.G. Vallee, *Eskimo of the Canadian Arctic*, pp. 218-227.

[18] T. Shibutani and K.M. Kwan, *Ethnic Stratification: A Comparative Approach* (Toronto: Collier-Macmillan Canada, 1965), p. 290. See also Frank Jones, "A Sociological Perspective on Immigrant Adjustment", *Social Forces*, Vol. 35 (October 1956), pp. 39-47.

[19] A. Ronald Gillis and Paul C. Whitehead, "Halifax Jews: A Community within a Community", in J.L. Elliott, ed., *Minority Canadians 2: Immigrant Groups*, pp. 84-94.

[20] Clifford J. Jansen, "Assimilation in Theory and Practise: A Case Study of Italians in Toronto", in J.E. Gallagher and R.D. Lambert, *Social Process and Institution: The Canadian Case* (Toronto: Holt, Rinehart and Winston of Canada, 1971), pp. 466-474.

[21] Ralph Piddington, "The Kinship Network among French-Canadians", in Gold and Tremblay, *Communities and Culture among French-Canadians*, pp. 123-141.

[22] Raymond Breton, "Institutional Completeness of Ethnic Communities and the Personal Relations of Immigrants", *American Journal of Sociology*, Vol. 70 (September 1964), pp. 193-205.

[23] Eva R. Younge, "Population Movements and the Assimilation of Alien Groups in Canada", *Canadian Journal of Economics and Political Science*, Vol. 10 (1944), pp. 372-380.

[24] This is known as Hansen's principle of third generation interest and asserts that "What the son wishes to forget, the grandson wishes to remember". The principle was constructed from the American immigration experience and probably overstates the case for the second generation in the Canadian context. Marcus L. Hansen, "Third Generation in America: The Problem of the Third Generation Immigrant", *Commentary*, Vol. 14 (November 1952), pp. 492-500. Isajiw speaks of this as the returning or rediscovery pattern. "The Process of Maintenance of Ethnic Identity: The Canadian Context", in Paul Migus, *Sounds Canadian: Languages and Cultures in Multi-Ethnic Society* (Toronto: Peter Martin, 1975), pp. 132-133.

[25] To most Canadians, the black population in Canada is almost non-existent since they are thinly dispersed across the continent. However, an important exception is the proportionately large black community

in Nova Scotia, particularly in Halifax. There is a growing literature on this topic; three recent and significant studies are: Robin W. Winks, "The Canadian Negro: A Historical Assessment", *Journal of Negro History*, Part I, Vol. 53 (1968), and Part 2 in Vol. 54 (1969); Donald H. Clairmont and Dennis W. Magill, *Africville: The Life and Death of a Canadian Black Community* (Toronto: McClelland and Stewart, 1974); and Frances Henry, *Forgotten Canadians: The Blacks of Nova Scotia* (Don Mills: Longman Canada, 1973).

[26] See particularly Chapter 8 and the tables in Chapter 9. The earlier chapters present a concise review of the racial minorities in Canada including Indians, Eskimos, Negroes, Chinese, Japanese; plus religious minorities such as the Doukhobors and Hutterites. Morris Davis and Joseph F. Krauter, *The Other Canadians: Profiles of Six Minorities* (Toronto: Methuen, 1971).

[27] For a good review of the relationship between language and ethnic relations see Stanley Lieberson, *Language and Ethnic Relations in Canada* (Toronto: John Wiley, 1970), Chapter 1.

[28] Asghar Fathi, "Mass Media and a Moslem Immigrant Community in Canada", *Anthropologica*, Vol. 15 (1973), pp. 201-230.

[29] This view of ethnic religion was proposed by Will Herberg, *Protestant-Catholic-Jew* (Garden City: Doubleday, 1955), particularly Chapter 2.

[30] Judith A. Nagata, "Adaption and Integration of Greek Working Class Immigrants in Toronto: A Situational Approach", *The International Migration Review*, Vol. 4 (1968).

[31] Harold B. Barclay, "A Lebanese Community in Lac La Biche, Alberta", in J.L. Elliott, *Minority Canadians 2: Immigrant Groups*, pp. 66-83.

[32] John A. Lee, "The Greendale Canadians: Cultural and Structural Assimilation in an Urban Environment", in B.R. Blishen et al., *Canadian Society: Sociological Perspectives*, 3rd abr. ed. (Toronto: Macmillan Co. of Canada, 1971), p. 440.

[33] Compare with Harold Cardinal, *The Unjust Society* (Edmonton: Hurtig, 1969), Chapter 8.

[34] For a good summary review of the nature of this conflict in Canada see J.K. Morchain, *Search for a Nation: French-English Relations in Canada since 1759* (Toronto: J.M. Dent and Sons(Canada), 1967). A good bibliography on this topic is *Selected Bibliography on Anglophone-Francophone Relations in Canada* (Ottawa: Department of the Secretary of State, 1973).

[35] Richard Jones, *Community in Crisis: French-Canadian Nationalism in Perspective* (Toronto: McClelland and Stewart, 1972), pp. 40, xviii.

[36] Daniel W. Rossides, *Society as a Functional Process: An Introduction to Sociology* (Toronto: McGraw-Hill Co. of Canada, 1968), pp. 173-182. Compare with David Kwavnick, ed., *The Tremblay Report: Report of the Royal Commission of Inquiry on Constitutional Problems* (Toronto: McClelland and Stewart, 1973), pp. 38-42. Excellent background reading to social change in Quebec is found in Marcel Rioux and Yves Martin, *French-Canadian Society*, Vol. I (Toronto: McClelland and

Stewart, 1964); E.C. Hughes, *French Canada in Transition* (Toronto: University of Toronto Press, 1963); and D.C. Thomson, ed., *Quebec Society and Politics: Views from the Inside* (Toronto: McClelland and Stewart, 1973).

[37] Daniel W. Rossides, *Society as a Functional Process: An Introduction to Sociology,* p. 180.

[38] Richard Jones, *Community in Crisis,* pp. 40-41.

[39] Hubert Guindon, "Two Cultures: An Essay on Nationalism, Class and Ethnic Tension", in R.H. Leach, *Contemporary Canada* (Durham, N.C.: Duke University Press, 1967), pp. 33-59.

[40] The year 1960 is considered the significant point because this was when Maurice Duplessis (the leader of the Union Nationale) died and the Liberals took over provincial power. Duplessis was considered an enemy of the intellectuals of the new middle class.

[41] For a good account of English dominance of these two spheres see the *Report of the Royal Commission on Bilingualism and Biculturalism,* Book III, Parts 2 and 3 (Ottawa: Queen's Printer, 1969).

[42] Hubert Guindon, "Social Unrest, Social Class, and Quebec's Quiet Revolution", *Queen's Quarterly,* Vol. 71 (Summer 1964), pp. 150-162. Guindon asserts that the Creditistes' sweep of rural Quebec was evidence that the separatist theme did not appeal to farmers, the semiskilled, or the lower classes in urban areas. Daniel Drache has brought together some working-class manifestoes which he identifies as the next stage in the Quebec independence movement after the arousal of the middle class. *Quebec — Only the Beginning* (Toronto: New Press, 1972).

[43] As this relates to advertising English products in Quebec, see an interesting account by Frederick Elkin, "Advertising Themes and Quiet Revolutions", *American Journal of Sociology,* Vol. 75 (July 1969), pp. 112-122.

[44] Joy's thesis is known as the Bilingual Belt Thesis. *Languages in Conflict: The Canadian Experience* (Toronto: McClelland & Stewart, 1972).

[45] Stanley Lieberson, *Language and Ethnic Relations in Canada* (Toronto: John Wiley and Sons Canada, 1970).

[46] For a good account by one who advocates separatism and who also happens to be a Quebecer and a sociologist, see Marcel Rioux, *Quebec in Question* (Toronto: James Lewis and Samuel, 1971). See also an interesting diary by a French Canadian who has no hope for Quebec in Canada: Solange Chaput Rolland, *My Country, Canada or Quebec?* (Toronto: Macmillan Co. of Canada, 1966). For an analysis of left-wing nationalism in Quebec see S.H. Milner and H. Milner, *The Decolonization of Quebec* (Toronto: McClelland and Stewart, 1973).

[47] Even in Quebec, more immigrants adopt English than French as their basic language: *Report of the Royal Commission on Bilingualism and Biculturalism,* Book I, *The Official Languages* (Ottawa: Queen's Printer, 1967), p. 31. This is a very interesting and informative document on the linguistic problem, including the experiences of other countries.

[48] For a recent study of the Canadian Indian see J.S. Frideres, *Canada's Indians: Contemporary Conflicts* (Scarborough: Prentice-Hall of Canada,

1974). An excellent reference source on the Indians and Métis of Canada has been put together by T.S. Abler, D. Sanders, and S.M. Weaver, *A Canadian Indian Bibliography 1960-1970* (Toronto: University of Toronto Press, 1974).

[49] A general theoretical statement on this concept can be found in G.D. Lenski, "Status Crystallization: A Non-Vertical Dimension of Social Status", *American Sociological Review*, Vol. 19 (August 1954), pp. 405-413.

[50] See his *The Unjust Society* (Edmonton: Hurtig, 1969).

[51] William I.C. Wuttunee, *Ruffled Feathers: Indians in Canadian Society* (Calgary: Bell Books, 1971), p. 107.

[52] Nathan Glazer and Daniel Moynihan, *Beyond the Melting Pot*, 2nd ed., (Boston: MIT Press, 1971).

[53] Allan Smith has pointed out that both of these terms are "a by-product of the kind of nationalism found in each country". In the United States, nationalism is built upon the conception of the existence of a common way of life and therefore the notion of a "melting pot" idealizes this nationalist imagery. However, the idea of conformity is foreign to Canada, for such insistence would probably burst the bonds of statehood. So the notion of a "mosaic" or the tolerance of differences more aptly describes what Canadian nationalism is all about. "Metaphor and Nationality in North America", *Canadian Historical Review*, Vol. 51 (September 1970), pp. 247-275.

[54] For a good account of the various types of assimilation see Milton M. Gordon, *Assimilation in American Life* (Oxford: Oxford University Press, 1964).

[55] David R. Hughes and Evelyn Kallen, *The Anatomy of Racism: Canadian Dimensions*, pp. 190-191.

[56] Isajiw points out that integration does not mean lack of conflict but the management and accommodation of groups through societal functioning. See "The Process of Social Integration: The Canadian Example", *Dalhousie Review*, Vol. 48 (1968), pp. 510-520.

[57] Frank E. Jones, "Some Social Consequences of Immigration for Canada", reprinted in Blishen et al., *Canadian Society: Sociological Perspectives*, 3rd abr. ed., p. 431.

5
Comparative Model

Learning about a society should not be restricted to studying that society alone. A comparative analysis of Canadian society with other societies should make us more conscious of the distinguishing features and specific character of Canadian society, and help us to place it in a world context. Such comparisons also help us to interpret events occurring in other societies in relation to our own society.

Through impressions based on personal experience and on information from the media, we form opinions about other societies. Our personal biases, which are based on selective perception, lead us to value judgments and defensive reactions that reinforce our stereotyped view of a particular society. For example, by asking students to describe their images of each society, Diemer and Dietz[1] formed profiles of Canadian students' stereotypes of Americans as outspoken, aggressive, paternalistic, and patriotic, and of Canadians as reserved, passive, courteous, and aloof. The authors linked the formation of these stereotypes to Canadian resentment of their position of dependency.

Because social scientists make comparisons based on hard data, their assertions ought not to reflect societal biases. Yet if we look at much of the literature involving comparisons of Canadian society with other societies, it becomes clear that hard data are often inadequate or lacking, that selective perceptions have frequently taken place, and that many of the comparisons are based on pure impressionism. As a result, there is no comprehensive study of Canadian society that specializes in comparative analysis.[2]

Problems of Societal Comparisons

There are numerous difficulties involved in making societal comparisons that are not merely due to social scientists having avoided this area of study.[3] The first problem is that there is a lack of uniform data from which adequate comparisons can be drawn. For example, the United States and Canada use different definitions of urban population, so comparisons cannot be made unless sufficient information is available to make the necessary adjustment of the statistics, and that may be virtually impossible.[4] The statistical designation "national origin" may be an important fact to note in Canadian society, but the computation of the ethnic background of the population of an older society such as the United Kingdom may be meaningless. Or, data may be unavailable, as in the case of religious preference in the United States where that question is not included in the census because it would violate the jealously guarded principle of the separation of church and state. In Canada that information is obtained as a matter of course. Projections may be used when data are lacking, but such estimates usually are not precise enough for firm comparisons. Every society collects its data in its own way and, while United Nations organizations are attempting to overcome the problems of non-uniform and insufficient data, they still present formidable difficulties to comparative researchers. Another problem is that of different time sequences in data collection and numerous time lags in compilation and release of data. When the data are released but are not printed in easily accessible publications, they are sometimes very awkward to retrieve.

More problems of comparative analysis need to be considered. Comparisons can be misleading and inadequate when non-contemporary time frames are used or when we are not alert to the time frame that the analysis covers. Canada in 1782 can be compared with the United States in 1782, but 1782 Canada cannot be legitimately compared with the United States today. In addition, we must keep in mind the problem of *place comparisons*. If we were to describe crime in Canada, would we base our description on the nature of crime in Quebec, Saskatchewan, Ontario or Newfoundland? Would we compare Canadian crime with crime in New York, Arkansas, or Montana? Comparisons easily lead one to suppose that a given phenomenon is relatively uniform within a particular society, but both studies and common sense lead us to conclude that this is seldom the case. Care must be taken therefore not to assume that a comparison is representative of all parts of the society.

With these difficulties in mind, we can easily see why comparative studies based on hard data are infrequently available. Furthermore, sociologists have been rather preoccupied with the analysis of Canadian society first and perhaps have postponed comparative work. All of these factors have reduced the possibility of giving a comprehensive view of Canadian society from a comparative perspective, and what follows is only a move in that direction.

The selection of appropriate countries with which to compare Canada is not difficult. Comparing Canada with the Honduras or with Algeria would have little point, for they are largely outside the Canadian frame of reference, are not in the same stage of development, and are part of another social tradition. Differences would likely be clear-cut. Of greater significance is how Canadian society differs from those societies that it most closely resembles.

The United States (as geographical and cultural neighbor), Great Britain (as "mother country" and Canada's greatest source of population), and Australia (as a Commonwealth country and also a recipient of large immigration) are most frequently compared to Canada. Other major countries with which Canada interacts can be included when appropriate.

In order to compare Canada with other countries, I have selected the following features which are major issues in Canadian society: population density, history, values, development, ethnicity, and language.

POPULATION DENSITY

Table 5.1 reveals that in comparison to other countries Canada has a large land surface area and a small population averaging 2 inhabitants per square kilometre. Of the countries in the table, only Australia has a smaller population and slightly smaller land area. Russia has the largest population as well as the largest land surface but a relatively low density. England and Wales has more than double Canada's population in a drastically smaller surface area with a density of 323 persons per square kilometre.

What general features does this table help us point out? First of all, most of Canada's immigration has been from societies of high densities such as the United Kingdom and West Germany. The appeal of Canada has often been the promise of open spaces

Table 5.1 Population Size, Land Area, and Population Density for Canada and Selected Countries, 1971

	Population	Area (Km²)*	Inhabitants Per Km²
Canada	21,786,000	9,976,139	2
United States	207,006,000	9,363,353	22
France	51,260,000	547,026	94
West Germany	59,175,000	247,973	239
United Kingdom	55,566,000	244,044	228
England and Wales	48,815,000	151,126	323
Australia	12,728,000	7,686,810	2
Russia	245,066,000	22,402,200	11
Japan	105,611,000	372,077	284

* 1 square Kilometre = 0.38614 square mile

Source: Reprinted by permission of Unesco from *UNESCO Statistical Yearbook, 1972*, ©Unesco 1973 (Table 1.1).

— although the population has tended to settle in a relatively narrow band on the southern border. Second, Canada shares with Australia (another recently settled country) a relatively low density that has encouraged migration. Third, Canada, Australia, and Russia share the phenomenon of large tracts of land that are not conducive to population settlement and therefore have the lowest densities. Fourth, countries such as Japan and the United Kingdom have both small land surfaces and large populations, indicating high densities and a general population problem that is unfamiliar to Canadian society.

Canada's small population residing in a large national territory clearly has been an important factor in Canadian social development.

HISTORY

Proximity has ordained that Canadian society would most frequently be compared with American society. The comparison is given impetus by the common start the two societies received through European migration and the guidance of European powers. The primary point of historical comparison, however, has been that the United States took a revolutionary course in relation to that colonial sponsorship whereas Canada did not. Such differences in historical beginnings have been used to contrast a whole range of societal attributes.

Lipset speaks of the United States as the "first new nation"[5] to emerge from the colonialist ventures of traditional European societies. What makes it new, according to Lipset, is the rejection of British control through the revolutionary activity of the American War of Independence. It was this act that severed the ties with the mother country and established the United States on its own course. It was also this act that created an ideology around which the members of the new society could rally and provided a set of folk heroes as reference points for the emerging society.

Whereas revolution characterizes the birth of American society, Lipset asserts that Canada was born of *counterrevolution.*[6] If revolution meant breaking the ties to the mother country, then counterrevolution meant retaining those ties. Two reasons are given for the counterrevolutionary tendency in Canada. The first is that thousands of British Loyalists flooded into Ontario and the Maritimes at the time of the American War of Independence in an attempt to retain British ties and to repudiate the aims of the Revolution. Secondly, in the ensuing years persistent fears developed about the threat of American expansion in the Canadian

West and perhaps even general absorption into the strengthening American nation. Lipset argues that in an attempt to resist absorption and to reinforce her societal distinctions, Canada used this threat to solidify counterrevolutionary ties with the "mother country". In other words, Canada sought to distinguish herself from the United States by reaffirming the ties that the United States had rejected.

Lipset's argument assumes that the decision to advocate revolution or counterrevolution was to have profound effects on the institutional structures of the two nations. For example, it meant that Canada would continue to accept British institutions and traditions which would sharply distinguish her from the United States. The maintenance of a close relationship with Britain would ultimately lead to the adoption of a parliamentary system of government as opposed to the congressional-presidential system of the United States. The monarchy and its representatives would be important symbols in Canadian society. The law and education would reflect British standards and traditions. Later, when the British Commonwealth replaced the declining British Empire, Canadian society would still operate under the influence of British-oriented relationships. In other words, Canadian society has never come to a juncture where the people "turned their backs on the past"[7] and therefore a social continuity has been maintained.

Whether Lipset made too much of Canadian fears of American expansion (as Truman has argued)[8] or whether the counterrevolutionary theme is still significant in contemporary Canada is debatable. It is important to note that the postwar Liberal governments have been busy phasing out many of the old British symbols (e.g. the Red Ensign and "God Save the Queen") and Canada has become more North American. Horowitz has pointed out the role of the major world wars in loosening the British relationship as Canada began to participate with other Allies including the United States.[9] Cooperation with other countries diluted the British influence. In criticizing Lipset, Horowitz also argues that if counterrevolution means loyalty to the British Crown, then the counterrevolution thesis has totally ignored French Canadians. Horowitz suggests that the differences that persist between Canada and the United States are the result of "a pecking order of power" in which the French are subordinate to the English in Canada and the English in turn are subordinate to American power. In fact, what is distinguishing Canada from the United States now, according to Horowitz, is not counterrevolution but *counternationalism* (developing a nationalism counter to that of the United States) in which Canadian society is aspiring toward economic independence and self-assertion.[10]

At the beginning of this chapter, I stated that one of the problems of comparisons is confusing time frames. It is acceptable to speak of the distinctions between Canada and the United States in their formative stages in counterrevolutionary terms provided that *contemporary* Canadian society is not assumed to be counter-revolutionary *and therefore conservative*. Obviously some elements of the British tradition still exist and may always persist, but that does not mean that the counterrevolutionary theme is still an adequate interpretive framework for contemporary Canada. On the other hand, counternationalism is clearly an inappropriate explanation of Canadian behavior in the days immediately following the American War of Independence. Therefore, Lipset's thesis must be applied with care so that the time frames are not confused in explaining differences between the two societies.

Louis Hartz has spoken of the new societies that were founded in the Western world as "fragments" of European culture and ideology.[11] For example, Latin America and French Canada were feudal fragments of more traditional societies such as Spain and France. The United States and English Canada, on the other hand, were bourgeois fragments of European societies bent on capitalist expansion. Thus, contemporary differences between societies in the New World can be traced at least partially to the sponsoring society. But Hartz suggests that inevitably the fragment society loses its European tradition and nationalism emerges. This nationalism may be a response to an external threat such as that posed by the United States to Canada or the result of social and ideological ideas held in opposition to the "Old Country" as in the case of Australia.[12]

The European influence in Canada has been and still is quite significant. Canada has never cut ties formally and sharply as the United States did, and this has made a difference to the institutional structure of the society. While elements of her "fragment" status still persist, Canada is coming more and more into her own as an independent unit, though cultivating ties with kin societies. In this way, Canada is similar to other nations whose sovereignty is clear but whose institutions and traditions bear the imprint of old alliances that are still maintained.

VALUES

Different reactions to historical events are not just important in themselves, according to Lipset, but are instrumental in the development of value patterns in each society. Lipset also notes that, even though Canada and the United States have many similar values, the counterrevolutionary tradition has perpetuated "old-world" values and given Canada a more *conservative* and traditional cast in comparison to American society.[13]

Lipset proceeds by analyzing the four English-speaking democracies: the United States, England, Australia, and Canada. He adopts four sets of dichotomous pattern variables: achievement/ascription, universalism/particularism, self-orientation/collectivity, and egalitarianism/elitism. He assumes that every society possesses a set of values that gives a particular orientation to social interaction. The orientation can be:

achievement ⟷ ascription
(basis of individual abilities)   (basis of inherited qualities)

universalism ⟷ particularism
(applying a general standard   (applying specific standards
for all)   of relationship)

self-orientation ⟷ collectivity-orientation
(emphasis on needs and   (emphasis on needs and
rights of the individual)   rights of the group)

egalitarianism ⟷ elitism
(equality of all persons)   (general superiority of some
persons)

Lipset concludes that the Canadian value orientation is more ascriptive, particularistic, collectivity-oriented, and elitist than that of the United States, which tends toward the opposite values.

Lipset's assumption is that the United States and Great Britain represent two contrasting value systems, with Canada and Australia somewhere in between. Britain emerged into the modern world with an aristocratic heritage consisting of a privileged class and a large lower class. This has meant that ascription, elitism, and particularism, based on inherited qualities, have abounded. In contrast, the ideology of the United States is replete with egalitarian themes and achievement goals of upward mobility made possible by such factors as a common school system. His argument is that both societies are democracies but are organized around different sets of value patterns. According to Lipset, Australia tends to be closer to the United States in her values (the left-hand side of the above scale), whereas Canada patterns herself more after England (the right-hand side of the above scale).

What evidence does Lipset give for his argument? First, he claims that the conservative nature of Canadian society is reflected in greater respect for law and order, which is part of the British tradition. For example, the settlement of the Canadian frontier was undertaken by organizations such as the Canadian Pacific Railway, the North West Mounted Police, and the churches. As a result, there was less of the lawlessness characterized by the typical American "westerns" in which settlers took the law into their own hands with vigilante groups and posses. Because the North West Mounted Police went before the settlers, no Canadian heroes of the order of the American Daniel Boone and Davy Crockett emerged in Canada. The ratio of police to population is also given as evidence of greater Canadian respect for the law. Using data for 1961 and 1962, Lipset points out that the United States had more than one third more policemen in proportion to the population as well as proportionately more lawyers, indicating that formal rather than informal methods of social control had to be utilized in the absence of a traditional, stable order. Lipset also gives higher crime and divorce rates as evidence of less respect for order in the United States. He uses these data to suggest that a more traditional and conservative society prevails in Canada.

Second, he argues that there is less equality of opportunity in Canada. Settlers of Australia and the United States were both fleeing from aristocratic Britain with its inequality, and sought to create a more egalitarian society. Australia put less stress on achievement than the United States did, but the idea of "mateship" in Australia fostered a sense of mutual equality and concern. Because of the distinct Canadian rejection of American values and her alignment with Britain, there has been a tendency in Canada for class privilege to prevail, with a large lower class and smaller middle class. Lipset argues further that levels of educational attainment are good indicators of whether achievement can overcome ascribed positions. Using data to show the number of persons in the 20-24 age cohort in institutions of higher learning, he concludes that the United States is considerably above Australia, Canada, and Great Britain in the percentage of persons in that group obtaining a higher education. Lipset feels that these figures indicate a basic difference in societal values, not just in economic development. If fewer people participate in the educational process, particularly at its highest levels, then it can be assumed that ascription will be more important than achievement.

Third, Lipset suggests that Canada is less individualistic than the United States and therefore more collectivist. The strength and control of the Anglican and Roman Catholic Churches in Canadian society tempered the individualism that was characteristic of much sectarian activity found in the United States, and helped to maintain the "blue laws" that reinforced traditional community values in Canada. Furthermore, the collectivist nature of government enterprises which challenge private industry has always been reprehensible to American society. But government participation in activity regarded as a threat to the individualism-capitalism creed dominant in the United States became quite commonplace in Canada. Canadian government involvement in activity such as railroads, airlines, and broadcasting has not been as a business venture but in the public interest. Lipset argues that fear of the loss of individualism is not as great in Canada because she possesses a value orientation more like that of Great Britain than of the United States. Lipset asserts that such contrasts in basic value orientations explain differences between the societies.

Thus ascription tends to dominate over achievement in Canada in comparison to the United States, and brings in its wake a more particularist and elitist society. These three characteristics (ascription, particularism, elitism) are more likely to be features of traditional societies and, according to Lipset, Great Britain is more traditional than the United States. Supposedly, a collectivity orientation is also more likely to be a feature of a "conservative" society; so the counterrevolutionary thesis is verified.

Critiques of Lipset. When Lipset deduces values from data such as crime rates, the per-capita number of lawyers, or divorce rates, he increases the risk of comparative societal analysis. Whether such data enable us to deduce with precision the dominant values in a society is a debatable point.[14] Furthermore, Lipset depends on data from 1950 to the early 1960s and therefore much of his analysis is dated, particularly in the light of considerable social change in Canada since that time.

Truman has taken Lipset to task for suggesting that on the egalitarian/elitist dimension, Australia is closer to the United States in being more egalitarian and that Canada is closer to Britain in being more elitist.[15] He presents data to show that the three Commonwealth countries are rather similar as a result of their more centralized system of government. For example, he argues that central government control over settlement of new territory in Canada and Australia was markedly different from the American attempt to construct law-enforcement procedures after self-government at the local level had been established. Also, the

British connection has produced concepts of equality in Canada and Australia that are different from those of the United States. Inherent in the American notion of equality is upward economic mobility, giving everybody the opportunity to "get ahead" or to improve his status position. The British working-class heritage has put greater stress on equality of living standards and income rather than on competitive achievement; this ideology has persisted in Australia and Canada in social democratic parties whose ranks have been filled by British working-class settlers. Continual reference to Great Britain through political communication and immigration leads Truman to conclude that Canada may have been more elitist than the United States in the nineteenth century but, at least in some respects, it is now decidely more egalitarian. The supposed greater egalitarianism of the United States must certainly be questioned in view of the inequalities between races and the great gaps between the wealthy and the poor. Even though egalitarianism may abound in American ideology, the theory should not blind us to the facts.[16]

Lipset has also argued that Canada is more particularistic and the United States more universalistic. Universalistic criteria such as education, income, and skills can easily be applied to all people, as opposed to particularistic standards of personal attributes or relationships. However, Pineo and Goyder found that there was little difference between the United States and Canada in the extent to which people used universalistic criteria to classify themselves in terms of social class.[17] Furthermore, the only empirical evidence of elitism in Canada has been a study that showed that professional and semiprofessional jobs rated a higher prestige level in Canada than in the United States.[18] In short, the values of contemporary Canada do not fit all of Lipset's stereotypes.

There are differences in divorce rates and crime rates between the United States and Canada, but perhaps they can be explained by factors that are less nebulous than values. For example, Horowitz suggests that in explaining differences in rates of divorce we must consider that Canada only liberalized her divorce legislation in 1968; since that time the difference between the two countries has narrowed.[19] Similarly, differences in crime rates could at least partially be attributed to the racial strife in the United States. Differences in levels of educational attainment are meaningless unless it is recognized that only since 1960 have great sums of money been put into higher education in Canada and enrollment figures have increased dramatically. According to Horowitz, the United States and Canada clearly have very similar norms, values, and aspirations. The differences between them are chiefly ideological in relation to institutional differences arising from the dependence-independence controversy and autonomous control. In Horowitz's view, it is at this political and economic level that we can speak of differences rather than in terms of values.

A recent study by Goldenberg[20] has suggested that the differences that persist between the United States and Canada are due not to cultural or value factors but rather to structural and environmental factors. Goldenberg gives as his example the tendency for U.S. colleges and universities to have a much higher residency rate than that of Canadian ones because of their cross-country appeal. Canadian schools at a comparable level tend to be more urban, commuter-oriented, and much more local in their appeal. Goldenberg is right in saying that if we compare the societies at this structural level, we are more likely to arrive at meaningful differences between them than by making general claims about values held by masses of people. Additional observations of this structural nature must await further research.

Rather than being overwhelmed by the difficulty of specifying societal values and reducing empirical data to such diffuse concepts, we can still use statistics on birth and divorce rates as meaningful indicators of comparative behavioral patterns. Cana-

Table 5.2   Crude Live Birth Rate and Crude Divorce Rates per 1,000 Population, Selected Countries, 1955 and 1971

	Crude Live Birth Rate		Crude Divorce Rates	
	1955	1971	1955	1971
Canada	28.1	16.8	.38	1.37
United States	24.7	17.3	2.30	3.72
France	18.6	17.2	.67	.93
West Germany	16.0	12.7	.85	1.31
United Kingdom (England & Wales)	15.0	16.0	.59	1.50
Australia	22.6	21.7	.73	1.02
USSR	25.7	17.8	.70*	2.63
Japan	19.4	19.2	.85	1.00

* 1956

Source: Compiled from United Nations, *1959 Demographic Yearbook*, Table 31; *1969 Demographic Yearbook*, Table 12; *1972 Demographic Yearbook*, Table 16 (New York). Reprinted by permission of the United Nations Information Center.

da's remarkably high birth rate in the past is noted in Table 5.2 for 1955. However, by 1971, it had fallen sharply below that of other countries listed, except for West Germany and the United Kingdom. To pinpoint the cause for this change as the secularization of values or new family values or just as a phenomenon common to industrial countries would require a much more comprehensive analysis with more evidence than these data provide. However, at the comparative statistical level, we can see that the Canadian birth rate has generally fallen, in line with those of other industrial societies, except for Japan and Australia which register higher rates. In terms of divorce rates, there are clear differences, particularly between Canada, Russia, and the United States in 1971 (Table 5.2). Whether the last two countries have made the mechanisms for divorce more easily available or whether Canada and similar countries harbor greater numbers of separations or unhappy marriages is a complex issue which we cannot resolve here.[21] But it is clear that Canadian society presently demonstrates only a moderate level of legal family breakup. All countries in Table 5.2 show an increase in the rate of divorce since 1955. Whatever such a trend might suggest about values, it does indicate changing behavior patterns and significant social change for Canada, the United States, the United Kingdom, and Russia in particular.

It could be argued that the urbanization and industrialization of societies has contributed to a *homogenization of values* among them.[22] If this were so, we might expect statistics of behavior patterns to be increasingly similar. However, such a similarity might never be verified as long as structural and cultural differences (e.g. divorce laws, norms of family size, norms of remarriage) confound the meaning of our statistics. Values are slippery concepts to identify and conclusive comparative studies of values present difficulties which increase when relatively similar societies are compared. Perhaps differences in the organization of the society (e.g. forms and styles of government) will help to perpetuate societal distinctions in spite of some value convergence.[23]

In an era of large-scale social change, it is to be expected that a statement of the nature of the Canadian value system must reflect this change. Vallee and Whyte, for example, described the Canadian "conservative syndrome" as being guided by tradition, emphasizing order, and accepting the inherited positions and decisions of elites.[24] Yet such a description of contemporary Canadian society now seems either grossly oversimplified or inaccurate. Though Canada and the United States are both basically capitalist societies, socialism has been a more frequent topic of conversation in Canada, and laborers have united with farmers to form socialist-oriented political parties. From these circles have emerged considerable challenges to tradition and numerous innovations that do not fit the conservative mold and make Canadian society appear quite radical and avant-garde.

Demographic data on a high birth rate, low divorce rate, and low levels of educational attainment have all been cited as measures of traditionalism within Canadian society. Such analyses always led to the observation that Canada was behind — which usually meant behind the United States. It is true that the educational system in Canada had a traditional orientation for a long time. Students were meticulously weeded through a rigorous examination system and few were urged to attend university. Courses were highly academic and vocational training was not stressed. As a result, there were high dropout rates. This phenomenon helped to maintain the status quo and the traditional nature of the society by limiting upward mobility. Yet things have changed drastically. Rich has pointed out that Canada's educational opportunities are more equitable than those of most countries of Western Europe.[25] Even countries such as Sweden where social democratic governments have been in power do not show a higher performance level. Furthermore, the gap between Canada and the United States has narrowed as the enrollment ratios in Table 5.3 demonstrate. Changes in the birth rate, the divorce rate, and in levels of education indicate that Canada cannot be described any longer as static, conservative, traditional, and maintaining the status quo. Few industrial societies could be described in that way.

Table 5.3   Secondary and University Enrollment Ratios, Canada and the United States

	1951-52	1965-66	Projected 1975-76
Secondary Enrollment	% of 14—17 Age Group		
Canada	46	80	94
United States	77	92	98
Full-time University Enrollment	% of 18—24 Age Group		
Canada	5	11	18
United States*	12	19	24

* Full-time degree credit enrollment in institutions of higher education.
Source: *Sixth Annual Review, Economic Council of Canada* (Ottawa: Queen's Printer, 1969), p. 126. Reprinted by permission of Information Canada.

DEVELOPMENT

One of the striking features of our world is the uneven economic development of its societies. The world leadership and dominance of the United States in fiscal programs and industrial growth is a phenomenon to which other less developed societies are forced to react. Whether a society abhors comparison with a more developed country or not, such a comparison, whether implicit or explicit, is invariably made.

Table 5.4 illustrates considerable differences in the Gross Domestic Product of selected countries in the world. The United States leads with the highest per-capita figure in 1971, with Sweden and Canada following. Among the industrial countries listed, the United Kingdom and Japan have the lowest figures. And then there is a proportionately even larger gap between the industrial countries and less industrialized countries (illustrated by the low numerical value for Yugoslavia). In a world context, Canada clearly ranks high in economic development.

Table 5.4 Gross Domestic Product per Capita in United States Dollars for Selected Countries*

	1961	1966	1971
Canada	2185	2911	4343
United States	2862	3859	5129
Japan	566	1036	2153
Australia	1543	2058	3044
France	1440	2190	3175
Germany	1471	2080	3551
Sweden	2009	3020	4409
United Kingdom	1442	1938	2428
Yugoslavia	276	456	762

* At current prices and exchange rates.

Source: National Accounts Statistics 1960-1971, Organization for Economic Cooperation and Development (OECD), (October 1973), p. 11. Reprinted by permission of the OECD.

The ability and freedom to purchase luxury items after subsistence concerns have been met is one indicator of a society's level of prosperity. Table 5.5 lists the number of radio and television receivers per 1000 population in selected countries. Generally, an obvious correlation exists between rank in terms of Gross

Table 5.5 Radio and Television Receivers per 1,000
Population in Select Countries, 1971

	Radios	Television Sets
Canada	773	349
United States	1623	449
France	313	227
West Germany	—	299
United Kingdom	—	298
Australia	212	224
Russia	408	160
Japan	568	223

Source: Reprinted by permission of Unesco from *UNESCO Statistical Yearbook*, 1972, ©Unesco 1973 (Table 13.2).

Domestic Product and rank in terms of ownership of radios and TV sets. As long as material possessions are a coveted goal, the desire to compare one's society with societies of higher economic development will persist. Canada finds herself near the top of the scale but still lower than the United States.

As long as economic development is a primary goal, there appears to be a dilemma whether to choose a higher standard of living or economic independence. Many societies have opted for a higher standard of living even if it means an influx of foreign capital, manpower, and technology. Perhaps an exception to this tendency is Red China who has sealed her borders and developed at her own pace without foreign influence.[26] Whatever immediate advantages it may have sacrificed by thwarting rapid development, the society gained in building a firm, long-term industrial base independent of more advanced societies. Of course, such a move was possible because of strong central government control and a large domestic market as well as plenteous resources that made the country relatively self-sufficient.

Canada has been less successful in opting for economic independence for several reasons. A large resource base and a small internal market have meant that there is less possibility of self-sufficiency. Perhaps most important of all, Canadian proximity to the United States encourages consumer comparisons that make gaps in the standard of living all the more obvious. Labor unions, for example, clamor for wage parity with their American counter-parts (i.e. equal pay for equal work) and a comparable standard of living becomes the goal. The role of the multinational corporation in providing capital and technology for the immediate develop-ment of Canada also reduces the likelihood of economic indepen-dence. As long as American society remains the object of com-parison in economic development, and as long as that society retains its economic leadership, it is likely that economic inde-pendence in Canada will be sacrificed in favor of a higher standard of living. Similar statements can be made about many other societies, although Canadian society may best exemplify this problem because of its strategic relationship with the United States.

As another country that borders the United States, Mexico has also found herself deluged with American influences. An inter-esting study of anti-Americanism found that this feeling was more restrained in Mexico than in Canada because of Mexican control of foreign enterprise.[27] While anti-Americanism was more prevalent in Canada, it was tempered by the compensation of a generally higher standard of living.

Porter has pointed out that in comparison to the United States there is a smaller proportion of persons in Canada who participate in stock ownership.[28] Particularly among the middle class, fewer people own stock and invest their money in corporations than in the United States where the wider dispersal of stock among more persons has tended to separate ownership from control to a greater extent. Needless to say, investment is a much more significant source of personal income in the United States than in Canada.[29] Capital investment is necessary for economic development, but the risk involved has generally not appealed to Canadians. When Canadians have invested, the risky new Canadian enterprise has not been as attractive as the established American corporation. Glazier refers to this perpetual flow of investment capital outside the country as the "capital drain".[30] Obviously, then, Canadian capital needs had to be met outside the country or measures had to be taken to encourage internal capital investment. Lipset noted that surplus Canadian capital in the past was more likely to be placed in insurance policies, as Canada reputedly has the highest per-capita rate of insurance investment in the world.[31]

Abundant natural resources necessary for industrial growth have attracted considerable foreign investment into Canada, parti-cularly from countries that lack these resources. Thus the Cana-dian economy evidences a solid growth rate that gives her a standard of living superior to that of most societies in the world.

Internal disparities in economic development have been a major problem for Canadian society. The Golden Horseshoe in Ontario is the center of financial and industrial activity in Canada, while the Maritimes and the Prairies lack this type of activity; such imbalances in the society create metropolis-hinterland relationships. But regional economic disparity is a problem that plagues many societies. Countries such as the United States have tried to decentralize industry by establishing numerous nodes of industrial activity in smaller centers to bridge this regional gap. Decentralization is also a major concern in Canada because much of the society is a hinterland to two or three metropolitan centers. Interestingly, Merritt has pointed out that Paris has had a similar dominant role in French society.[32] Spain has also experienced tensions between the industrial and rural sectors. In contrast to Canada, however, where the rural underdeveloped areas feel exploited, in Spain it is the developed regions that feel alienated because they have economic power without political power.[33] The rural and more traditional areas of Spain have thus far resisted control by the industrial areas.

In comparison to other industrial countries, Canada's development has been more recent and more directly in the shadow of a dominant power. Her comparatively high standard of living has made the nation attractive to migrants from less developed countries. The regional disparities that industrial development has produced within the country, however, are not necessarily a unique phenomenon.

ETHNICITY

Canada shares with other countries of the "New World", such as the United States and Australia, the distinction of having been highly dependent on migrated populations from overpopulated European countries for the settlement of spacious territory. Primarily the countries of Northern Europe provided the new residents for all three societies in contrast, for example, to the Spanish influence in South America. The majority of Northern European migrants settled in North America rather than South America.

Several other points about the similarities of these three receiving societies stand out. First, immigration was a long-term process rather than a one-wave affair and it was multinational in origin. People came from numerous countries and for various reasons. Secondly, in spite of the variety of countries represented, people of British origin tended to dominate and their language served as the foundational language. Furthermore, all three societies possessed a native population which was later displaced by the more dominant Europeans.[34]

Table 5.6 attempts to illustrate the differences in the European ethnic composition of the three societies. Comparable data are very difficult to obtain as neither the United States nor Australia gathers data on ethnic origin in the same way that Canada does. The United States is not as concerned with tracing ethnicity as Canada is (which perhaps lends some support to the American melting pot idea) and Australia views ethnicity in terms of

Table 5.6 Percentage Distribution of the Population of European Ethnic Origin in Canada, the United States, and Australia

	Canada (1971)	United States (1971)**	Australia (1966)***
English	44.62	23.32 (incl. Irish)	95.57
French	28.65	2.55	*
German	6.10	12.65	.37
Italian	3.38	4.30	1.32
Ukrainian	2.69	*	*
Netherlands	1.97	*	.43
Scandinavian	1.78	*	*
Polish	1.46	2.43	.11
Hungarian	.61	*	.04
Greek	.57	*	.92
Yugoslavian	.48	*	.33
Spanish	*	4.41	*

* Blank spaces are not necessarily indicative of a lack of population in that category but show that the percentage was relatively small or data were unavailable.

** The largest percentage (41.75%) for the United States is listed in a nondescript "Other" category.

*** Australian figures were computed on the basis of "national allegiance". 81.55% of the total 95.57% English declared themselves to have been born in Australia.

Source: Compiled and computed from 1971 Census of Canada, Statistics Canada, Vol. I, Part 3, Cat. 92-723; United States Bureau of the Census, 1973 Statistical Abstract of the United States, Table 41 (Washington, D.C.); Commonwealth Bureau of Census and Statistics, 1972 Australia Yearbook (Canberra, Australia), p. 139.

national allegiance. Therefore, the data in Table 5.6 are only a rough comparison. In contrast to Canada, the American population of French descent is a very small minority. Of the three societies, only Canada has a large proportion of French persons; the United States has a significant population of Spanish extraction, and Australia has a minimal number of other European nationalities and a predominance of those of British descent (though it is not clear whether this figure is really as meaningful since national allegiance is a different category from ethnic origin). Clearly, the United States and Canada have been the major recipients of European migration in all its variety, whereas Australia does not have the same degree of ethnic pluralism.

Statistics of religious affiliation further indicate British domination in Australia.[35] Fully one third of the population claims affiliation with the Church of England, and denominations of British origin such as Methodists and Presbyterians are also sizeable. On the other hand, continental European churches such as the Lutheran and the Greek Orthodox are poorly represented in Australia.

Neither of the two countries with which Canada is compared has two strikingly large ethnic groups that closely rival each other. Social strain is more likely when ethnic groups are large and competition is as prevalent as in Canada.

In the preceding chapter, I indicated that societal strain can also be fostered by physical or racial differences among members of a society. Table 5.7 demonstrates why racial strain is a greater issue in the United States than in Canada. Even though both societies are dominantly white, the United States contains a large

Table 5.7   Percentage Distribution of the Population of Canada and the United States by Racial Group

	Canada (1971)	United States (1970)
White	97.08	87.46
Indian and Eskimo	1.45	.39
Chinese	.55	.21
Japanese	.17	.29
Negro	.15	11.11
Other Asian (e.g. Indian, Pakistani, Filipino)	.60	.51

Source: Compiled from 1971 Census of Canada, Statistics Canada, Vol. I, Part 3, Cat. 92-723; United States Bureau of the Census, 1973 Statistical Abstract of the United States, Table 32 (Washington, D.C.).

segment which is black, whereas the black population in Canada is proportionately minute. The largest nonwhite racial groups in Canada are the Indians and Eskimos; current events reveal that most societal tensions of a public and racial nature have been between Indians and whites. However, the source of these racial conflicts is somewhat different in each society. The blacks in the United States are demanding equal participation in American society because of their mobility deprivation, while the Indians in Canada are insisting on their right to search for and control their own destiny apart from the white society. The geographical separation of the aborigine population from the white population in Australia has been one of the factors minimizing racial conflict there.

LANGUAGE

Although there are 2,500 languages in the world, there are only approximately 150 nations.[36] Therefore it is obvious that the problem of linguistic plurality is not new. The Commission on Bilingualism and Biculturalism has pointed out that, in contrast to many other societies, both of Canada's major languages are international. Countries such as India have a diversity of languages many of which are only local and have little worldwide impact. We have come to expect that large industrial societies usually will evolve one major language to serve as the *lingua franca* for the whole society.

The strength of two rival, major ethnic groups brings us to the uniquely Canadian characteristic of bilingualism. Although the United States has also been the recipient of large-scale in-migration, one language predominates. It is not uncommon for immigrants to maintain their native tongue for two or three generations, or for the society to harbor numerous dialects; but in most of these situations, one language serves as the medium of communication. Some countries, such as Belgium and Switzerland, use more than one language because of proximity to foreign borders, facilitating population and language interchange. In contrast, Francophones in Canada are alone on a continent where English predominates.

If language is an ethnic group's major mechanism to thwart assimilation, then an ethnic group will be most successful in maintaining its language and independent identity if it has regional concentration. What gives the French language strength in Canada is its rootage in Quebec. Thus, bilingualism in Canada does not mean that all persons speak two languages. It means that the dominant language of Quebec (French) and the dominant language of the rest of Canada (English) are to have equal status. As I have shown earlier, in Canada bilingualism in practice means the dominance of one language or the other in different parts of the society.

In comparing Switzerland with Canada we see how language choice relates to the *territorial dominance* of a specific language. Switzerland has four national languages (German, French, Italian, and Romansch); all are designated "official" languages except Romansch which is used by less than 1% of the population.[37] About 74% of the people speak German, 20% French, and 4% Italian. How can language rights and the existence of minority languages be guaranteed?

Switzerland is composed of a loose federation of almost completely autonomous cantons. The Constitution advocates the idea of *territoriality*. Every canton is entitled to preserve its own language and all in-migrants must learn the language used in that canton. Language boundaries are guaranteed and cannot be changed. Each canton writes its laws and documents in its own language. Education and the military are the responsibility of individual cantons and use their own language.

German is the language found in most cantons, but French and Italian cantons also thrive. The use of German in numerous dialects weakens its dominance which is also offset by the greater prestige of French, particularly for official business. In addition, many Swiss can speak more than one language, which facilitates communication.

Decentralized federalism like that of Switzerland is a concept that Francophones have always advocated in Canada. It would give them a chance to maintain linguistic control of their territorial unit in the face of homogenizing pressures. Thus Quebec has recently reasserted the principle of territoriality by declaring French the official language of the province. Perhaps it is the only way that languages can be protected against the threat of assimilation.

In contrast to Canada, Russia has one major language but numerous dialects and languages with a certain degree of regional autonomy. It remains to be seen whether a society such as Canada can successfully enter world politics and business using two languages equally when territorial control is demanded at the local level.

CANADIAN SOCIETY IN COMPARATIVE PERSPECTIVE

A number of distinguishing features set the population of Canada apart from other societies in the world: the multi-ethnic mixture, constitutional bilingualism, a high standard of living (slightly lower than her neighbor's), colonial ties, and a heavy reliance on foreign input for economic development. All of these factors differentiate Canadian society from other societies with which it is ordinarily ranked. With these comparisons in mind, we can discuss the formation of Canada's identity.

QUESTIONS FOR FURTHER EXPLORATION

1. *Why do Europeans frequently visualize Canadian society and American society as essentially the same or very similar? Is such an observation correct?*
2. *Compare British society with its four major national groups with Canadian society and its numerous national groups.*
3. *Is it accurate to say that Canadian society is a "hybrid" of British, French, and American societies?*

NOTES

[1] A.H. Diemer and M.L. Dietz, "Canadian University Students' Stereotypes of Canadians and Americans", *McGill Journal of Education,* Vol. 5 (1971), pp. 29-37.

[2] One excellent study of a specific area — the social origins of differences in the political structure of the major English-speaking countries — is Robert R. Alford's *Party and Society: The Anglo-American Democracies* (Chicago: Rand McNally, 1963). In other comparative studies Canada is frequently only briefly discussed or totally ignored. C.C. Hunt and L. Walker, for example, compare ethnic relations in many countries, but fail to discuss the Canadian case: *Ethnic Dynamics: Patterns of Intergroup Relations in Various Societies* (Homewood, Ill.: Dorsey Press, 1974).

[3] For a fuller discussion of the problems involved in comparative social research see Robert M. Marsh, *Comparative Sociology* (New York: Harcourt, Brace and World, 1967), pp. 261-286.

[4] In Canada the basic urban population base is 1000, whereas in the United States it is 2,500; in Japan 30,000, and in South Africa 555. United Nations, *1972 Demographic Yearbook* (New York, 1972), pp. 147-153.

[5] S.M. Lipset, *The First New Nation: The United States in Historical and*

Comparative Perspective (New York: Basic Books, 1963).

6 S.M. Lipset, "Revolution and Counter-Revolution: The United States and Canada" in *Revolution and Counter-Revolution: Change and Persistence in Social Structures*, rev. ed. (Garden City, N.Y.: Doubleday, 1971). Lipset is not the only analyst to speak of the counterrevolutionary tradition in Canada [e.g. S.D. Clark, *The Developing Canadian Community* (Toronto: University of Toronto Press, 1962), pp. 185-198] but he has developed it most fully in a comparative framework.

7 S.M. Lipset, p. 198.

8 Tom Truman, "A Critique of Seymour M. Lipset's Article 'Value Differences, Absolute or Relative: The English Speaking Democracies' ", *Canadian Journal of Political Science*, Vol. 4 (December 1971), pp. 513, 525.

9 Irving L. Horowitz, "The Hemispheric Connection: A Critique and Corrective to the Entrepreneurial Thesis of Development with Special Emphasis on the Canadian Case", *Queen's Quarterly*, Vol. 80 (1973), pp. 336-337.

10 I.L. Horowitz, p. 354. Horowitz suggests that the liberation of Canada developed without a revolutionary war, though the major world wars curiously served as a "surrogate revolutionary war effort".

11 Louis Hartz, ed., *The Founding of New Societies* (New York: Harcourt, Brace and World, 1964), Chapter 1. For a critique of Hartz on minimizing differences between the United States and Canada, see G. Horowitz, "Conservatism, Liberalism, and Socialism in Canada: An Interpretation", *Canadian Journal of Economics and Political Science*, Vol. 32 (May 1966), pp. 143-150.

12 Richard N. Rosecrance, "The Radical Culture of Australia" in Louis Hartz, ed., *The Founding of New Societies*, pp. 275-318.

13 S.M. Lipset's comparison of Canada and the United States can be found in *Revolution and Counter-Revolution: The United States and Canada* and in "Canada and the United States — A Comparative View", *Canadian Review of Sociology and Anthropology*, Vol. I (November 1964), pp. 173-185. For his comparative analysis of the four English-speaking democracies, see "The Value Patterns of Democracy: A Case Study in Comparative Analysis", *American Sociological Review*, Vol. 28 (August 1963), pp. 515-531, and *The First New Nation*, Chapter 7. Much of the analysis and data presented are the same or overlap in all four accounts.

14 Horowitz cites John Shiry who also argues that the values of a society cannot be deduced from the indicators Lipset uses. "The Hemispheric Connection: A Critique and Corrective to the Entrepreneurial Thesis of Development with Special Emphasis on the Canadian Case", p. 337.

15 "A Critique of Seymour M. Lipset's Article, 'Value Differences, Absolute or Relative: The English Speaking Democracies' ", pp. 513, 525.

16 A.K. Davis makes a similar point that what might be ideologically true about the United States needs revision in actuality. He notes that the United States is "hierarchical" and "racist" contrary to its "middle-class

liberal self-image". "Canadian Society and History as Hinterland versus Metropolis" in R.J. Ossenberg, ed., *Canadian Society: Pluralism, Change and Conflict* (Scarborough: Prentice-Hall of Canada, 1971), p. 16.

[17] Peter Pineo and John Goyder, "Social Class Identification of National Subgroups" in J.E. Curtis and W.G. Scott, *Social Stratification: Canada* (Scarborough: Prentice-Hall of Canada, 1973), p. 194.

[18] Peter Pineo and John Porter, "Occupational Prestige in Canada", *Canadian Review of Sociology and Anthropology*, Vol. 4 (February 1967), p. 31.

[19] I.L. Horowitz, "The Hemispheric Connection", p. 340.

[20] Sheldon Goldenberg, *"Composition or Character? — Structural Alternatives to Cultural Explanations of Canadian-American Institutional Differences"*, Ph. D. dissertation, Northwestern University, 1974.

[21] In a study of Canadian and American university students, Whitehurst and Plant found it paradoxical that Canadians should report higher alienation levels toward marriage at the same time that they were supposed to be conservative and conventional. Canadians were more ready to accept alternatives to conventional marriage forms and wanted more liberal divorce laws while Americans wanted stricter laws. Robert N. Whitehurst and Barbara Plant, "A Comparison of Canadian and American University Students' Reference Groups, Alienation, and Attitudes towards Marriage", *International Journal of Sociology of the Family*, Vol. 1 (March 1971). For a somewhat dated account of U.S.-Canadian differences see Arthur P. Jacoby, "Some Family Problems in Canada and the United States: A Comparative Review" in R. Laskin, *Social Problems: A Canadian Profile* (Toronto: McGraw-Hill Co. of Canada, 1964), pp. 280-284.

[22] George Grant speaks of the universalizing power of technology which destroys particularisms. *Technology and Empire* (Toronto: House of Anansi, 1969), Chapter 1.

[23] Dennis N. Wrong, *American and Canadian Viewpoints* (Washington: American Council on Education, 1955), p. 56.

[24] Frank Vallee and Donald R. Whyte, "Canadian Society: Trends and Perspectives" in B.R. Blishen et al., *Canadian Society: Sociological Perspectives*, 3rd abr. ed. (Toronto: Macmillan Co. of Canada, 1971), p. 559.

[25] Harvey Rich, *"The Vertical Mosaic Revisited"*, mimeographed paper, University of Calgary, 1974.

[26] Gerhard Lenski and Jean Lenski, *Human Societies: An Introduction to Macro-Sociology* (Toronto: McGraw-Hill Co. of Canada, 1970), p. 458.

[27] C.S. Tai, E.J. Peterson, T.R. Gurr, "Internal Versus External Sources of Anti-Americanism", *Journal of Conflict Resolution*, Vol. 17 (September 1973), pp. 455-488.

[28] John Porter, *The Vertical Mosaic*, p. 241.

[29] Jerry R. Podoluk, "Some Comparisons of the Canadian-U.S. Income Distributions" (Ottawa: Statistics Canada, 1969), unpublished paper, p. 9.

[30] Kenneth M. Glazier, "Canadian Investment in the United States:

Putting Your Money Where Your Mouth Is", *Journal of Contemporary Business,* Vol. 1 (1972).

[31] S.M. Lipset, *Revolution and Counter-Revolution,* p. 51.

[32] R.L. Merritt, "West Berlin — Center or Periphery?" in R.L. Merritt and Stein Rokkan, eds., *Comparing Nations: The Use of Quantitative Data in Cross-National Research* (New Haven: Yale University Press, 1966),p.322.

[33] J.J. Linz and A. De Miquel, "Within Nation Differences and Comparisons: The Eight Spains", in Merritt and Rokkan, eds., *Comparing Nations: The Use of Quantitative Data in Cross-National Research,* pp. 267-319.

[34] S.D. Clark points out that in South America the native culture was absorbed by the invading society, which fostered a sense of social continuity. On the other hand, little borrowing from the native culture took place in North America as Indians were relegated to the background. "The Canadian Community" in G.W. Brown, *Canada* (Toronto: University of Toronto Press, 1950), p. 377.

[35] Commonwealth Bureau of Census and Statistics, *1972 Australia Yearbook* (Canberra, Australia, 1972), p. 139. Based on 1966 figures.

[36] *Report of the Royal Commission on Bilingualism and Biculturalism:* Book I, *The Official Language,* pp. 6-16.

[37] Kenneth D. McRae, *Switzerland: Example of Cultural Co-existence* (Toronto: Canadian Institute of International Affairs, 1964).

6
Identity Model

The preceding chapters have uncovered problem areas within Canadian society. The colloquial expression that Canada has yet to "get it all together" seems appropriate, for the population found within Canadian political and geographic borders lacks a sufficiently unified character to give the society cohesiveness. Undoubtedly, if loyalties to the collectivity are weak, the national image projected to the world will be weak.

Alford's comparative political study of the Anglo-American democracies noted that Canada does not have the unifying loyalties and the consciousness of nationality that are taken for granted in American and British society.[1] W. L. Morton argued that Canada's hope for independence as a nation depends upon the society's achieving a clearer self-definition.[2] Mildred Schwartz stated the Canadian problem very succinctly:

> Ninety-eight years after its formation as a viable state, Canada was only beginning to cope with problems most nations meet (though not necessarily solve) at their birth. Canada's late start in acquiring the symbols of nationhood is indicative of the larger problems it faces as a creation of Britain, a neighbor of the United States, and a nation peopled by groups that somehow had never developed many unifying bonds.[3]

And even Ronald Manzer's recent work laments that a sense of national identity is more intense and more widely shared in most other countries than in Canada.[4] The conclusion is that Canadian society either lacks an identity or possesses such a diffuse sense of identity that its members are not very concerned about maintaining their common bonds against divisive forces. While a number of factors have contributed to change this situation somewhat in recent years, clearly Canadian society is still in the process of self-definition or identity formation.

Identity as a Concept

In spite of the frequency with which the term "identity" is used in a sociological context, the concept more properly belongs in the province of social psychologists who are concerned with human personality development. A nation in the process of identity formation, then, is merely *like* or *similar* to an individual experiencing identity formation.[5] Needless to say, an identity is very difficult to define and it is virtually impossible to determine the fine line between lack of an identity and the existence of an identity.

The matter of identity is of sociological concern because sense of *self* is only attained through social interaction. A child learns who he is by noting how others see him. Through the judgments of others, particularly those with whom the child interacts most frequently ("significant others"), the child becomes aware of himself and differentiates himself from others. The self is continuously redefined throughout life as the feedback from social interaction helps a person to readjust his self-image. An identity is not automatically obtained at birth; rather, it is a process of self-discovery from interaction with others.

The early identity of a child is influenced and sponsored by parents and close relatives. This identity is more or less handed to him until the teenage years when identity formation reaches critical moments in the emergence of an independent personality. At this point decisions must be made about what aspects of the sponsored identity to retain as the person develops his own ideas, attitudes, and values. Identity formation does not come easily, but is full of confusion and conflict which we label "growing up".

An analogy from childhood and youth to the development of a nation may be tenuous but nevertheless worthwhile in giving us our final perspective on Canadian society. A *national identity* is the collective identity of all the participants within that society. But it is only as the members of the society interact that they learn what unites them. A sense of cohesion or belonging is attained when individuals see each other in relation to the collectivity and, on this basis, distinguish their society from other societies. *A national identity,* then, is obtained through a process of self-discovery whereby members of a society evolve a collective awareness of their unity and of the differentiation of the in-group from the out-group. The national self-image is adjusted and readjusted as the result of interaction both within the society and with members of other societies.

To carry the analogy further, a national identity was not automatically obtained when Canada officially became a nation in 1867. Britain, the sponsor of the early identity of the nation, maintained strong parental attachments with Canada in her infancy. But as childhood has been outgrown, former parental ties are being reevaluated and an independent identity is emerging. It is possible that the conflicts and struggles of youth which Canada is now facing are part of this process of identity formation. With the presupposition that the society is currently in a period of identity formation, this chapter will explore the forces that have retarded and contributed to the formation of a Canadian identity.

When we use the term "national or societal identity", we refer to the way members of a society see themselves as a collectivity set apart from other collectivities. In this interpretation, identity is largely the product of mutual reflection and interaction by those within a society, which solidifies their existence together and results in their own unique bonds of consensus. Many of the matters already discussed in this book can be brought to bear on this theme.

FACTORS RETARDING THE EMERGENCE OF AN IDENTITY

It is not to be suggested that Canada has no identity — that she is a faceless land with faceless people. Our concern instead is with what has delayed the emergence of a societal self-concept. Furthermore, an awareness of the factors that have retarded identity formation does not carry with it a condemnation of their essentially negative character or an implication that change is necessary. The reader can make his own value judgments about these points. In any case, whatever positive value the four factors discussed below may have, they have reduced the sense of Canadian unity necessary for the development of a societal identity.

Perpetuation of symbols of colonialism. Identity formation has been slowed down through the use of symbols connected with the British monarchy. For many years there was a general lack of interest in establishing distinctive Canadian symbols because of the desire to maintain British ties. The Queen's picture appeared on all Canadian money, "God Save the Queen" was sung at important Canadian events, the Union Jack was flown, and the Queen sent her representatives at the head of both provincial and federal governments in the person of the Lieutenant-Governors and the Govenor General. Retaining ties with the British government may have been beneficial for many reasons but it obviated the necessity for Canada to develop her own symbols. Leonard Doob has pointed out how important symbols are in evoking feelings of nationalism.[6] Canadian dependence on foreign symbols made it more difficult for residents of this society to perceive what differentiated Canadian society from British society.

A study by the Canadian Institute of Public Opinion in 1971 revealed that 40% of the Canadians polled felt that the monarchy should play a less important role in Canadian life.[7] However, the durability of colonial ties was shown by the same poll; 42% felt that the British monarchy should *not* become less important in Canadian life. Women were more likely to uphold the monarchy than men, and residents of the Maritimes and the West were slightly more interested in retaining the monarchy than residents of Ontario. Not unexpectedly, all these regions were much more interested in retaining these ties than Quebec was. It is clear that Canadians are quite divided over what influence this symbol of colonialism or social tradition ought to have in Canadian society.

The lack of a revolutionary origin myth. On the one hand, revolution means rejecting dependencies on other countries and severing intimate relationships. On the other hand, revolution means the affirmation of the independent destiny of one's society. From a historical perspective, revolutions have been an important factor in molding the independent character of national societies.[8] Revolutions usually include the promulgation of an ideology through the drafting of historic documents and the emergence of leading personalities who become national heroes. These features become part of a mythology about national origins and destiny that is transmitted to succeeding generations. A national mythology differentiates a society and can contribute to the arousal of patriotic feelings.

Lack of a decisive separation and of a mythology replete with heroes has undoubtedly contributed to Canada's diffuse identity.[9] Canada's foundational document is called not the "Canada Act" but the *British North America Act* and was passed by the British Parliament with all amendments requiring ratification by that body. Political independence may have come by peaceful evolution rather than by revolution[10] but the price was entanglement in a web of alliances that could only delay Canada's process of self-discovery.

Internal cleavages. Cleavages based on language, culture, region, and standard of living have hampered the attainment of a Canadian identity. Chapter 1 pointed out how waves of immigration and emigraton have produced a heterogeneous population, many of whom still possess Old-Country loyalties with few bonds to unite them with other residents of Canada. The cultural and linguistic dualism represented in the French-English relationship has divided Canadian society.[11] The existence of regional disparities in industrialization and economic development has been a source of conflict. All of these factors have engendered deep hostilities that have made it difficult for the society to establish consensus and common loyalties.

As a relatively new society, Canada has experienced more obvious cleavages than a more mature society. Traditions take time to develop, and people must live together and even struggle together to form common bonds that assist in the coagulation of identity. And yet we must be careful not to assume that differences within this heterogeneous society are all solvable. For example, it appears that two languages will continue to divide the society. However, what we might expect in time is the evolution of a truer bilingualism whereby continuous exposure would enable more Canadians to converse in both languages. If this were to happen, then we might expect less conflict, though the seemingly enduring dualistic nature of Canadian society may make us quite pessimistic about the outcome.

While linguistic dualism and cultural pluralism may give Canada a unique character,[12] they thwart the development of a societal identity insofar as they are barriers to interaction. When interaction does occur, it only serves to remind persons of their differences. And as long as members of the society lack common commitments, identity will be quite diffuse.

Proximity to the United States. This is the fourth factor that has been responsible for the delay in the specification of a Canadian identity. I have already shown that historically the United States was an attractive destination for migrants from Canada. The combination of employment opportunities and warmer climate has been an incentive for disaffected members of Canadian society to resettle. In addition, as Chapter 3 has illustrated, American finance, technology, and culture have infiltrated and influenced Canadian society. While it might be argued that this American influence is worldwide, geographical proximity has facilitated a greater impact on Canada. Proximity makes comparisons between the two societies more natural, and Canada has often found herself caught up in playing "follow the leader" and copying standards set in another society.

It is not just American strength as a world power that is significant to Canadian society but similarities of values, language, and standard of living. S.D. Clark has pointed out that an emerging Canadian identity has encouraged feelings of anti-Americanism.[13] Yet the curious paradox remains that Canadian society has become more and more like American society. As the differences between the two societies become more obscure, small distinctions are overplayed as the only means of preventing Canadian society from feeling overwhelmed.[14]

Proximity also encourages frequent interaction with Americans. As an example of the volume of this interchange, in 1970 approximately 37 million U.S. residents visited Canada, while over 35 million Canadian residents visited the United States. Since Canada's total population is almost 22 million and since over 35 million Canadians visited the United States in the year, many Canadians evidently made multiple crossings. It might be expected that the primary reason for most of these crossings was for business, but a voluntary questionnaire distributed by immigration officials at Canadian border points in the same year showed that business was a minor reason for visiting the United States. For 55.9%, holiday or recreation was the reason for entering the United States; 26.9% crossed to visit friends and relatives, and only 9.2% indicated business as the purpose for their travel.[15] Such data illustrate how proximity encourages intermingling and increases the effect that American society has on Canadian society.

The acquisition of an identity does not mean that the members of a society should form a homogeneous mass. Rather a nation as a multi-bonded group requires a shared understanding of its members' mutual existence. Some persons might consider the factors hindering the formation of an identity that were discussed above as the "best" aspects of Canadian society. A people may actually prefer a very diffuse identity and weak sense of commitment to the collectivity, and perhaps this stance has been preferable to many Canadians. Yet all of these factors have had particular consequences and effects in making members of the society more aware of what divides them than of what unites them.

FACTORS THAT CONTRIBUTE TO IDENTITY FORMATION

Even though identity formation has been a rather lengthy process for Canadian society, several factors can be pointed out that have more recently contributed to the crystallization of the Canadian identity.

The decline of the British Empire. Less able to maintain her colonialist posture, Britain formed closer economic alliances with European nations, increasing Canada's independence. The Commonwealth of Nations reduced the central and paternalistic role of Britain and substituted an alliance of countries which met on an autonomous and equal basis. The position of Governor General was first filled by a Canadian in 1952 when Vincent Massey was appointed as the Queen's representative. Even though the "mother country" was given deference by Canadian society, parental attachments were loosening. Canada was being allowed to control her own destiny even while she was actively appropriating this control.[16]

Britain's move to the European Common Market might have increased Canada's sense of autonomy but for her switch in orientation to the United States in a new dependency which undoubtedly again retarded identity formation. However, as we will see, persistent reevaluations of this dependency have helped to renew the society's attempts to differentiate itself, even if in very limited ways.

More positive assessment of their own society by Canadians.   In comparing themselves to Britain, Canadians can observe that their own higher standard of living makes Canada a preferable place to live. In fact, Schwartz argues that it is "the high level of material satisfaction" in Canadian society that helps contain its divisive elements.[17]   Instead of using Britain, the United States, or any other more dominant society as the standard of reference, Canadians are developing confidence in the intrinsic worth of their own society. Similarly, negative features of American society such as racial struggles, high crime rates, or the Viet Nam War have encouraged Canadians to make comparisons that downgrade their neighbor and contribute to a feeling of superiority. In addition, the contemporary demand for Canadian natural resources that other countries require because of scarce world supplies contributes to an inflation of the national ego. The notion that Canadian society has to take a back seat to more dominant societies is slowly disappearing as Canadian society becomes aware of and defends its advantages and positive features.

Anti-imperialist sentiment around the world.   Members of Canadian society have been encouraged to be more aware of foreign influences from dominant societies because the demands for independence by colonial countries of the Third World have underscored the issues of national sovereignty and internal control over national destiny. Schwartz found that as late as the 1950s, public approval of economic ties with the United States and of U.S. investment in Canada had been as high as 68%, which indicates the recency of expression of the anti-imperialist sentiment in Canada.[18]   The reverberations from independence movements throughout the world have no doubt been felt in Canada to the point of encouraging greater participation in and internal control of the society. When an out-group is interpreted as a threat to one's existence, that out-group becomes an important mechanism in establishing one's identity.

Government sponsorship of communication links that span the nation.[19]   The Canadian Broadcasting Corporation is a crown corporation operated for the explicit purpose of tying the nation together. The network makes possible the gathering and dissemination of news from all parts of the society. Such government involvement was more vital in an earlier stage of Canadian history when without government action no such unitive tie would have been shared by Canadians. Even though private economic interests might be willing to move into these areas now, such concerns as the CBC, the National Film Board, and Air Canada have become Canadian institutions that have an integral role in the development of a Canadian identity. These communication links have helped Canadians, at least to a certain extent, to understand and experience what is occurring in other parts of their society. It is probable that without government initiative such unitive links would have been developed much later.

The specification of unique societal symbols.   Two symbols that have finally been accepted are a flag and a national anthem. A uniquely Canadian flag with a maple leaf at its center was adopted in 1965 in a storm of controversy, particularly from hard-core supporters of the British Union Jack.[20] As a national anthem, "God Save the Queen" had been particularly offensive to French Canadians and to those who stressed Canadian independence. English Canadians often sang "The Maple Leaf Forever" (written in 1867); but the fact that it recalled historical events which were variously interpreted by persons in different parts of the society reduced its usage. The popular acceptance of "O Canada" (written in 1880) as a general expression of nationhood by both English and French Canadians has led to its adoption as the national anthem.[21] Both the flag and the national anthem provide a common frame of reference for the collectivity and assist in the crystallization of a national identity.

The five forces which we have discussed are all playing an important role in assisting Canadian society in identity formation. Individuals are more likely to be conscious of the existence of the national society as an entity when loyalties to the collectivity are established. Because loyalties have tended to be more regional than national, the concept of Canadian society has often appeared meaningless. In fact, Lower viewed Confederation as merely "an artificial conjunction of local loyalties".[22] Thus, because the means whereby a societal bonding might occur have taken considerable time to develop, it is appropriate to speak of a Canadian societal identity in formation.

The Concept of Nationalism

If a societal identity emerges as the result of social interaction among the society's members, then loyalty to the unit that binds them together is likely to develop. A societal consciousness or crystallized societal identity has the potential of contributing to the emergence of a sense of nationalism in which loyalties to the collectivity are dominant.

In a poll of Canadians in 1971, 59% of the respondents agreed with the idea of Canadian nationalism while only 8% disagreed, stating that it was bad for the country; 33% were undecided.[23] It is clear from this evidence that not all Canadians feel that nationalism is an important requirement of being a member of this society, and even when they do support nationalism, the concept means different things to different people.

Part of the problem lies in the definition of nationalism. To some it conjures up a psychological state involving mass hysteria, intolerance, or ethnocentrism. To others it may primarily mean defense of the nation as a unit, particularly in light of the threat of separation in Canada or of foreign control. The Gallup Poll found that one half of the adult respondents could not even express what nationalism meant to them.

Nationalism is often fused with patriotism but there is a significant difference. Patriotism literally means a "love of country" and is an age-old phenomenon. People have always identified with the place of their birth or place of residence and have been loyal to it. They have usually been conscious of their nationality in terms of the group to which they belonged. But Carlton Hayes has argued that nationalism is a recent phenomenon because it is coextensive with the independent nation-state and demands exclusive loyalty.[24] This loyalty toward a particular state rather than just to a geographic locale is so exclusive that other loyalties are crowded out by the belief in the "surpassing excellence" or superiority of the sovereign state. Hayes points out that it is just another step to claim that nationalism is the new religion because of its all-encompassing belief in the strength of the nation beyond the individual.

Christian and Campbell refer to this type of nationalism as "full-blown nationalism" because of its extreme view of the state and its claims on its citizens.[25] The individual loses himself to the state and subordinates all other interests and loyalties to the nation. It is the sort of enthusiasm and commitment that produced slogans such as *Deutschland über alles* (Germany above everything else). Such nationalism has never been characteristic of Canada, according to Christian and Campbell, because linguistic and ethnic loyalties have moderated nationalist sentiment.

The idea of a Canadian nationalism has developed most specifically among English-speaking Canadians. Many new immigrants could not identify with nationalist sentiments for they were perceived as an attempt to force new bonds of loyalty and to destroy the old national loyalties. In other words, Canadian nationalism was perceived as a tool of assimilation and therefore was frequently rejected. French Canadians also reacted to the collectivist nature of Canadian nationalism because it seemed to destroy their particularisms. In consequence, they have usually withheld overt forms of loyalty to the nation-state. If nationalism subordinates other loyalties, then it is clear how and why its coercive power would be objectionable to minorities.

Obviously, Confederation did not bring a sense of nationalism to Canada[26] because the focus of loyalties for most residents was outside the country. For Francophones, it was France and perhaps the Roman Catholic Church, while for Anglophones, it was usually Great Britain. The "Canada First" movement of the 1870s was a short-lived campaign to forge a nationalism based on British culture.[27] Resistance to this and other similar attempts at destroying the pluralist loyalties of Canadians has prevented the emergence of an overarching sense of nationalism. And these feelings still continue. In the 1971 Public Opinion Poll referred to earlier, 63% of English-speaking Canadians accepted Canadian nationalism as a good thing, whereas only 49% of French-speaking Canadians did. 57% of those of other ethnic groups agreed with the idea of Canadian nationalism. While it is important to note that few were opposed to nationalism, a large percentage of persons were undecided on this issue.

FRENCH-CANADIAN NATIONALISM

The same forces that have retarded the emergence of a Canadian identity have also inhibited the development of nationalism. Sectionalism and ethnicity continue to be divisive, particularly when they coincide. They have been the source of a nationalism that has recently flowered in Quebec.

French-Canadian nationalism is not really a new phenomenon: the goal of Francophones in Canada has always been "la survivance". Under the British crown, the defense of religion, language, and culture in general sought to insulate the French-Canadian community. This has been referred to as "defensive nationalism" because it was rigidly protective in nature.[28] But Charles Taylor has argued that the *new nationalism* among French Canadians is not so much a defense of an old way of life as an attempt to create something new in building a modern French society on this continent.[29] The only thing the old nationalism has in common with the new nationalism is the maintenance of the French language. Traditional nationalism supported an agricultural society which had religion at its center and a desire to carry the French-Canadian culture throughout the continent. The new nationalism emerges from a rising middle class who are suspicious of federal nationalism as an assimilationist technique. The desire to industrialize and modernize Quebec without assimilation has produced a nationalism which has separatism as its theme. Nationalism in this sense is not primarily a feeling of cultural superiority but a desire for non-interference from Anglophones. To that extent, French-Canadian nationalism is an ethnic and regional response to social change in which those who belong to the group want to control the direction and nature of that change.[30]

Separatism is an attempt to create sufficient loyalty to the regional unit so that national ties will be rejected. The view of Quebec nationalism adopted here is that, at the grass-roots level, it is more of a cultural and economic nationalism concerned with restructuring relationships than a political nationalism of independence.[31] This assertion is borne out by a study sponsored by the Canadian Institute of Public Opinion in 1971 that determined that there was more support for Quebec's right to separate in all other regions of Canada than in Quebec itself.[32] For example, 49% of the respondents in the West thought Quebec should have the right to separate, whereas only 30% in Quebec thought so. Conversely, more people in Quebec thought that Quebec should *not* be permitted to separate than residents in any other region in Canada. This indicates that while ethnicity has become a powerful basis for a nationalist sentiment among French Canadians, it has not developed to the point of severing relationships with the nation as a whole.

THE NATURE OF CANADIAN NATIONALISM

Porter has observed that whatever national unity exists in Canada has been preserved by retaining the pluralist status quo as intact as possible in order to minimize conflict.[33] If Canada is really only a loose federation of local loyalties, then the idea of a demanding nationalistic loyalty is contrary to what the society is all about.

Hugh Hood argues that everybody in Canada possesses the psychology of a member of some minority group.[34] Minorities are zealous to maintain their rights as well as their independence, and this produces a minimal commitment to the collectivity that makes a "full-blown nationalism" almost impossible to achieve.

In this context, it is not surprising that Canadian society evidences so little nationalist feeling. If nationalism involves authoritarian demands for loyalty that reduce individual freedom, then it is to be expected that whatever collective sentiment would exist in Canada would be low-key. Heiman says a heightened sense of nationalism is undesirable because it produces bigotry and ethnocentrism,[35] and Bay calls it a "noxious weed" that produces a "phony euphoria" impairing our concern for all mankind.[36]

And yet we speak of a growing nationalism in Canada that is related to hositility toward foreign intrusions and to growing identification with the country. We also speak of economic nationalism and cultural nationalism. If these forms have been largely absent from Canada in the past, there is every indication that they are now developing rapidly. In Chapter 3, I referred to the negative side of nationalism or the "anti-spirit" found in Canadian society. We can now consider its more positive side. The divisions in Canada notwithstanding, *nationalism* has come to mean the mutual affirmation of the significance and destiny of the collectivity. It is *the reaffirmation of the right of Canadian society to continue to exist and for its members to control the nature of that existence.*

Of course, the danger persists that nationalism will produce the narrow-mindedness and ethnocentrism characteristic of any obsessive loyalty. But thus far the moderate nationalism that has been expressed has been an attempt to ensure that the society works for the good of all its inhabitants without demanding exclusivist loyalties to the state. Given the pluralist nature of the society, any extreme demands at the moment would probably be rejected.

Whether this moderate form of nationalism is based on a love of the land[37] or on mutual agreement to accept the political structure,[38] its primary concern is to ensure that the national society does not disintegrate. Heiman suggests that instead of blind commitment and intolerant zeal, the patriotic individual develops a nationalist sentiment naturally and spontaneously because the society is conducive to his personal preferences and aspirations.[39] Sociologically, nationalism is more likely to develop when frequent interaction between members of a national society makes them aware of each other. But nationalism is more than mere awareness; it is the concerned *action* that results from embracing the collectivity.[40]

HOW DOES NATIONALISM ARISE?

To suggest that nationalism arises spontaneously is perhaps over-stating the case, as important mechanisms do play an integral role in its development. A sense of nationalism is chiefly fostered by those agents that socialize the members of the society into the goals and traditions of the collectivity. *Socialization* is the process whereby individuals learn what the society expects of them. The Canadian problem is not only that the society must teach its younger members about their relationship to the societal unit, but also that it must *resocialize* many of its older migrated members into identification with the national society — and that has proved a difficult task. The primary socializing agents that teach and encourage members of a society to develop nationalist feeling are the educational system, intellectuals, citizens who find nation-alism advantageous, and political leaders and parties.[41] Through-out our discussion it is assumed that the mass media are important in disseminating the information that fosters a nationalist senti-ment.

One of the major building blocks for a societal identity and a sense of nationalism is the *educational system* for it socializes the young into the societal tradition.[42] The schools teach what it means to be a member of the society through instruction in societal history and geography, the celebration of societal holi-days, and the interpretation of current national events.

The Royal Commission on Bilingualism and Biculturalism dis-covered that one of the problems in developing a Canadian identity was the presentation of two different views of Canadian history in the textbooks of the two dominant languages.[43] The French-language textbooks stressed the survival of French-Canadian society, and one half of the text was usually devoted to the period prior to the English Conquest. Such events as the Durham Report and Confederation were presented from the point of view of a minority facing English domination. English-language textbooks, on the other hand, stressed the Conquest as a beginning rather than an ending, and emphasized the need for a strong Canadian society on the continent. Thus, the schools were perpet-uating two historical traditions in Canada and were contributing to a rift in Canadian society.

A recent study of Anglophone and Francophone school children in Quebec was designed to test these conclusions empirically.[44] The children were asked to name an important person whom they admired in the country's history. Francophones and Anglophones overwhelmingly identified with the heroes of their own culture and the ethnocentric selection increased with the age of the child. Francophone heroes were drawn primarily from the pre-1760 era, whereas Anglophone heroes were drawn primarily from the post-1760 period. The investigator concluded that there were relatively few "reconciliation symbols" shared by the two groups that could serve as unitive forces. The educational system was ensuring a cultural gulf in Canada through the way it was socializing the children.

Even though there are two different views, it could be argued that it is still Canadian history that is being taught and that students are being socialized into an awareness of the Canadian societal unit. Nevertheless, a study of civic education programs across Canada by Hodgetts has severely indicted most Canadian schools for not contributing to the development of a national understanding and a national identity.[45] Not only were different views of national history presented in French and English textbooks, but the emphasis was placed on the bland facts of history prior to the 1930s with little attention given to contemporary issues. When current events were discussed, Hodgetts found the focus was more likely to be on non-Canadian events such as the Viet Nam War, the black problem in the United States, or the United Nations' debate on the admission of The People's Republic of China. The Canadian educational system has not been as significant as it could be in the forging of a national unity.

The second agent in fostering a nationalist sentiment is the *intellectual*. The historian, for example, in researching, interpreting, and writing about history, enables the member of a society to be more aware of his country's heritage and usually stimulates him to personal reflection about its identity. Literary figures write about the land and its people in romantic or thought-provoking ways. It has been argued that nationalism is the product of print technology[46] and undoubtedly the dissemination of views of the society through books, newspapers, and magazines evokes both emotional and intellectual responses toward the society. Intellectuals can also serve as critics, for their study and research may uncover trends or anticipate consequences harmful to the society that are not readily accessible to the general public. Since most of the society's leaders have a university education, the perspectives of the academic intellectual undoubtedly have wide scope and influence. Less academic but more popular writers such as Pierre Berton and James Gray become symbols of the society's search for itself through their widely read books of the Canadian past.

Thirdly, nationalism is promulgated by those *citizens for whom nationalism is personally advantageous.* S.D. Clark points out that in the early years there was little support for a nationalist sentiment among the people, but Canada's "most ardent patriots" were her dignitaries — business leaders, bishops, ministers of the Crown, and military officers — whose well-being and superior position were connected to the independent existence of Canada and to a strong Canadian society.[47] In another instance, he argues that nationalism was deliberately encouraged by the Canadian Manufacturers' Association whose financial soundness depended upon the protection of internal markets.[48] The dubious origin for such societal feeling is expressed by Levitt, who labels these individuals "misguided nationalists" in that they advocated policies that were personally beneficial, often at the expense of the consumer or the general public.[49] Even French-Canadian nationalism could be viewed as a movement by those who would benefit by drawing hard lines between the in-group and the out-group. The skilled and professional middle class in Quebec wanted the opportunities that were previously given primarily to the out-group. Tremblay's study of the Maritime Acadian society found that the more affluent Francophones stressed the maintenance of cultural distinctiveness, whereas those who were preoccupied with merely making a living wanted the easiest route to that end without concern for their ethnic tradition.[50] Nationalism will be vociferously advocated by those who stand to benefit from the existence of such a feeling in the society.

S.D. Clark has argued that the most recent wave of nationalism is a product of the post-war baby boom in that the new generation of middle class youth are anxious about creating "a place for themselves" in the Canadian business, labor, political and educational world.[51] Clark rejects the idea that such nationalism is based solely on self-interest, but observes that it is merely a progressive stage in the development of the society, particularly in the broadening of the middle class.

The fourth means whereby the residents of the society are socialized into nationalist sentiment is *political leaders and political parties.* In a democratic society, political parties require participation at the grass-roots level through election campaigns and interaction with elected officials; many persons have developed interest in societal issues through such involvement. Furthermore, political leaders articulate national issues for the public, and the variety of appeal and expression of these leaders, often in opposition to each other, stimulates public awareness. Doob refers to politicians as "professional patriots" on whom the average citizen who has little inclination to dwell on political issues depends for the construction of a national consciousness.[52] Here again, the impact of the mass media is great in making the members of the society aware of political personalities and societal issues that they all share.[53]

THE CANADIAN IDENTITY

It is debatable whether nationalism or a societal identity can ever crystallize without a common culture, a common language, or a common sense of history.[54] Undoubtedly a common language, for example, would facilitate interaction among members of a society. Yet none of these common bonds appear to be present or even forthcoming in Canadian society. A basic duality is confounded by a complex plurality that is encouraged by federal policy.

Paradoxically, there persists a vague feeling among the majority of the members of the society that they belong together. Surely French Canadians are more Canadian than they are French, and Ukrainian-Canadians are by now more Canadian than Ukrainian.[55] If, as Porter argues, French Canadians are struggling to retain their identity while other Canadians are looking for an identity,[56] the entire struggle is still taking place in a Canadian context. And from these struggles of maturation (a developmental task in obtaining an identity) a new nationality may eventually emerge in which all members of the society will participate.

The search for a national identity is a good perspective from which to end this macro-sociological study of Canadian society. After discussing cleavages within the society and pressures from without, it is useful to come back to the question with which we began: "What enables us to speak of the population residing in Canada as a society, and what holds the society together?" In the search for an answer to such a complex question, we have considered the forces that are producing a nationalist spirit and a sense of mutual identification with the societal collectivity. Nevertheless, whether we will ever feel comfortable in speaking of the population of Canada as a society in the full sense of the term discussed in Chapter 1 remains to be seen.

QUESTIONS FOR FURTHER EXPLORATION

1. *What are the advantages and dangers of a stronger nationalist feeling in Canadian society?*
2. *Is the attainment of a clear national identity really important? Why or why not?*
3. *Study Canadians who are outspoken in their nationalist statements and determine what their reasons may have been for speaking out.*

NOTES

[1] Robert R. Alford, *Party and Society: The Anglo-American Democracies* (Chicago: Rand McNally, 1963), p. 254.

[2] W.L. Morton, *The Canadian Identity* (Madison: University of Wisconsin Press, 1965), p. vii.

[3] Mildred A. Schwartz, *Public Opinion and Canadian Identity* (Berkeley: University of California Press, 1967), p. ix. Reprinted by permission of the University of California Press.

[4] Ronald Manzer, *Canada: A Socio-Political Report* (Toronto: McGraw-Hill Ryerson, 1974), p. 329.

[5] Schwartz gives a similar warning that to speak of a nation's identity is to use a metaphor, *Public Opinion and Canadian Identity*, p. 9.

[6] Leonard W. Doob, *Patriotism and Nationalism: Their Psychological Foundations* (New Haven: Yale University Press, 1964), p. 50.

[7] Canadian Institute of Public Opinion, *the Gallup Report* (July 17, 1971).

[8] See Don Martindale, "The Sociology of National Character", *The Annals of the American Academy of Political and Social Science*, Vol. 270 (March 1967), p. 32.

[9] An early account of Canadian identity termed the War of 1812 Canada's War of Independence and in many ways the account is probably correct. However, the War did not generate the same mythology or the same break as the American War of Independence did for the United States. The War of 1812 served to emphasize British ties and to reaffirm a distance from the United States. See W. Stewart Wallace, *The Growth of Canadian National Feeling* (Toronto: Macmillan Co. of Canada, 1927), pp. 14-15; and also A.R.M. Lower, *Colony to Nation: A History of Canada* (Don Mills: Longman Canada, 1964), Chapter 14.

[10] K.A. MacKirdy, "Canada and the Commonwealth", *Queen's Quarterly*, Vol. 74 (1967), p. 453.

[11] The perpetuation of dualism in Canadian society is the theme of R.J. Ossenberg, "The Conquest Revisited: Another Look at Canadian Dualism", *Canadian Review of Sociology and Anthropology*, Vol. 4 (November 1967), pp. 201-219.

[12] For a more elaborate discussion of these factors as they relate to the lack of a societal identity see John Porter, "Canadian Character in the Twentieth Century", *The Annals of the American Academy of Political and Social Science*, Vol. 370 (March 1967), pp. 48-56.

[13] S.D. Clark, "Canada and her Great Neighbor", *Canadian Review of Sociology and Anthropology*, Vol. 1 (November 1964), pp. 193-201.

[14] S.F. Wise and R.C. Brown, *Canada Views the United States* (Seattle: University of Washington Press, 1967), p. 95.

[15] *Canada Yearbook 1972* (Ottawa: Statistics Canada), pp. 1114-1115.

[16] W.L. Morton asserts that Canadian nationhood in 1867 was not obtained as a result of Canadian demands but as a result of British policy: *The Canadian Identity*, p. 47. Also consider his statement that the monarchy serves as the pivotal point of Canadian unity (p. 111).

[17] M.A. Schwartz, *Public Opinion and Canadian Identity*, pp. 251-252. See also Kenneth M. Glazier, "The Surge of Nationalism in Canada Today", *Current History* (April 1974), p. 150.

[18] M.A. Schwartz, *Public Opinion and Canadian Identity*, p. 67.

[19] See Frank W. Peers, "Broadcasting and National Unity", in Benjamin D. Singer, ed., *Communications in Canadian Society* (Toronto: Copp Clark, 1972), pp. 202-230. Peers argues that the media both mirror and contribute to problems in crystallizing the Canadian identity. See also, Frank Peers, "The Nationalist Dilemma in Canadian Broadcasting", in Peter Russell, ed., *Nationalism in Canada* (Toronto: McGraw-Hill Co. of Canada, 1966), pp. 252-267.

[20] For an account of the debate regarding the flag see Blair Fraser, *The Search for Identity* (Toronto: Doubleday, 1967), Chapter 23.

[21] Schwartz discovered a greater hard core of support for the Union Jack than for "God Save the Queen". But widespread acceptance was registered for "O Canada". *Public Opinion and Canadian Identity*, pp. 106-112.

[22] A.R.M. Lower, *Canada: Nation and Neighbor* (Toronto: Ryerson Press, 1952), p. 119.

[23] Canadian Institute of Public Opinion, *the Gallup Report* (January 2, 1971).

[24] Carlton J. Hayes, *Essays on Nationalism* (New York: Russell and Russell, 1966), p. 26. For a good history of the rise of nationalism see pp. 30-60. Hayes relates the emergence of nationalism to the rise of political democracy, the industrial revolution, and philosophical romanticism.

[25] W. Christian and C. Campbell, *Political Parties and Ideologies in Canada* (Toronto: McGraw-Hill Ryerson, 1974), pp. 159-161. Chapter 6 of this book contains a good study of Canadian nationalism particularly in its historical development. Another readable statement on nationalism with particular reference to Canada is David Cameron, *Nationalism, Self-determination and the Quebec Question* (Toronto: Macmillan Co. of Canada, 1974).

[26] Gerald M. Craig, *The United States and Canada* (Cambridge: Harvard University Press, 1968). Compare Craig with Hubert Guindon who sees Confederation as the birth of Canadian nationalism and links it with

geographic expansion into the West: "Two Cultures: An Essay on Nationalism, Class and Ethnic Tension" in R.H. Leach, *Contemporary Canada* (Durham, N.C.: Duke University Press, 1967), p. 53.

[27] For a good discussion of the Canada First Movement see A.G. Bailey, *Culture and Nationality* (Toronto: McClelland and Stewart, 1972), Chapter 9.

[28] J.C. Bonenfant and J.C. Falardeau, "Cultural and Political Implications of French-Canadian Nationalism", in Ramsay Cook, ed., *French-Canadian Nationalism: An Anthology* (Toronto: Macmillan Co. of Canada, 1969), p. 19. Cook's book is a good reference on the topic of French-Canadian nationalism.

[29] Charles Taylor, "Nationalism and the Political Intelligentsia", *Queen's Quarterly*, Vol. 72 (1965), pp. 150-168. Taylor points out that French-Canadian nationalism repudiates English Canadians without denying many of their values.

[30] For the best account of this expression of nationalism see Hubert Guindon, "Two Cultures: An Essay on Nationalism, Class and Ethnic Tension". A good account of the crystallization of French-Canadian nationalism in historical and sociological perspective is Fernand Dumont and Guy Rocher's "An Introduction to a Sociology of French Canada", in M. Rioux and Yves Martin, eds., *French-Canadian Society*, Volume I (Toronto: McClelland and Stewart, 1964), pp. 178-200; and Michael Brunet "The French Canadians' Search for a Fatherland", in Peter Russell, ed., *Nationalism in Canada*, (Toronto: McGraw-Hill Co. of Canada, 1966), pp. 47-60.

[31] Compare with William P. Irvine, "Recruitment to Nationalism: New Politics on Normal Politics", *Canadian Journal of Political Science*, Vol. 5 (December 1972), pp. 503-520. This is not to ignore the minority who advocate a political nationalism.

[32] Canadian Institute of Public Opinion, *the Gallup Report* (April 17, 1971).

[33] John Porter, "Canadian Character in the Twentieth Century", p. 54.

[34] Hugh Hood, "Moral Imagination: Canadian Thing", in William Kilbourn, ed., *Canada: A Guide to the Peaceable Kingdom* (Toronto: Macmillan Co. of Canada, 1970), pp. 31-32.

[35] George Heiman, "The Nineteenth Century Legacy: Nationalism or Patriotism?", in Peter Russell, ed., *Nationalism in Canada*, p. 339.

[36] Christian Bay, "The Perils of Patriotism", in V. Nelles and A. Rotstein, *Nationalism or Local Control* (Toronto: New Press, 1973), p. 21.

[37] See Blair Fraser, *The Search for Identity* (Toronto: Doubleday, 1967), p. 314, and Carl Berger, "The True North Strong and Free", in Peter Russell, ed., *Nationalism in Canada*, pp. 3-26.

[38] Donald V. Smiley suggests that nationalism must be established on political rather than racial (ethnic) grounds: *The Canadian Political Nationality* (Toronto: Methuen, 1967), p. 130.

[39] George Heiman, "The Nineteenth Century Legacy: Nationalism or Patriotism?" in Peter Russell, ed., *Nationalism in Canada*, p. 325.

[40] I am following L.W. Doob here in noting that patriotism is more of

a feeling, whereas nationalism is the action that results from that feeling: *Patriotism and Nationalism: Their Psychological Foundations*, p. 6.

[41] Compare Carlton Hayes, *Essays on Nationalism*, p. 62, and Mildred A. Schwartz, *Public Opinion and Canadian Identity*, pp. 15-23.

[42] For a study of the political socialization of children in British Columbia, with specific emphasis on parental influence, see Elia T. Zurick, "Children and Political Socialization", in K. Ishwaran, *The Canadian Family: A Book of Readings* (Toronto: Holt, Rinehart and Winston of Canada, 1971), pp. 186-199.

[43] *Report of the Royal Commission on Bilingualism and Biculturalism*, Book II: *Education*, p. 275.

[44] Jean Pierre Richert, "The Impact of Ethnicity on the Perception of Heroes and Historical Symbols", *Canadian Review of Sociology and Anthropology*, Vol. 11 (May 1974), pp. 156-163.

[45] A.B. Hodgetts, *What Culture? What Heritage? A Study of Civic Education in Canada* (Toronto: Ontario Institute for Studies in Education, 1968).

[46] Melville Watkins, "Technology and Nationalism" in Peter Russell, ed., *Nationalism in Canada*, p. 284.

[47] S.D. Clark, "Canada and Her Great Neighbor", p. 195.

[48] S.D. Clark in H.F. Angus, ed., *Canada and Her Great Neighbor* (Toronto: Ryerson Press, 1938). Clark reports the President of the CMA as wanting to inculcate in children the same reverence for country that is found in the United States.

[49] Kari Levitt, *Silent Surrender: The Multi-National Corporation in Canada* (Toronto: Macmillan Co. of Canada, 1971), p. 18.

[50] M. Tremblay, "The Acadian Society of Tomorrow: The Impact of Technology on Global Social Structure", in G.L. Gold and M. Tremblay, eds., *Communities and Culture in French Canada* (Toronto: Holt, Rinehart and Winston of Canada, 1973), pp. 62-74.

[51] S.D. Clark, "The Post Second World War Canadian Society", *Canadian Review of Sociology and Anthropology*, Vol. 12 (February 1975), pp. 30-31.

[52] Leonard W. Doob, *Patriotism and Nationalism: Their Psychological Foundations*, p. 239.

[53] The importance and effectiveness of political leaders in Canada might be questioned, however, in that in 1974, 52% of Canadians questioned were unable to name the member of Parliament that they admired the most. Canadian Institute of Public Opinion, *the Gallup Report* (January 2, 1974).

[54] For a discussion of this debate and its role in nationalism see Karl W. Deutsch, *Nationalism and Social Communication* (Boston: MIT Press, 1953), pp. 3-14.

[55] For a discussion on the relationship between ethnicity and nationalism see James Lightbody, "A Note on the Theory of Nationalism as a Function of Ethnic Demands", *Canadian Journal of Political Science*, Vol. 2 (1969), pp. 327-337.

[56] John Porter, *The Vertical Mosaic*, p. 35.

7
Conclusion

I have stressed conflict and problem areas within Canadian society in order to reveal important clues about the nature of the social unity and disunity that exist within the national entity. There have been no hidden value judgments in this approach to suggest that either conflict or a homogeneous national unity is the ultimate desired good. Furthermore, the identification of conflicts and differences is not meant to indicate either that they are irresolvable or that they ought to be resolved. My approach has been to cultivate an appreciation for the uniqueness and the diversity of Canadian society.

Societies are not static entities and Canadian society is no exception. Any description of the society is likely to be changed by events that generate new conflicts or heal old ones. For example, spiralling inflation could reinforce class cleavages in contemporary society by forcing the working class to perpetually fight for a minimum level of economic security. Furthermore, in a world of rapid social change, Canadian society is also in a position of continuous flux. The processes of urbanization, assimilation, and secularization have weakened old or traditional social patterns and created new social bonds, values, and behavior patterns. S. D. Clark has recently argued that not only French Canada has experienced a Quiet Revolution but English Canada has just undergone a similar process.[1] Since the Second World War the society has become less rural and unskilled working-class and more urban and middle-class with profound implications for the structure of the society. Therefore, any sociological understanding of a society requires continual modification in the light of changing relationships and events.

Nevertheless, it is possible to extract from Canada's relatively short history several recurring issues that have circumscribed and continue to circumscribe the development of Canadian society. Each of the different models of the society that I have presented isolated and focused on one of these issues. Relevant data were introduced and a general discussion of the sociological dimensions of the issue specified the consequences and significance of each feature of the society for understanding the society as a whole.

I began with the assumption that the population within the geographic and political borders of Canada formed, in some loose sense, a national society. My task, then, was to determine the nature of this society through six different approaches or perspectives. It is now incumbent on me to assess the contributions and limitations of each of these models to our understanding of Canadian society.

Organismic Model

In the Organismic Model, Canadian society was perceived as a social organism with specific boundaries distinguishing it from other national societies. The characteristics of the population varied considerably from region to region within the national society, showing that it was not a uniform, homogeneous social group. Certainly no modern society is expected to possess a homogeneous population devoid of constituent regions. Yet, because Canada is a young society with a relatively recently settled population of diverse origins, of uneven national distribution, and of changing residence, regional differences loom much larger. The Canadian social organism is divided by regional differences and regional loyalties that make it difficult for Canadians to identify with the whole national social unit. Thus, instead of contributing to the functioning of the whole, the parts have at least the potential of serving as barriers to the welding together of the national society. Even though the parts of a biological organism possess different characteristics and functions, they still work together for the maintenance of the entire organism. If the parts were in tension or at odds with each other, the unit would be in danger of collapsing. In contrast to physical bodies, it is certainly not necessary for Canadian society to be a homogeneous unit in order to function as a national society. As long as the regional parts work together at some minimal level of harmony, the national social unit can survive. But frequently the regional subunits have expressed their hostilities to each other in such a way that the existence of the national society is threatened.

The advantage of looking at Canadian society in terms of these regional differences is that it forces the student to grapple with the question of what we mean when we speak of Canadian society. In what sense is there cohesion or a feeling of belonging together and to what extent are these elements necessary? If a society is only what its constituents make of it and want it to be, then perhaps Canadian society will remain, and even ought to remain, a loose federation of regional units.

Another advantage of this way of looking at Canadian society is that it puts into context the federal-provincial struggles that have always been strong within the nation. The articulation of regional demographic differences has enabled us to see why regional suspicions and stereotypes have arisen and provide a basis for further conflict. The student may want to examine his own regionally attained biases and his attitudes to other regions, and note how such viewpoints hamper the development of a cohesive national society. The fact that the goal of a national society is rejected by many is additional evidence of a persisting regionalism.

The presentation of this model as disjunctive parts detracting from a cohesive national society ought not to mislead us into thinking that a consensus is either needed or desired. Clearly no society has a complete consensus. The nagging question that arises, however, is what minimal level of consensus is needed in order to sustain the national unit? While some would argue for the necessity of a high level of consensus, others would respond negatively to such a goal in that its collectivist emphasis would be likely to suppress individuality. A further problem with a focus on regionalism is that it makes regions appear to be more homogeneous than they really are. Caution ought to be exercised in order not to minimize differences within regions or misunderstand problems that may easily span regions.

It appears that some sort of regulation of our mutual societal world is necessary and for that reason the skeleton of government was constructed to hold the society together. But to assume that these bare bones are sufficient is to take a particular position about what Canadian society is or ought to be. If a true sense of society is to exist, a deeper feeling of belonging together must develop. This model points out that regionalism has been one factor in inhibiting a sense of togetherness and in promoting an associative federalist type of society.

Stratification and Internal Power Model

The Stratification and Internal Power Model presents another perspective on the society by noting divisions and conflicts that arise as the result of class differences and of a system of rank. What can we learn about Canadian society by observing variations in levels of income, education, and prestige of occupations that tend to place the population in an informal ranking arrangement?

The first thing we learn is that a stratification system does exist and that equality — at least in its economic sense — just does not exist. Along with the differences in rank go differences in power. Those at the top of the stratification system have an inordinate amount of power, not only over their own lives but over the lives of others, because they are the decision makers for the society.

This differential in rank and power serves as an extremely

helpful analytical tool, for it puts many of Canada's societal issues into perspective. For example, it helps us see that ethnic hostilities are often based not just on differences in language or culture but on differences in rank and power. I have pointed out how the French-English conflict involved a sense of exploitation and subordination on the part of Francophones in Canada. Rank and power differentials also help to explain why regions become antagonistic because of the sense of exploitation and dominance.

The Stratification and Internal Power Model forces us to look at Canadian society *critically* to observe the sociological ramifications of particular aspects of the society that have been taken for granted for so long. For example, we might be far more critical than we have been of the elitist conception of education that has prevailed in Canada for many years and continue to press for more educational reforms. This perspective also enables us to understand why some segments of Canadian society (e.g. the working class) are critical of the society and have joined parties such as the New Democratic Party which provides an alternative to the mainline parties.

The model makes economic factors the central variable for understanding any issue in Canadian society. Although it is certainly useful to point out the cleavages that exist within the population, it is easy to become obsessed with this one-sided view of the society. There is something exhilarating in exposing decision makers and persons in control, or the exploitation of the poverty-stricken. At the same time, there is something naive and simplistic in taking the next logical step to say that power roles ought to be abolished or even to imply that they can be abolished. The reader is warned to consider his personal conclusions carefully.

As long as a given stratified society is accepted by most of its members as legitimate, the status quo can be preserved and the society will function adequately. But when the legitimacy of the stratification system is questioned, considerable social conflict can be expected. More than any other model, this model stirs our consciences, for it asks what type of society should Canadian society be. It makes us aware of the limited control that many people have over their lives. Does the differential in rank and power detract from the democratic nature of the society or is it in itself an expression of democracy? Is it inevitable? What do we do about it? No simple solution to these questions can be offered but we must seek more conscionable alternatives that are at the same time realistic.

External Power and Domination Model

The External Power Model considered the penetrating influence of other societies on Canadian society. Other societies continue to affect many aspects of life in Canada, including employment, prices, standard of living, what we read and hear, who are our heroes, where we spend holidays, what we eat, how the goods we buy are packaged, and what we decide is important. Even though no contemporary national society lives in isolation in the modern world, Canadian society has been affected by external influences to an undeniable extent throughout her history.

Not all parts of Canada have been equally influenced by foreign societies or by the same foreign societies. For example, the Niagara Peninsula and Vancouver are heavily influenced by the United States, whereas Victoria has a strong British influence. Therefore, settlement patterns and regional and economic factors must also be considered in discussing the effect of foreign influences.

The External Power Model gives us good reasons for the difficulty Canadian society is having in developing in its own way. Particularly problematic is the fact that we can see that external influences are not just a hazard but have had short-term benefits for the society, putting them in the category of mixed blessings.

There are three limitations to the use of this model. First, care must be taken not to make external power the scapegoat for anything that goes wrong internally. Looking for the source of a problem elsewhere might be a convenient way of sidestepping internal remedies or internal causes which resist change. Secondly, finding the source of the problem externally can contribute to a defeatist attitude or a sense of pessimism because it is difficult to control that which is outside one's society. Such an attitude ignores the constructive remedies which might be attempted internally. Thirdly, there is a danger that the removal of the external influence will be seen as a panacea. Whatever is wrong with Canadian society will not necessarily be corrected just by eliminating these foreign influences, even if this were possible in the modern world.

So it is not just regionalism or class differences which divide the society. The inability to develop internal unity and to become a society in a true sense is further affected by having dominant external foci which contribute to an increasing homogenization of culture. As if to seal the fate of the society, some Canadian industries and investors are also becoming multinational in the scope of their activities. The difficulty is to determine how isolated a country can be from foreign influence and control in this age, and what the maximum level of this influence ought to be for the good of the host country.

Ethnic Group Conflict Model

It could easily be argued that it is impossible to understand Canadian society without understanding the role of ethnicity. The Ethnic Group Conflict Model looked at the relationships between the ethnic groups that make up the society. Because ethnicity is not just a characteristic of individual persons but refers to groups to which individuals belong, the study of ethnicity has implications for societal unity. The fact is that for many people, participating in Canadian society is not as important as participating as a member of a sub-society, or in some cases, being a member of another national society simultaneously. Being a Canadian, then, is diluted in significance by other loyalties and identities.

The advantage of this approach is that it links ethnicity with belonging to a group and indicates how ethnic groups might be more important than the idea of a national society for at least some persons. Therefore, the demands for conformity that ethnic groups may make on their members may lessen the significance of the larger society. However, there is considerable variation in the extent to which ethnicity is personally important in Canadian society, and even when it is important, overt conflict is not necessarily the result. What is frequently noticeable is the extent to which ethnic groups bargain with each other to ensure their mutual existence. The dominant ethnic groups agree to guarantee the existence of minority groups in exchange for their acceptance of the status quo. Nevertheless, ethnicity in Canadian society hardly means that intact foreign cultures are existing side by side. In the hierarchy of ethnic groups within the society, the dominant group ostensibly encourages the maintenance of fragments of foreign culture while at the same time demanding and receiving considerable Anglo-conformity.

The limitation of this model is that it gives the appearance that all ethnic groups are welded into identifiable social units when they actually are not. Some persons have left their ethnic traditions behind them long ago and have embraced the dominant Anglo-Canadian culture. Secondly, while suspicions and hostilities are expressed on occasion, ethnic group conflict occurs infrequently.

While conflict may always be possible theoretically, it seldom materializes.

It might also be argued that in studying Canadian society too much has been made of ethnicity. Many societies can distinguish subgroups and even nationalities within their borders. The British Isles contain the English, the Welsh, the Scottish, and the Irish. Russia has a great number of subgroups. Nevertheless, because Canadian society consists largely of migrated persons with varying lengths of residence and degrees of assimilation, frequently mixed together in the same territory, and surrounded by persons who belong to other ethnic groups, ethnicity is a significant source of division within the society.

Perhaps this perspective on the society gives us a clue to why an ethnically diverse society fails to be too upset about foreign influences. How can you be aroused by the effect of external powers when you have external loyalties yourself? Or how can you be concerned about class conflict when class loyalties and interests are subverted by ethnic loyalties and interests? Furthermore, how can you know what it means to be a Canadian when official government policy encourages people to retain their ethnic ties and culture? How is it possible to promote a sense of "belonging together" in this context?

Ishwaran has argued that pluralism may effectively increase rather than decrease unity because all groups can bargain for their own rights and recognition.[2] He asserts that there is no necessity for a high degree of integration or for strong feelings of mutuality among the members of Canadian society, and that the self-interest of each of the groups as well as their mutual security will hold them together in a loose federation. The problem with this conception is that some ethnic groups have more bargaining power than others and a completely pluralist model assumes an equality among all ethnic groups, which is certainly not the case in Canada. Clearly, whatever national integration does exist is influenced by ethnic allegiances and as a result is rather incomplete.

Comparative Model

It is helpful to clarify what type of society Canada possesses by comparing Canadian society with other societies. Comparing whole units to whole units is difficult because whole units are usually very diverse internally. In addition, stressing characteristics held in common must not be done at the expense of the differences. For instance, both Canada and the United States were recipients of large migration flows. Both countries, therefore, house many ethnic groups, and yet Canada is very different in having no large racial problem, and the United States has no non-English ethnic group dominating one linguistic area such as Quebec.

The Comparative Model is useful to point out that many Canadian problems are not unique to this society — even though they may seem to be from an inside view. For example, bilingualism or multilingualism is shared by societies such as Belgium and Switzerland. External dominance, sparsely populated land areas, and linguistic arealism are problems that have been met by other societies. Canada can learn from the experience of other societies, although she must seek her own indigenous solutions to her problems (such as those answers propounded by the Royal Commission on Bilingualism and Biculturalism).

Comparative sociological data enable us to explain why countries develop differently and why some events become issues in one country and not in others. Why are there linguistic problems in Canada and not in the United States? Why are Canadians more anti-American than Australians? These are the kind of questions that comparisons help to clarify.

More comparative sociological studies are urgently needed. Each of the perspectives on Canadian society already discussed needs to be dealt with in a more thorough comparative framework. For example, how does elitism in Canada differ from elitism in the United States? What has been the effect of external powers on Australia? Is there more poverty in Canada than in Great Britain? We get a better idea of the uniqueness of Canadian society or its similarity with other societies when these comparisons can be explicitly drawn. More comparisons involving Canadian society may help the society in establishing its own identity both in the minds of its citizens and in the minds of persons in the rest of the world. Thus, comparisons are valuable because they bring out the distinctive aspects of each society.

Identity Model

The concept of a national identity is frequently batted about as though we knew what it was or that we would at least recognize it when we obtained it. An identity is very diffuse and intangible; yet all books on Canadian society refer to it as though it were an understood reality. I initially asked the question whether the members of Canadian society possessed any sense of belonging together. I concluded that a feeling of belonging may be developing but is presently very diffuse.

The search for a national identity implies that an identity has not yet been crystallized. The idea persists that Canadian society has not yet matured and is still in the process of becoming. The purpose of the Identity Model was to point out the problems that prevent the society from, emerging with a commonly accepted character. The quest for an identity is basically an attempt to develop an indigenous culture with stronger internal interdependencies.

Of all the perspectives on the society discussed in this book, this model requires the most value judgments about Canada's future. If you feel a weak identity should be the national preference, then the idea of nationalism will be reprehensible. If, on the other hand, you want an identity crystallized around a strong cohesive unit, you might like more nationalist sentiments to counteract the regional tendencies, the class conflicts, or the ethnic tensions discussed in earlier models.

The limitation of this perspective on Canada is that it can be construed to mean that all members of the society are equally agreeable to and participant in this search for an identity. This is certainly not the case. French Canadians or Western Canadians or hyphenated Canadians may be perfectly happy with the diffuse identity the society possesses; or if they do accept the quest for an identity as a legitimate exercise, their idea of what that identity should be might conflict with the ideas of others.

It is difficult to determine what the social climate of the world will be in the future with regard to the existence of national societies. In a postnational world, the solidarity of a nation-state required for a clear identity may be obsolete. On the other hand, with the proliferation of nation-states in recent years, nationality may become even more important. There is also the rather appealing view that Canadian society as a loose conjunction of regional and ethnic units for mutual survival serves as an appropriate world model for national social relations.

All of these models or pictures of Canadian society are equally important. Together they give us different ways of understanding the society even if one perspective such as the Internal Power Model or the External Power Model may be personally preferred over the others. Combined, however, they yield a macro-sociological portrait of the society. The fact that some persons might prefer to stress one model over all others as an explanatory variable leads us to the final section on values, science, and the sociologist.

Values, Science, and the Sociologist

I have struggled through considerable data and discussion in order to present alternative ways of perceiving Canadian society. Can a sociologist pretend that he has given an objective analysis of the society at hand?

Sociology is a young discipline, particularly in the Canadian setting.[3] As a social science, sociology was born largely in response to social crises or social problems that prompted systematic inquiries for their resolution. For instance, the rapid growth of sociology in the United States was actually fostered by the urban problems and migration flow of numerous ethnic groups into the city of Chicago. Similarly, in Canada, the theme of social reform was intimately tied to the early development of sociology as a discipline.[4] But as sociology struggled for a legitimate place in the scientific community, impetus was given to the idea that the sociological enterprise must become value-free. Sociologists were to stand dispassionately by and describe and analyze given phenomena without letting their own values intrude. Thus, sociology was understood as *pure science* — the acquisition of knowledge for its own sake by a neutral, trained observer.

In an address in 1966, sociologist Howard Becker claimed that the choice between being value-free and being value-committed in sociological research was really an imaginary one.[5] He claimed that to think that any human being could do uncontaminated research was unrealistic. A researcher studying prisoners over a period of several months would be likely to develop some sympathy for his subjects. Similarly, a study of elites would be likely to evoke feelings within the researcher. Perhaps your own reading of this book has stirred feelings of both hostility and sympathy toward certain aspects of Canadian society. Human beings dealing with human phenomena cannot be cold and calculating in research. Some sociologists would even argue that any researcher who claims to be detached has no business studying human activity.

If no sociologist can be value-free, is sociology then a mass of subjectivity? A distinction must be made between the researcher and his method of research: The sociologist himself may not be value-free, but his method ought to be. Particular techniques of sociological research exist which he must use consistently and systematically in order to obtain fair and accurate results. However, the way the research program is set up, the subjects chosen, and the subjects rejected for analysis reflect the sociologist's judgment — to say nothing of the interpretation of the data with which he concludes his study. Keyfitz argues that while the method has objective elements, even the choice of a basic topic or subject for investigation reflects particular values.[6]

Keyfitz, Clark,[7] and others have asserted that sociology in Canada needs more researchers with Canadian values to choose topics that are important to Canadian society and to interpret them within the Canadian context rather than imposing on Canadian data an interpretive framework which is more appropriate to another society. It is particularly in the selection and interpretation of data that the values of the researcher need to be fully expressed in the development of a Canadian sociology. The scientific procedures of sociology may make sociology universal,[8] but the specification of problem areas and issues and their treatment within this societal context make sociology Canadian.

This leads to the last question: science for what and knowledge for whom? Sociologists do not research and write to entertain themselves, but to inform and to influence. In addition, any scientific analysis is bound to uncover evidence which can easily lead to a critique of that aspect of society. Thus, while sociology is not a science of social reform, its investigations frequently lead in that direction. The results of sociological research can be used to support the status quo or to incite rebellion. Knowledge tends to be put to use. Nevertheless, there is some debate within the discipline whether the sociologist should be the critic, the reformer, or the prophet, or whether he should search for pure knowledge with no concern for its practical use. While the latter alternative is in truth unlikely, it is quite correct that most sociologists in Canada have eschewed a prophetic role in favor of a priestly role in which they do the research and leave the crusading for others.[9]

This study of Canadian society ought to have evoked value judgments from the reader. If knowledge is not just for its own sake, the presentation of the data should have stimulated a response. Social policy ought to be formulating in your mind regarding questions such as these:

Should Canadian society be more united and integrated?
If so, how can this sense of belonging together be created?

Should elites have control and power?
If not, how can a more democratic society be achieved?

*Should external influence on Canada be as strong as it is?
If not, is it possible for the society to develop on its own? How?*

*Should ethnicity be encouraged? If so, how can cultural units
be maintained without assimilation?*

Whatever you decide Canada is and should be will determine how
you will respond to the problems of regionalism, stratification,
external dominance, group conflict, and the search for a national
identity. Sociology does not bring you merely academic information; it challenges you to put information to use to create a better
society.

NOTES

[1] S.D. Clark, "The Post Second World War Canadian Society", *Canadian
Review of Sociology and Anthropology*, Vol. 12 (February 1975),
p. 29.

[2] K. Ishwaran, "The Canadian Family: An Overview", in K. Ishwaran,
ed., *The Canadian Family* (Toronto: Holt, Rinehart and Winston,
1971), p. 20.

[3] For brief histories of sociology in Canada see B.Y. Card, *The Expand-
ing Relation: Sociology in Prairie Universities* (Regina: Canadian Plains
Study Center, 1973) and S. Crysdale and C. Beattie, *Sociology Canada*
(Toronto: Butterworth, 1973), Chapter 15.

[4] Dennis Forcese and Stephen Richer, "Social Issues and Sociology in
Canada", in Forcese and Richer, *Issues in Canadian Society: An Introduction to Sociology* (Toronto: Prentice-Hall of Canada, 1975), pp.
453-464.

[5] Howard S. Becker, "Whose Side Are We On?", *Social Problems*, Vol.
14 (Winter 1967), pp. 239-247.

[6] N. Keyfitz, "Sociology and Canadian Society", in T.N. Guinsberg and
G.C. Reuber, *Perspectives on the Social Sciences in Canada* (Toronto:
University of Toronto Press, 1974), p. 33.

[7] S.D. Clark, "The American Takeover of Canadian Sociology: Myth or
Reality", *Dalhousie Review*, Vol. 53 (1974), pp. 205-218.

[8] It has recently been argued in somewhat of a polemic that the idea
that sociology possesses no national boundaries has its origin in a form
of imperialism propagated by American sociology. Especially the emphasis on empiricism and quantitative research in American sociology
is said to be a diversion from getting a wholistic, objective view of Canadian society. James Stolzman and Herbert Gamberg, "The National
Question and Canadian Sociology", *Canadian Journal of Sociology*,
Vol. 1 (Spring 1975), pp. 91-106.

[9] The prophet-priest distinction is Robert W. Friedrich's: *A Sociology of
Sociology* (New York: Free Press, 1970).

A Select Bibliography on Canadian Society

Abler, T.S., D.Sanders and S.M. Weaver. *A Canadian Indian Bibliography 1960-1970.* Toronto: University of Toronto Press, 1974.

Adams, I. *The Poverty Wall.* Toronto: McClelland and Stewart, 1970.

Adams, I. W. Cameron, B. Hill and P. Penz. *The Real Poverty Report.* Edmonton: M.G. Hurtig, 1971.

Adams, W. *The Brain Drain.* Toronto: Macmillan Co. of Canada, 1968.

Aitken, H.G.J. et al. *The American Economic Impact on Canada.* Durham, N.C.: Duke University Press, 1959.

Alford, R.R. *Party and Society: The Anglo-American Democracies.* Chicago: Rand McNally, 1963.

Anderson, G.M. *Networks of Contact: The Portuguese in Toronto.* Waterloo: Wilfred Laurier University, 1974.

Angus, H.F., ed. *Canada and Her Great Neighbor.* Toronto: Ryerson Press, 1938.

Armstrong, J. "Canadians in Crisis: The Nature and Source of Support for Leadership in a National Emergency", *Canadian Review of Sociology and Anthropology*, Vol. 9 (November 1972), pp. 299-324.

Bailey, A.G. *Culture and Nationality.* Toronto: McClelland and Stewart, 1972.

Beattie, C., J. Désy and S. Longstaff. *Bureaucratic Careers: Anglophones and Francophones in the Canadian Public Service.* Ottawa: Information Canada, 1972.

Beattie, C. *Minority of Men in a Majority Setting.* Toronto: McClelland and Stewart, 1975.

Blishen, B.R. "The Construction and Use of an Occupational Class Scale", *Canadian Journal of Economics and Political Science*, Vol. 24 (1958), pp. 519-531.

Blishen, B.R., F.E. Jones, K.D. Naegele and J. Porter, eds. *Canadian Society: Sociological Perspectives*, 3rd abr. ed. Toronto: Macmillan Co. of Canada, 1971.

Boldt, M. "Images of Canada's Future in *The Vertical Mosaic*", in W. Bell and J.A. Mau, *The Sociology of the Future.* New York: Russell Sage Foundation, 1971.

Boydell, C.L., C.F. Grindstaff and P.C. Whitehead, eds. *Critical Issues in Canadian Society.* Toronto: Holt, Rinehart and Winston of Canada, 1971.

Breton, R. "Institutional Completeness of Ethnic Communities and the Personal Relations of Immigrants", *American Journal of Sociology*, Vol. 70 (1964), pp. 193-205.

———— "The Socio-Political Dynamics of the October Events", *Canadian Review of Sociology and Anthropology*, Vol. 9 (1972), pp. 35-56.

———— *Social and Academic Factors in the Career Decisions of Canadian Youth.* Ottawa: Department of Manpower and Immigration, 1972.

Burchill, C.S. "The Multi-National Corporation: An Unsolved Problem in International Relations", *Queen's Quarterly*, Vol. 77 (1970), pp. 3-18.

Cameron, D. *Nationalism, Self-determination and the Quebec Question.* Toronto: Macmillan Co. of Canada, 1974.

Camu, P., E.P. Weeks and Z.W. Sametz. *Economic Geography of Canada.* Toronto: Macmillan Co. of Canada, 1964.

Card, B.Y., ed. *Perspectives on Regions and Regionalism.* Edmonton: University of Alberta Press, 1969.

_____ *Trends and Change in Canadian Society.* Toronto: Macmillan Co. of Canada, 1968.

Cardinal, H. *The Unjust Society.* Edmonton: M.G. Hurtig, 1969.

Christian, W., and C. Campbell. *Political Parties and Ideologies in Canada.* Toronto: McGraw-Hill Ryerson, 1974.

Clairmont, D.H., and D.W. Magill. *Africville: The Life and Death of a Canadian Black Community.* Toronto: McClelland and Stewart, 1974.

Clark, S.D. "Canada and Her Great Neighbor", *Canadian Review of Sociology and Anthropology*, Vol. 1 (1964), pp. 193-201.

_____ "The American Takeover of Canadian Sociology: Myth or Reality", *Dalhousie Review*, Vol. 53 (1974), pp. 205-218.

_____ *The Developing Canadian Community.* Toronto: University of Toronto Press, 1962.

Clement, W. *The Canadian Corporate Elite: An Analysis of Economic Power.* Toronto: McClelland and Stewart, 1975.

Cook, R., ed. *French-Canadian Nationalism: An Anthology.* Toronto: Macmillan Co. of Canada, 1969.

Craig, G.M. *The United States and Canada.* Cambridge: Harvard University Press, 1968.

Croll, D.A. *Poverty in Canada: Report of the Special Senate Committee on Poverty*, pp. 1-8. Ottawa: Information Canada, 1971.

Crysdale, Stewart, and Chris Beattie. *Sociology Canada: An Introductory Text.* Toronto: Butterworth, 1973.

_____ *Sociology Canada: Readings.* Toronto: Butterworth, 1974.

Curtis, J.E., and W.G. Scott. *Social Stratification: Canada.* Scarborough: Prentice-Hall of Canada, 1973.

Dales, J.H. *The Protective Tariff in Canada's Development.* Toronto: University of Toronto Press, 1966.

Davies, D.I., and K. Herman, eds. *Social Space: Canadian Perspectives.* Toronto: New Press, 1971.

Davis, M., and J.F. Krauter. *The Other Canadians: Profiles of Six Minorities.* Toronto: Methuen, 1971.

Denton, F.T. *An Analysis of Interregional Differences in Manpower Utilization and Earnings* (Staff Study No. 15). Queen's Printer, 1966.

Diemer, A.H., and M.L. Dietz. "Canadian University Students' Stereotypes of Canadians and Americans", *McGill Journal of Education*, Vol. 5 (1971), pp. 29-37.

Drache, D., ed. *Quebec — Only the Beginning: The Manifestoes of the Common Front.* Toronto: New Press, 1972.

DuWors, R.E., J. Beaman and A. Olmsted. *Studies in the Dynamics of the Residential Populations of Thirteen Canadian Cities.* Winnipeg: Center for Settlement Studies, University of Manitoba, 1972.

Elkin, F. "Advertising Themes and Quiet Revolutions", *American Journal of Sociology*, Vol. 75 (July 1969), pp. 112-122.

Elliott, J.L., ed. *Minority Canadians 1: Native Peoples.* Scarborough: Prentice-Hall of Canada, 1971.

——— *Minority Canadians 2: Immigrant Groups.* Scarborough: Prentice-Hall of Canada, 1971.

Elton, D.K., ed. *One Prairie Province? A Question for Canada.* Lethbridge: Lethbridge Herald, 1970.

Engelmann, F.C., and M.A. Schwartz. *Political Parties and the Canadian Social Structure.* Scarborough: Prentice-Hall of Canada, 1967.

Fathi, A. "Mass Media and a Moslem Immigrant Community in Canada", *Anthropologica*, Vol. 15 (1973), pp. 201-230.

Fearn, Gordon. *Canadian Social Organization.* Toronto: Holt, Rinehart and Winston of Canada, 1973.

Ferguson, Edith. *Immigrants in Canada.* Toronto: University of Toronto Guidance Center, 1974.

Finnigan, Bryan, and Cy Gonick, eds. *Making It: The Canadian Dream.* Toronto: McClelland and Stewart, 1972.

Fisher, E.A.S. "Financial Accessibility to Higher Education in Canada during the 1960s", *CAUT Bulletin*, Vol. 18 (1970), pp. 92-106.

Frankfurter, G. *Baneful Domination.* Don Mills: Longman Canada, 1971.

Fraser, B. *The Search for Identity.* Toronto: Doubleday, 1967.

Frideres, J.S. *Canada's Indians: Contemporary Conflicts.* Scarborough: Prentice-Hall of Canada, 1974.

Gajda, R.T. "The Canadian Ecumene — Inhabited and Uninhabited Areas", *Geographical Bulletin*, 15 (1960).

Gallagher, J.E., and R.D. Lambert, eds. *Social Process and Institution: The Canadian Case.* Toronto: Holt, Rinehart and Winston of Canada, 1971.

Gentilcore, R.L., ed. *Geographical Approaches to Canadian Problems.* Scarborough: Prentice-Hall of Canada, 1970.

George, M.V. *Internal Migration in Canada: Demographic Analyses.* Ottawa: Statistics Canada, 1970.

Glazier, K.M. "Canadian Investment in the United States: Putting Your Money Where Your Mouth Is", *Journal of Contemporary Business*, Vol. 1 (1972).

Goldenberg, S. *"Composition or Character? — Structural Alternatives to Cultural Explanations of Canadian-American Institutional Differences",* Ph.D. dissertation, Northwestern University, 1974.

Goodspeed, D.J. "The Canadian Revolution: The Bourgeoisie Versus Marx", *Queen's Quarterly*, Vol. 64 (1957), pp. 521-530.

Gordon, W.L. *A Choice for Canada.* Toronto: McClelland and Stewart, 1966.

——— *Troubled Canada.* Toronto: McClelland and Stewart, 1961.

Government of Canada. *Foreign Direct Investment in Canada* (Gray Report). Ottawa: Information Canada, 1972.

Grant, G. *Lament for a Nation.* Toronto: McClelland and Stewart, 1965.

——— *Technology and Empire: Perspectives on North America.* Toronto: House of Anansi, 1969.

Gregorovich, A., ed. *Canadian Ethnic Groups Bibliography.* Toronto: Ontario Department of the Provincial Secretary and Citizenship, 1972.

Grindstaff, C.F., C.L. Boydell and P.C. Whitehead, eds. *Population Issues in Canada.* Montreal: Holt, Rinehart and Winston of Canada, 1974.

Guindon, H. "Social Unrest, Social Class, and Quebec's Quiet Revolution", *Queen's Quarterly,* Vol. 71 (1964), pp. 150-162.

Harp, J., and J. Hofley, eds. *Poverty in Canada.* Scarborough: Prentice-Hall of Canada, 1971.

Hartz, L., ed. *The Founding of New Societies.* New York: Harcourt, Brace and World, 1964.

Heap, J.L., ed. *Everybody's Canada: The Vertical Mosaic Reviewed and Re-examined.* Toronto: Burns and MacEachern, 1974.

Henry, F. *Forgotten Canadians: The Blacks of Nova Scotia.* Don Mills: Longman Canada, 1973.

Hodgetts, A.B. *What Culture? What Heritage? A Study of Civic Education in Canada.* Toronto: Ontario Institute for Studies in Education, 1968.

Horowitz, G. "Conservatism, Liberalism, and Socialism in Canada: An Interpretation", *Canadian Journal of Economics and Political Science,* Vol. 32 (1966), pp. 143-150.

Horowitz, I.L. "The Hemispheric Connection: A Critique and Corrective to the Entrepreneurial Thesis of Development with Special Emphasis on the Canadian Case", *Queen's Quarterly,* Vol. 80 (1973), pp. 336-337.

House of Commons Standing Committee on External Affairs and National Defence, *Proceedings* No. 33, "Special Committee Respecting Canada-U.S. Relations" (July 1970), pp. 33-58.

Hughes, D.R., and E. Kallen. *The Anatomy of Racism: Canadian Dimensions.* Montreal: Harvest House, 1974.

Hughes, E. *French Canada in Transition.* Chicago: University of Chicago Press, 1943.

Hurley, J.R. "Federalism, Coordinate Status, and the Canadian Situation", *Queen's Quarterly,* Vol. 73 (1966), pp. 147-166.

Irvine, W.P. "Recruitment to Nationalism: New Politics or Normal Politics", *Canadian Journal of Political Science,* Vol. 5 (1972), pp. 503-520.

Isajiw, W.W. "The Process of Social Integration: The Canadian Example", *Dalhousie Review,* Vol. 48 (1968), pp. 510-520.

Ishwaran, K. *The Canadian Family: A Book of Readings.* Toronto: Holt, Rinehart and Winston of Canada, 1971.

Jackson, J.D. "A Study of French-English Relations in an Ontario Community: Toward a Conflict Model for the Analysis of Ethnic

Relations", *Canadian Review of Sociology and Anthropology*, Vol. 3 (1966), pp. 117-131.

Jones, R. *Community in Crisis: French-Canadian Nationalism in Perspective.* Toronto: McClelland and Stewart, 1972.

Joy, R. *Languages in Conflict.* Toronto: McClelland and Stewart, 1972.

Kalbach, W. *The Impact of Immigration on Canada's Population.* Ottawa: Statistics Canada, 1970.

Kalbach, W.E., and W.W. McVey. *The Demographic Bases of Canadian Society.* Toronto: McGraw-Hill Ryerson, 1971.

Kilbourn, W., ed. *Canada: A Guide to the Peaceable Kingdom.* Toronto: Macmillan Co. of Canada, 1970.

Krueger, R.R., F.O. Sargent, A. DeVos and N. Pearson, eds. *Regional and Resource Planning in Canada.* Toronto: Holt, Rinehart and Winston of Canada, 1963.

Kubat, Daniel, and David Thornton. *A Statistical Profile of Canadian Society.* Toronto: McGraw-Hill Ryerson, 1974.

Lanphier, C.M., and R.N. Morris. "Structural Aspects of Differences in Income between Anglophones and Francophones", *Canadian Review of Sociology and Anthropology*, Vol. II (February 1974), pp. 53-66.

La Pierre, L., et al. *Essays on the Left: Essays in Honour of T.C. Douglas.* Toronto: McClelland and Stewart, 1971.

Laskin, R. *Social Problems: A Canadian Profile.* Toronto: McGraw-Hill Co. of Canada, 1964.

Laxer, R., ed. *Canada Ltd.: The Political Economy of Dependency.* Toronto: McClelland and Stewart, 1973.

Leach, R.H., ed. *Contemporary Canada.* Durham, N.C.: Duke University Press, 1967.

Levitt, K. *Silent Surrender: The Multi-National Corporation in Canada.* Toronto: Macmillan Co. of Canada, 1971.

Lieberson, S. *Language and Ethnic Relations in Canada.* Toronto: John Wiley & Sons Canada, 1970.

Lightbody, J. "A Note on the Theory of Nationalism as a Function of Ethnic Demands", *Canadian Journal of Political Science*, Vol. 2 (1969), pp. 327-337.

Lipset, S.M. "Canada and the United States — A Comparative View", *Canadian Review of Sociology and Anthropology*, Vol. 1 (1964), pp. 173-185.

―――― *The First New Nation: The United States in Historical and Comparative Perspective.* New York: Basic Books, 1963.

―――― *Revolution and Counter-Revolution: Change and Persistence in Social Structures.* Garden City: Doubleday, 1971.

―――― "The Value Patterns of Democracy: A Case Study in Comparative Analysis", *American Sociological Review*, Vol. 28 (August 1963), pp. 515-531.

Lithwick, N.H., and G. Paquet. *Urban Studies: A Canadian Perspective.* Toronto: Methuen, 1968.

Lithwick, N.H. "Poverty in Canada: Some Recent Empirical Findings",

Journal of Canadian Studies, Vol. 6 (May 1970), pp. 27-41.

Litvak, I.A., C.J. Maule and R.O. Robinson. *Dual Loyalty: Canadian-U.S. Business Arrangements.* Toronto: McGraw-Hill Ryerson, 1971.

Lower, A.R.M. *Colony to Nation: A History of Canada.* Don Mills: Longman Canada, 1964.

Lucas, R.A. *Minetown, Milltown, Railtown: Life in Canadian Communities of a Single Industry.* Toronto: University of Toronto Press, 1971.

Lumsden, I., ed. *Close the 49th Parallel: The Americanization of Canada.* Toronto: University of Toronto Press, 1970.

MacKirdy, K.A. "Canada and the Commonwealth", *Queen's Quarterly,* Vol. 74 (1967).

Macpherson, C.B. *Democracy in Alberta: Social Credit and the Party System,* 2nd ed. Toronto: University of Toronto Press, 1962.

Mann, W.E. *Canada: A Sociological Profile,* 2nd ed. Toronto: Copp Clark, 1971.

Manzer, R. *Canada: A Socio-Political Report,* Toronto: McGraw-Hill Ryerson, 1974.

Marsden, Lorna. *Population Probe: Canada.* Toronto: Copp Clark, 1972.

Mathews, R., and J. Steele. *The Struggle for Canadian Universities.* Toronto: New Press, 1969.

Mathias, P. *Forced Growth.* Toronto: James Lewis and Samuel, 1971.

McCormack, T. "Poverty in Canada: The Croll Report and Its Critics", *Canadian Review of Sociology and Anthropology,* Vol. 9 (November 1972), pp. 366-372.

Meyers, G. *A History of Canadian Wealth.* Chicago: Charles Kerr, 1914.

Morchain, J.K. *Search for a Nation: French-English Relations in Canada since 1759.* Toronto: J.M. Dent and Sons (Canada), 1967.

Morton, W.L. *The Canadian Identity.* Madison: University of Wisconsin Press, 1965.

Milner, S.H., and H. Milner. *The Decolonization of Quebec.* Toronto: McClelland and Stewart, 1973.

Nagata, J.A. "Adaptation and Integration of Greek Working Class Immigrants in Toronto: A Situational Approach", *The International Migration Review,* Vol. 4 (1968).

Nelles, V., and A. Rotstein. *Nationalism or Local Control.* Toronto: New Press, 1973.

Oliver, M., ed. *Social Purpose for Canada.* Toronto: University of Toronto Press, 1961.

Ossenberg, R.J. "The Conquest Revisited: Another Look at Canadian Dualism", *Canadian Review of Sociology and Anthropology,* Vol. 4 (1967), pp. 201-219.

_____ , ed. *Canadian Society: Pluralism, Change and Conflict.* Scarborough: Prentice-Hall of Canada, 1971.

Pankhurst, K.V. "Migration between Canada and the United States", *The Annals of the American Academy of Political and Social Science,* 367 (September 1966), pp. 53-62.

Park, L.C., and F.W. Park. *Anatomy of Big Business.* Toronto: Progress Books, 1962.

Pavalko, R.M. "Socio-Economic Background, Ability, and the Allocation of Students", *Canadian Review of Sociology and Anthropology*, Vol. 4 (1967), pp. 250-259.

Perry, R.L. *Galt, U.S.A.: The American Presence in a Canadian City.* Toronto: Maclean-Hunter, 1971.

Pineo, P.C., and J. Porter. "Occupational Prestige in Canada", *Canadian Review of Sociology and Anthropology*, Vol. 4 (1967), pp. 24-40.

Podoluk, J.R. *Incomes of Canadians.* Ottawa: Statistics Canada, 1968.

Porter, John. *Canadian Social Structure: A Statistical Profile.* Toronto: McClelland and Stewart, 1967.

―――― *The Vertical Mosaic.* Toronto: University of Toronto Press, 1965.

―――― "Canadian Character in the Twentieth Century", *The Annals of the American Academy of Political and Social Science*, Vol. 370 (1967), pp. 48-56.

Porter, M.R., J. Porter and B. Blishen. *Does Money Matter? Prospects for Higher Education.* Toronto: York University Institute for Behavioral Research, 1974.

Presthus, R. *Elite Accommodation in Canadian Politics.* Cambridge: Cambridge University Press, 1973.

Putnam, D.F., and R.G. Putnam. *Canada: A Regional Analysis.* J.M. Dent and Sons (Canada), 1970.

Report of the Royal Commission on Bilingualism and Biculturalism: Book I, *The Official Languages;* Book II, *Education;* Book III, *The Work World;* Book IV, *The Cultural Contribution of Other Ethnic Groups.* Ottawa: Queen's Printer, 1969.

Richardson, B. *James Bay: The Plot to Drown the North Woods.* Toronto: Clarke, Irwin, 1972.

Richert, J.P. "The Impact of Ethnicity on the Perception of Heroes and Historical Symbols", *Canadian Review of Sociology and Anthropology*, Vol. II (1974), pp. 156-163.

Richmond, A.H. "Social Mobility of Immigrants", *Population Studies*, Vol. 17 (July 1964).

―――― *Post-War Immigrants in Canada.* Toronto: University of Toronto Press, 1967.

Rioux, M., and Y. Martin. *French-Canadian Society*, Vol. I. Toronto: McClelland and Stewart, 1964.

Rocher, G. *A General Introduction to Sociology.* Toronto: Macmillan Co. of Canada, 1972.

Rolland, S.C. *My Country, Canada or Quebec?* Toronto: Macmillan Co. of Canada, 1966.

Rossides, D.W. *Society as a Functional Process: An Introduction to Sociology.* Toronto: McGraw-Hill Co. of Canada, 1968.

Rotstein, A., ed. *Power Corrupted: The October Crisis and the Repression of Quebec.* Toronto: New Press, 1971.

Rotstein, A., and G. Lax. *Independence: The Canadian Challenge.* Toronto: The Committee for an Independent Canada, 1972.

Russell, P., ed. *Nationalism in Canada.* Toronto: McGraw-Hill Co. of Canada, 1966.

Ryan, T.J. *Poverty and the Child: A Canadian Study.* Toronto: McGraw-Hill Ryerson, 1972.

Safarian, A.E. *Foreign Ownership of Canadian Industry.* Toronto: McGraw-Hill Co. of Canada, 1966.

_____ "Some Myths about Foreign Business Investment in Canada", *Journal of Canadian Studies*, Vol. 6 (1971), pp. 3-21.

Schlesinger, B. *What about Poverty in Canada?* Toronto: University of Toronto Guidance Center, 1972.

Schwartz, M.A. *Politics and Territory: The Sociology of Regional Persistence in Canada.* Montreal: McGill-Queen's University Press, 1974.

_____ *Public Opinion and Canadian Identity.* Berkeley: University of California Press, 1967.

Simmons, R., and J. Simmons. *Urban Canada.* Toronto: Copp Clark, 1969.

Sinclair, Peter, and Kenneth Westhues. *Village in Crisis.* Toronto: Holt, Rinehart and Winston of Canada, 1974.

Singer, B., ed. *Communication in Canadian Society.* Toronto: Copp Clark, 1972.

Smiley, D.V. *The Canadian Political Nationality.* Toronto: Methuen, 1967.

Smith, A. "Metaphor and Nationality in North America", *Canadian Historical Review*, Vol. 51 (1970), pp. 247-275.

Smith, D., and L. Tepperman. "Changes in the Canadian Business and Legal Elites, 1870-1970", *Canadian Review of Sociology and Anthropology*, Vol. II (May 1974), pp. 97-109.

Stone, L.O. *Urban Development in Canada.* Ottawa: Statistics Canada, 1967.

_____ *Migration in Canada: Regional Aspects*, pp. 22-26. Ottawa: Statistics Canada, 1969.

Taylor, C. "Nationalism and the Political Intelligentsia", *Queen's Quarterly*, Vol. 72 (1965), pp. 150-168.

Taylor, D.M., L.M. Simard and F.E. Aboud. "Ethnic Identification in Canada: A Cross-Cultural Investigation", *Canadian Journal of Behavioral Science*, Vol. 4 (January 1972), pp. 13-20.

Teeple, G., ed. *Capitalism and the National Question in Canada.* Toronto: University of Toronto Press, 1972.

Truman, T. "A Critique of Seymour M. Lipset's Article 'Value Differences, Absolute or Relative: The English Speaking Democracies' ", *Canadian Journal of Political Science*, Vol. 4 (1971), pp. 513-525.

Valentine, V.F., and F.G. Vallee, eds. *Eskimo of the Canadian Arctic.* Toronto: McClelland and Stewart, 1968.

Vallières, P. *White Niggers of America.* Toronto: McClelland and Stewart, 1971.

Wade, M. ed. *Regionalism in the Canadian Community, 1867-1967.* Toronto: University of Toronto Press, 1969.

Wallace, W.S. *The Growth of Canadian National Feeling*. Toronto: Macmillan Co. of Canada, 1927.

Warkentin, J. *Canada: A Geographical Interpretation*. Toronto: Methuen, 1968.

Watkins, M.H. *Foreign Ownership and the Structure of Canadian Industry*, (Report of the Task Force on the Structure of Canadian Industry). Ottawa: Privy Council, 1968.

Weir, T.R. "Population Changes in Canada, 1867-1967", *The Canadian Geographer*, Vol. II, No. 4 (1967).

Whittingham, F.J. *Educational Attainment of the Canadian Population and Labour Force: 1960-1965* (Special Labour Force Studies, No. 1), pp. 10-11. Ottawa: Statistics Canada, 1966.

Winks, R.W. "The Canadian Negro: A Historical Assessment", *Journal of Negro History*, Part I, Vol. 53 (1968), and Part II, Vol. 54 (1969).

Wise, S.F., and R.L. Brown. *Canada Views the United States*. Seattle: University of Washington Press, 1967.

Wrong, D.N. *American and Canadian Viewpoints*. Washington: American Council on Education, 1955.

Wuttunee, W. *Ruffled Feathers: Indians in Canadian Society*. Calgary: Bell Books, 1971.

Younge, E.R. "Population Movements and the Assimilation of Alien Groups in Canada", *Canadian Journal of Economic and Political Science*, Vol. 10 (1947), pp. 372-380.

Zimmerman, C.C., and S. Russell, eds. *Symposium on the Great Plains of North America*. Fargo: North Dakota Institute for Regional Studies, 1967.

Index

Achieved traits, 104, 135-41
Aggrandizement effect, 59
Air Canada, 97, 162
American War of Independence, 132, 134
Anglo-Canadian society, 59
   French-Canadian society, differences from, 38-39, 58-62, 69-70, 111
   identity, 7
Anglo-conformity, 115, 181
Anti-Americanism, 98, 144, 159
Ascribed traits, 104, 111, 122, 135-41
Assimilation, 28, 105, 164, 176, 182
   definition, 121
   to the English language, 23, 148-49
   of French Canadians, 24, 115, 165

Banks, 67, 69
Biculturalism, 38, 108, 117
Bilingualism, 24-25, 69, 108, 118-19, 148-50, 159, 183
Birth rate, 27-28, 30, 32, 34, 117, 139-41
Blue laws, 137
Brain drain, 64, 87
Brain gain, 64
Brain swamp, 87
Brain trade, 65
Branch plant, 94, 96
British North America Act, 2, 158
British tradition, 132-34, 136

Canada Development Corporation, 95
Canada First movement, 164
Canadian Broadcasting Corporation, 89, 97, 162
Canadian Football League, 88
Canadian Manufacturers' Association, 169
Canadian National Railways, 97
Canadian Pacific Railway, 9, 69, 136
Canadian Radio-Television Commission, 97
Capital drain, 144
Capitalism, 74, 116, 134, 137, 140
Census metropolitan area, 34-36
Charter group, 107
Church-state relations, 116, 130

Civil servants, 68-70
Clergy, 116, 117
Cocacolonization, 91
Cold War, 97
Collectivity-orientation, 135-41
Colleges,
   community, 54, 65
   technical, 55, 65
Colonialism, 84-86, 90, 97, 132-34, 150, 157-58, 160, 161
Committee for an Independent Canada, 86
Common market, European, 161
Commonwealth, 131, 160
Community, 109, 112, 113, 115, 164
Confederation, 162, 167
Conflict,
   French-English, 116-19, 179
   institutionalized, 109-10
   out-group, 109-12, 159, 161, 169
Conformity, 112, 113, 181
Consciousness of difference, 108
Consciousness of kind, 108
Conservatism, 134-37, 140-41
Continentalism, 96-97
Cooperatives, Eskimo, 111
Corporations, 67, 119
   crown, 162
   multinational, 69, 92-95, 96, 180
Crime, 136-37, 161
Cultural diffusion, 85-86, 89, 91
Cultural penetration, 86
Cybernetics, 4

Defense policy, 97
Demography, definition, 13
Depressions, 30, 38
Dialects, 148-49
Directorships, interlocking, 68, 69
Discrimination, 69, 107, 114
Distant Early Warning System, 97
Divorce, 136-41
Domination, 86-90
   athletic, 88
   cultural, 88-89
   economic, 86-87
   educational, 87-88
   political, 87
   resource, 90
   technological, 89-90

Durham Report, 167

Ecology, human, 12
Ecumene, definition, 16
Education, 167 (see also social class)
    changes in, 76, 117, 141
    conflict in, 109-10, 168
    foreign, 87-88, 149
    mobility with, 64-66
    reform in, 64-65, 138, 141, 179
Elections, 169
Elites/elitism, 9, 67-73, 75-76,
    116-17, 135-38, 140, 179, 185
Emergency Measures Act, 39, 109
Emigration, 7, 28, 30-32, 34, 38,
    39, 64, 87, 105, 158, 159
Empire, American, 91-92
Equality/inequality, 47, 48, 67,
    75-76, 110-11, 118, 135-41, 178
Ethnic associations, 114-15
Ethnic dispersion, 21-23, 26
Ethnicity, 104-22, 129, 146-48, 165,
    181-83
    employment opportunities and, 66
    religion and, 25-26, 115
Ethnic sovereignty, 105, 146
Ethnic stratification, 59-63, 66,
    165, 169, 182
Ethnic tensions, 108, 164
Ethnocentrism, 163, 166, 168
Exclusivism, 70-71, 166
Exploitation, 85, 179
Extraterritoriality, 93

Federalism, 149, 178
Flag, Canadian, 162
FLQ crisis, 73, 109
Folk heroes, 7, 132, 136, 158, 168
French-Canadian society, 59
    English-Canadian society,
        differences from, 38-39, 58-62,
        69-70, 111
    identity, 7, 115
Frontier, 136
Functional analysis, 4, 8-10

"God Save the Queen", 133, 157, 162
Gray Report, 89, 92-93, 95
Gross Domestic Product, 142-43
Gross National Product, 96
Group awareness, 111-12
Group conflict, 105
Group consciousness, 107

Hinterland, 33, 37, 39, 72-73, 85,
    90, 96, 97, 145
Homogenization of culture, 85, 95,
    117, 149, 180
    of values, 140
Hyphenated Canadians, 8, 104, 184

Identity, 30, 39, 104
    ethnic, 109-13, 115, 119, 148
    national, 150, 155-70, 183-85
Immigration, 7, 22, 28-34, 38, 39,
    62-66, 87, 105, 107, 113, 115,
    131, 138, 145-49, 158, 160
Immigration policy, 9, 28-29, 62-65,
    106-7
Imperialism, 95, 161
Income (see also social class),
    discretionary, 74
    guaranteed annual, 75
    regional differences in, 72
Indian Act, 105
Indians,
    associations of, 110, 113, 119-20
    exploitation of, 9, 84
    expressions by, 111
    religion and, 115
Indian-White conflict, 119-20, 148
Industrialization, 32-34, 36, 37, 39,
    57, 58, 90, 140-45, 158
    education and, 51-53
    ethnic stratification and, 61-63, 165
    of Quebec, 117
Industry, domestic, 90, 95
Inequality (see equality)
Inferiority complex, 98, 107
Inflation, 76, 176
Institutional completeness, 112-13
Integration, 121
Interaction,
    environment, effect of, 5-6, 12,
        21, 38, 139
    migration, effect of, 33, 36, 38, 105
    values, effect of, 134-41
Intermarriage, 70, 112
Investment, foreign, 86-87, 94, 144,
    150, 161
    direct, 86
    portfolio, 86
Iron law of oligarchy, 70

James Bay Project, 110

Kinship, 108, 112

Labor drain, 64
Labor unions, 143-44
Language, 23-24, 26, 69, 104, 105,
    108, 109, 111, 114, 116, 118,
    146, 148-50, 158, 159, 164-65,
    167, 170, 179
Legislation, 87, 114, 119, 136-37, 149
Legislators, 68
Linguistic dualism, 158-59, 170
Loyalists, 132

Maîtres chez nous, 118
Majority, oppressed, 62
Marginality, 98
Marginal man, 120
Marriage, 140
Mass society, 104
Media, 88, 129, 167, 168, 170
Melting pot, 23, 120-22, 146
Métis, 9
Metropolis, 72-73, 145
Migration, 66, 132, 182-83, 185
    definition, 33
    interprovincial, 33-34, 36
    interurban, 36, 37
    rural-urban, 36-37, 117
Military, the, 149, 169
Miniature replica effect, 96
Minority, oppressed, 119
Minority complex, 116
Minority groups, 106, 109-12, 114,
    118, 147, 164, 166
Mobility, geographical, 32, 66
Mobility deprivation, 65, 118, 148
Monarchy, 133, 157
Multiculturalism, 38, 108, 121

National anthem, 162
National Energy Board, 97
National Film Board, 162
Nationalism, 98-99, 134, 157, 163-70,
    184
    counternationalism, 133-34
    French-Canadian, 164-65, 169
National origin (see ethnicity)
National unity, 8, 27, 39-40, 97, 155,
    165, 168, 176, 180
Native peoples, 105, 107
Natural increase, 27-28, 30-32, 34
Natural selection, 4
Neighborhood, 108

"O Canada" (see national anthem)

Occupation (see social class)
Ownership, foreign, 86, 94, 95, 97,
    144, 150

Parish, 116
Parliament, British, 158
Parliamentary system, 133
Particularism, 135-41
Paternalism, 98, 129, 160
Patriotism, 163, 169, 170
Pattern variables, 135-41
Peer group, 113
Pluralism, 104, 159, 164, 166, 170
    definition, 121
    ethnic, 38, 147, 150, 165, 182
    linguistic, 148-50
Police, the, 136
Polls, 163-65
Population,
    ageing, 30, 32
    change, 27-32, 38
    composition, 21-26, 106
    density, 17-18, 33, 131-32
    distribution, 13-21, 33
    drain, 19
    drift, 33
    durability, 6-7, 27, 30, 32, 39
    internal shifts, 33-37
    organization, 6, 33, 38, 76
    settlement, 5-6, 16, 33-34, 38, 132
    turnover, 27, 36, 37, 105
    uniqueness, 7-8, 38
Poverty, 73-75
Prejudice, 114
Pressure group, 108
Primary group, 112
Primordial event, 116
Proletariat, 62

Quebec Bill 22, 118
Québecois, 7
Quiet Revolution, 117-18, 176

Race, 104, 105, 114, 138, 147-48, 161
Reactionism, hostile, 98
Red Ensign, 133, 157, 162
Red Power movement, 119
Reference group, 62, 113
Regionalism, 10-40, 165, 177-78
    definitions, 11-13
    identification with, 38-39
    power differences, 71-73, 145,
    158, 164, 179

Relative deprivation, 111-12
Religion, 25-26, 115, 129-30, 137, 147, 163-65
Resources, natural, 90, 143-44, 161
Revolution, 132, 158
counterrevolution, 132-35, 137
Royal Canadian Mounted Police, 8-9, 136
Royal Commission on Bilingualism and Biculturalism, 64, 69-70, 148, 167, 183

Satellite society, 90-91
Secession, 10
Secularization, 140, 176
Segregation, 121
Self-orientation, 135-41
Separatism, 165
Shadow society, 86-87, 99, 145
Social change, 3, 5, 32, 116, 117, 140, 165
Social class, 25, 47-48, 63, 65, 67, 72, 75, 91, 135-36, 144, 178-79
conflict and, 76, 176
education and, 51-55, 57, 61, 65, 68, 119, 135
ethnicity and (see ethnic stratification)
income and, 48-51, 55, 57, 119
industrialization and, 61
occupation and, 51, 55-57, 58-60, 61-62, 68, 117-19, 138
subjective indices, 58-60, 138
Social cohesion, 10, 12, 32, 156, 177-78
lack of, 23, 30, 37-40, 111, 112, 155
Social continuity, 133
Social control, 71-73, 109, 136
Social differentiation, 46, 55, 104, 114, 156
Social distance, 113
Socialism, 73, 141
Sociality, 104
Socialization, 74, 111, 112, 167-70
Social mobility, 63-66, 71, 117, 135, 138, 141
intergenerational, 64
intragenerational, 64
Social power, 67-73, 109, 111, 133, 178-79
Social pressures, 115

Social reform, 185-86
Social status, 58-60, 63, 66, 71, 105, 119-20, 138
entrance, 63, 66
subordinate, 108, 111, 118
Social stratification, 46-76, 178-79
ethnic, 59-63
Society,
characteristics, 5-8
definition, 2-3, 8, 38
Solidarity, group, 109, 110
Solidarity, Pan-Eskimo, 111
Spillover effect, 87
Sport, national, 88
Standardization, 95
Standard of living, 50, 66, 74, 76, 90, 92, 96-97, 143-45, 150, 158, 159, 161, 180
Status crystallization, 119
Status dislocation, 66
Stereotypes, 114, 129, 138, 177
Stock ownership, 144
Subsidiaries, 94-95, 96
Subsistence, 73-74, 110, 142
Symbols,
British, 133, 157-58
Canadian, 7, 133, 157-58, 168

Tariffs, protective, 6, 10, 96
Technology, imported, 89
Territorial dominance, 149
Territory, 107, 145
Textbooks, 7, 167-68
Trading with the Enemy Act, 93
Transfer payments, 50
Treaty mentality of dependence, 120
Truncation, 94

Unilingualism, 118-19
Universalism, 135-41
University faculty, 87
Urbanization, 3, 31, 39, 61, 117, 129, 140, 176
provincial variations, 18-21, 33-37

Values, 134-41, 185-86
Viet Nam War, 161, 168

Wage parity, 144
Welfare, 50, 112